To Randy
Best Wishes

Roger L Galatas
7/12/05

The WOODLANDS

The Inside Story of Creating a Better Hometown

Roger Galatas with Jim Barlow

ULI–the Urban Land Institute
1025 Thomas Jefferson Street, N.W.
Suite 500 West
Washington, D.C. 20007-5201

Galatas, Roger
     The Woodlands: The Inside Story of Creating a Better Hometown
Washington, D.C.: ULI–the Urban Land Institute, 2004

ISBN: 0-87420-931-5
Library of Congress Control Number: 2004110835

Printed in the United States of America.
10 9 8 7 6 5 4 3 2 1

To my family: Ann, Susan, Bob, Richard, Carrie, Mason, Molly, Max, and Grace—all live in The Woodlands.

—Roger Galatas

To Samantha, Saul, Paolo, Sofia, and especially to Susan. She knows why. And in memory of Joe Kutchin.

—Jim Barlow

CONTENTS

Foreword ix

The Woodlands Chronology of Development xi

The Woodlands Location Map xvii

Introduction xix

Part I: The Beginning 1

Chapter 1: The Mitchell Story 3

Chapter 2: The HUD Experience 13

Chapter 3: Land Acquisition 21

Chapter 4: Planning and the Environment 30

Part II: Commitment to Develop 43

Chapter 5: A Challenging Start 45

Chapter 6: The Turnaround Begins 53

Chapter 7: Success Emerges 60

Part III: Building Institutions 69

Chapter 8: Interfaith 71

Chapter 9: Governance 79

Chapter 10: Health Care 86

Chapter 11: Education 93

Chapter 12: The Name Game 102

Part IV: Productive Relationships 107

Chapter 13: Homes in the New Community 109

Chapter 14: Affordable Housing and Affirmative Action .115

Chapter 15: Research Forest 121

Chapter 16: Town Center 125

Chapter 17: Transportation and Mobility 133

Chapter 18: Golf 135

Chapter 19: YMCA 140

Chapter 20: The Pavilion 142

Chapter 21: Art in Public Places 144

Chapter 22: The Woodlands and Its Neighbors 146

Chapter 23: Hometown Heroes 152

Part V: The Woodlands After Mitchell 153

Chapter 24: Sale of The Woodlands 155

Chapter 25: Future of The Woodlands 165

Chapter 26: Lessons Learned 173

ACKNOWLEDGMENTS

Books like this one are not solely the product of the author, or in our case, the coauthors. The story of The Woodlands could not have been written without the patience and encouragement of many people. We wish to express our appreciation to those who spent many hours talking with us about the community and their part in its growth. So special thanks go to Dave Bumgardner, Jim and Wanda Cochran, Tom D'Alesandro, Burt Darden, Joe Davis, Mickey Deison, Joel Deretchin, Don Gebert, Pat Goodpastor, Robert Heineman, David Hendricks, Earl Higgins, Gary Kappler, John Landrum, Tom Ledwell, Dr. Jack Lesch, Charles Lively, Jim McAlister, Steve McPhetridge, George Mitchell, Pat Moritz, Mike Page, Plato Pappas, John Pipkin, Michael Richmond, Frank Robinson, Terry Russ, Ken Stockton, Coulson Tough, Jim Veltman, Susan Vreeland, Paul Wahlberg, Ken Ward, Ted Washington, and Jack Yovanovich.

The authors also owe a large debt to the late Joe Kutchin, who compiled an oral history of Mitchell Energy & Development Corporation that helped the authors with their research for this book. We also wish to thank Robert Heineman, Michael Richmond, and Mike Page, who reviewed some of the chapters, and Wayne Hyatt, Richard Peiser, and Dan Van Epp, who reviewed the entire manuscript. They all provided excellent advice and constructive criticism. If errors remain, they are ours.

A special thanks to Harry Frampton for his thoughtful foreword to the book. Our thanks to Abby Bussel of Engine Books, the consulting editor, and to Jo Allen Gause of the Urban Land Institute for helping us to understand the ways of editors and publishers. All of the photography, except where noted, is the work of Ted Washington, who has chronicled the growth of The Woodlands for decades. A special thank you goes to Kristen Weaver, who transcribed several hundred hours of interviews, despite being hampered by the technical limitations of one of the authors. Working well beyond her original assignment, she corrected our grammar and spelling and provided useful criticisms about the book's contents.

We also wish to thank Larry and Sandy Woodard of BST Timberlands, LP, the Southwest Bank of Texas; Mitchell Mortgage Company, LLC; Roger Galatas, LLC; and Stewart Title Company of The Woodlands for their generous help in funding the transcription, research, and writing costs of this project. And The Woodlands Operating Company, LP, provided access to its historical records and photo collection.

Finally, we would be remiss if we did not acknowledge George P. Mitchell. It was his intelligence, determination, and desire that made The Woodlands a reality.

Roger Galatas
Jim Barlow

FOREWORD

"The Woodlands is an attractive new town that successfully integrates all the necessary elements of a vibrant, healthy community: a diversity of housing types; employment centers; a town center; a research park; and cultural, educational, medical, and recreational facilities. Its success is directly attributed to the vision, courage, and financial commitment of its developer."

Official Jury Statement on The Woodlands
1994 ULI Awards for Excellence
New Community Category

There are many people in the land use profession who have long believed that it is admirable, but not possible, to apply smart growth development practices to the suburbs. Fortunately, George Mitchell never believed that—not even 30 years ago, when "best practice" in outlying development meant sticking to a low-density, land-consumptive approach.

The Woodlands—which George conceived as an antidote to the rather haphazard building environment prevailing at the time—was truly an ambitious undertaking. The fact that George would even propose a master-planned community in which one could live, work, shop, learn, and play illustrates his incredible vision. The fact that he persevered to make The Woodlands a reality is a testament to his unwavering belief that his vision would ultimately result in a better community.

I first heard about The Woodlands at an Urban Land Institute conference in the late 1960s. It was part of a unique group of new towns, including Reston, Virginia, and Columbia, Maryland, that were turning traditional development notions upside down by employing a mix of land uses with a design built for people, not cars. I found the concept intriguing, as it enhanced what I had learned from Charles Fraser about land-efficient, environmentally conscious, sustainable development.

Several years later, I met Roger Galatas after he became president of The Woodlands, and was incredibly impressed with his ability to forge productive public/private partnerships—another example of the foresight and incredible capability of those creating this trendsetting community. Roger and his team worked with a broad range of government entities, resulting in the construction of schools, cultural facilities, and infrastructure—the underpinnings of any successful community.

The story told in *The Woodlands: The Inside Story of Creating a Better Hometown* is about beating the odds and achieving success. But The Woodlands story is also a tribute to the business acumen of George Mitchell and Roger Galatas. In 1994, I was privileged to serve on the jury for the ULI Awards for Excellence program, when The Woodlands was a finalist. During the judging process, it was gratifying to revisit this community, which I had seen being shaped so many years earlier, and to see that vision as reality. As part of that experience, I discovered what separates great projects from those that are just good enough. Behind every great project—and The Woodlands is a great project—there is one champion who is passionate about the project, who is devoted to it, and who provides unique leadership. The Woodlands has been doubly fortunate to have two champions in George and Roger.

All of us at ULI can learn from the precedent set by The Woodlands. As ULI members, we have a responsibility to lead collectively in building better communities by building better suburbs.

During my time as ULI chairman, one of my priorities has been to continue the Institute's advocacy of smart growth development, with a particular emphasis on suburban smart growth. George figured it out long before the rest of us, but we all need to recognize that we cannot keep using more land than is necessary for development and expect to preserve land at the same time. Our organization needs to lead the effort in finding ways to develop land more efficiently in outlying urban areas, where most future growth will occur.

The logical solution is smart suburban growth, and The Woodlands is solid proof that it works. In promoting this concept, we can apply the same themes that apply to smart growth in general: conservation of open space and parkland; more choices in living and working environments; more choices in transportation; and more inclusive, public/private decision making.

Even though we are making progress, the reality is that there are not yet enough communities like The Woodlands. Restoring our suburban landscape will take many years. Consider that The Woodlands has been 30 years in the making. However, as each chapter of *The Woodlands: The Inside Story of Creating a Better Hometown* so clearly illustrates, today's pursuit of sustainable growth patterns will set the course for better communities in the future.

Harry H. Frampton III
ULI Chairman
Managing Partner
East West Partners
Beaver Creek, Colorado

The Woodlands Chronology of Development

On October 19, 1974, The Woodlands celebrated its grand opening and the introduction of this new master-planned community to the Houston marketplace. Progress over the years has been achieved through the collaborative efforts of our employees and residents, governmental agencies, houses of worship, civic organizations, financial institutions, and business leaders. Working together, we have created a unique community—the result of many defining events.

1964   George Mitchell purchases the Grogan Cochran Lumber Company land, including 2,800 acres that were to become the first piece of The Woodlands property.

1964–1974   An additional 300 transactions produce the original 17,455 acres.

George Mitchell hires environmental planner Ian McHarg to join the master-planning team. His concept for "developing in harmony with nature" emphasizes the preservation of existing vegetation and a natural drainage system.

1971   The community's first public school, Lamar Elementary, opens.

1972   The U.S. Department of Housing and Urban Development agrees to provide $50 million in loan guarantees to a Mitchell Energy subsidiary for development of The Woodlands.

On September 6, the federal government issues $50 million in 7.1 percent New Community Debentures.

1972–1976   The OPEC oil embargo and high interest rates lead to an economic downturn for the country.

1974   The Woodlands opens on October 19.

The Woodlands Corporation's Real Estate Division completes its move to 2201 Timberloch Place in The Woodlands.

Houston Golf Association signs a ten-year contract to hold the PGA Houston Open at The Woodlands.

1975   Interfaith, a nondenominational religious organization, is established.

1976	Jack Eckerd Drug purchases land and develops first distribution facility in Trade Center, a rail-served business park for the new town.
	McCullough High School opens.
1978	Jamail's, the town's first supermarket, opens.
1979	The MEDC headquarters building breaks ground.
1980	Construction of The Woodlands National Bank Building begins.
1982	Houston Advanced Research Center constructs its first building and announces plans to develop a research campus.
	The Research Forest is established.
1983	Total investment in The Woodlands reaches $1 billion.
	Village of Cochran's Crossing opens.
1983–1987	Severe economic downturn as energy prices collapse and Houston market crashes. The Woodlands increased its share of the housing market.
1984	Village of Indian Springs opens.
	Agreement signed to establish a Tournament Players Course golf course, which is designated as the site of the Houston Open Tournament.
1985	The Woodlands Hospital opens.
	Lake Woodlands is filled with water.
1986	Harmony Bridge opens, providing an alternate route into Harris County.
	South County YMCA opens its new building in The Woodlands.
1987	Hardy Toll Road opens.
	First Venture Technologies Building opens in the Research Forest.
1988	The John Cooper School opens.

1990   The Woodlands' population tops 30,000.

        The Cynthia Woods Mitchell Pavilion opens in April.

        The Woodlands ranks number one in new home sales and closings in
        Houston for first time.

        Total investment exceeds $2 billion.

        The Arnold Palmer Golf Course opens.

1991   Hughes Tool moves its world headquarters to The Woodlands.

1992   All The Woodlands united in the same school district.

        The Woodlands Community Association transitions to resident control.

        Original $50 million in HUD debentures retired.

1993   Construction of The Woodlands Mall begins.

        Formal announcement of Town Center, a commercial, retail, and urban
        residential center designed to serve as the downtown for 1 million–plus
        residents of the North Houston region.

        Community college campus announced.

1994   Town Center Improvement District formed.

        State Highway 242 opens.

        Cemetery and funeral home announced.

        Cochran's Crossing Shopping Center opens.

        Population of The Woodlands exceeds 40,000.

        The Woodlands Mall opens.

        The Village of Alden Bridge celebrates its grand opening.

1995   Montgomery Community College opens.

               The Woodlands is first in new home sales in the region for the sixth con-
               secutive year.

               Jobs in The Woodlands top 15,000.

               Cynthia Woods Mitchell Pavilion expands seating capacity to 13,000.

1996   University Center building breaks ground.

               The Woodlands High School opens.

               Population exceeds 45,000.

               First car drives across new Woodlands Parkway overpass above Grogan's
               Mill Road.

               New information center opens on Woodlands Parkway.

               Shell Learning Center initiates operations.

               The 17-screen Tinseltown Cinema in Town Center shows its first movie.

               1,053 new homes sold, setting a calendar year record.

               Seventh consecutive year The Woodlands is number one in new home
               sales in the region.

1997   Population exceeds 50,000.

               JCPenney becomes The Woodlands Mall's fifth anchor store.

               Construction begins on Alden Bridge Shopping Center.

               Plans unveiled for a 150,000-square-foot, six-story office building in
               Town Center.

               The Woodlands Corporation and all of its assets are purchased by a part-
               nership of Morgan Stanley and Crescent Real Estate Equities for $543
               million on July 31.

1999   The Woodlands celebrates its 25th anniversary.

First Hometown Heroes are inducted.

Harper's Landing, a community of 1,300 homes, opens.

Construction of The Woodlands Waterway begins.

Town Center Two office building is occupied.

2000   Windsor Hills "active adult" neighborhood opens.

Woodlands resident Laura Wilkinson wins diving gold medal at Olympic Games in Sydney, Australia.

Waterway Plaza One office building completed.

All-time record of 1,679 new home sales set.

Hike and bike trails reach 100-mile milestone.

2001   Jack Nicklaus Signature Golf Course opens in Carlton Woods.

Sterling Ridge Village Center opens.

College Park Retail Center opens.

Maersk Sealand's 100,000-square-foot Customer Resource Center opens in the Research Forest.

Opening of the Palmer Clubhouse celebrated.

Waterway Plaza Two office building is occupied.

The Woodlands' new signature entryway is unveiled.

2002   Lake Woodlands Drive extended over Lake Woodlands, providing third major east-west artery.

Gosling Road Bridge opens, providing connector to Harris County.

Gary Player Signature Course opens in the Village of Sterling Ridge.

The Woodlands Waterway Marriott Hotel & Convention Center opens.

The 800,000-square-foot Anadarko Tower, the tallest building between Houston and Dallas, is occupied.

Chevron Phillips Chemical Company occupies its new 200,000-square-foot building in Town Center.

The Urban Land Institute's *Great Planned Communities* features The Woodlands.

The Club at Carlton Woods ranked "best new private course in Texas" by *Golf Digest*.

Population of The Woodlands exceeds 70,000.

2003   First urban residential projects open on the Waterway in Town Center.

CBI completes and occupies its new building on Lake Woodlands.

Market Street pedestrian-oriented project underway in Town Center.

Memorial Hermann, The Woodlands Hospital, completes $78 million expansion.

St. Luke's Woodlands Community Medical Center opens.

The World Championship LPGA event played on the Tournament Players Course.

A 53,000-square-foot clubhouse opens at The Club at Carlton Woods.

New YMCA opens in Sterling Ridge.

Construction of Indian Springs Village Center begins.

Fazio Course announced for the Village of Creekside Park.

Rouse Company purchases Crescent Real Estate Equities's 52.7 percent interest in The Woodlands on December 31.

THE WOODLANDS LOCATION MAP

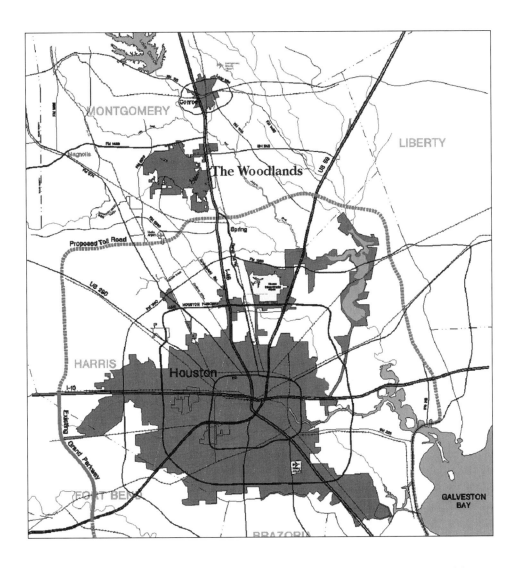

The Woodlands, Texas, is a 27,000-acre master-planned community located 27 miles north of downtown Houston. It is home to 75,000 residents and 3,000 employers, and the population is expected to reach 125,000 when the community is completely built out by 2014.

Courtesy of The Woodlands Operating Company, LP

INTRODUCTION

This book tells the story of The Woodlands, one of the most successful master-planned communities in the United States. Developed on a 27,000-acre site north of Houston beginning in 1974, the community has won international acclaim for its successful mix of commercial, retail, and residential components; its ability to attract and sustain jobs; and its protection of the natural environment. The Woodlands isn't just another suburban housing development. It's a hometown where people not only live, but also work, shop, and become involved in their community in a way not often seen in modern-day America.

This book, however, is more than an account of a real estate investment. While planning and money are vital parts of any business endeavor, success, in the end, comes down to the people involved. It is the story of decisions made and difficulties—often self-imposed—overcome by the developer and his team of professionals. It is also the stories of those who chose to live in The Woodlands and how they interacted with and sometimes changed the decisions of the planners and implementers of this new town.

So what exactly are master-planned communities? Jim Heid, a real estate consultant and developer who wrote a paper for the Urban Land Institute on the role of planned communities in greenfield development, offers a useful answer. He defines *planned* as "a comprehensive approach to analysis, programming, construction, development, and management." Community, he says, is "a creation of a balanced and vibrant set of uses that not only creates place, but also provides the attendant benefits of allowing people to live, work, and play in their local environs, socialize formally or informally with their neighbors, and most of all be part of a place they take pride in."

Master-planned communities are not new. In fact, they date back to the 14th century. But in the United States they are largely a phenomenon of the post–World War II era. Iconic figures of the planned community movement include Jim Rouse, who initiated the development of the new town of Columbia, Maryland, in 1967; Robert E. Simon, the mastermind behind Reston, Virginia, where the first homes were sold in 1964; Charles E. Fraser, the environmentally minded creator of Hilton Head, South Carolina; Ray Watson of the Irvine Ranch in Orange County, California; and George Mitchell, the man who envisioned The Woodlands.

The Woodlands set the pattern for suburban growth in the Houston area. It is the primary economic generator for Montgomery County, the largely suburban and preferred residential area for much of the growing population of the Greater Houston area. After an infancy that can only be described as shaky and a toddler stage that threatened severe financial consequences for a successful oil and gas company, The Woodlands grew into a healthy adulthood and a solid business success. It has led the Houston area in new home sales every year since 1990, and ranks first in new home sales in Texas and among the leaders in the nation.

Today, The Woodlands' 27,000 acres is home to over 75,000 people living in more than 20,000 single-family homes and 5,000 apartments and townhomes. What makes it a real hometown is more than just where people sleep at night, but where and how they spend the rest of the day: The Woodlands has more than 20 million square feet of commercial and institutional space. Today, 3,000 employers provide jobs for more than 30,000 people. And it's still growing. Eventually, The Woodlands is projected to be home to some 125,000, with jobs for 65,000 people in 33 million square feet of commercial and institutional space.

The Woodlands, however, would not have gotten off the ground without loan guarantees from a federal government program meant to enable new town development, removing people from the supposed evils of declining central cities. The instigators of The Woodlands did not completely share that utopian view. But they did take the loan guarantee and used it to build the only viable master-planned community in the federal new town program.

Success did not come easily. The challenges The Woodlands met and conquered included wrangles with the federal government, local municipalities, and school districts. There were failures in planning and execution and a financial crisis that came close to bankrupting its parent company, Mitchell Energy & Development Corporation , and ending one of the more remarkable careers in the oil and natural gas business.

Any large, complicated enterprise such as The Woodlands must employ a talented team of planners, construction experts of all kinds, sales personnel, and managers. This book seeks to tell the story of The Woodlands by looking at the individual stories of many of those involved in building the community. It examines their missteps and subsequent corrective actions, demonstrating what works and what does not. This is not just the tale of a housing development, a new town, or a company. It is a human story.

Like most such efforts, it started with the vision of one man, in this case George Mitchell. Mitchell exemplifies what America is all about. The son of poor immigrant parents, he became one of the richest men in America. He achieved his wealth through skill, education, perseverance, intelligence, and, most important, the ability to dream big and make those dreams come true. One of the better geologists in Texas—in a state full of good ones—he made his first fortune in the oil and gas business. Then he turned to real estate development in an effort to diversify the petroleum business. The result was The Woodlands, the only successful outcome of an otherwise failed social experiment by the federal government to build new towns outside the central cities of the United States.

While The Woodlands is a unique property development, especially for the Houston area, it can best be understood in the context of master-planned communities. They are more than housing developments. They are efforts to build communities, not just homes. And how are communities built?

John W. Gardner, former Secretary of Health, Education, and Welfare (1965–1968) and later professor of public service at Stanford University, offered some parameters in a 1991 paper, "Building Community," which was prepared for the Leadership Studies Program of the Independent Sector in Washington, D.C. "Families and communities are the ground-level generators and preservers of values and ethical systems. No society can remain vital or even survive without a reasonable base of shared values—and such values are not established by edict from lofty levels of society. They are generated in the family, school, church, and other intimate settings in which people deal with one another face to face. The ideals of justice and compassion are nurtured in communities. Where community exists it confers upon its members identity, a sense of belonging, a measure of security. Humans need communities—and a sense of community." As Gardner rightly points out, successful master-planned communities focus on the human side of development and include institutions and programs that nurture people.

During the past four decades, large-scale master-planned communities have become a major force in promoting better-quality suburban development in the United States. When conceived with strategic development and design guidelines, they offer an alternative to the suburban sprawl that engulfs much of our countryside today. They use land more efficiently, maintain public open space, conserve valuable environmental assets, and support a range of housing types, employment opportunities, economic benefits to local governments, and a potential reduction in vehicular travel. And if all goes as planned, they are profitable for the sponsor.

Master-planned communities must have long-term commitments of land, capital, and human resources. They require advance planning and thoughtful fiscal review. They need a degree of cooperation between the public sector and the community developer. They are always market sensitive. Lessons learned in large-scale master-planned communities can be applied to smaller projects, too. Master-planned communities range in size from several hundred to more than 20,000 acres. While any community, regardless of size, can use the concepts of master planning, communities of more than 2,000 acres provide an opportunity to achieve more housing diversity in terms of design, density, and affordability. They have the potential to produce a resident population sufficient to support an elementary school and a neighborhood shopping center with a supermarket anchor tenant and retail shops that create local jobs. They can reduce travel outside the community for daily family needs.

Large-scale master-planned communities are generally divided into villages, with each village offering its own individual character but sharing the benefits of community-wide systems of parks, open space, and schools, as well as a greater selection of shopping choices.

This collection of smaller villages promotes a sense of community found in small towns of the past where neighbors knew one another. Smaller residential neighborhoods within each village are threads of community fabric. Large-scale communities with multiple villages have the greater potential to develop commercial town centers that offer regional shopping, entertainment, and job creation, expanding the tax base for the community and surrounding region. Large-scale master-planned communities support the development and operation of houses of worship, community colleges, museums, hospitals, performing arts venues, community centers, civic clubs, public agencies, and charitable organizations.

While a number of master-planned communities have tens of thousands of acres, including The Woodlands, it is more likely that future larger-scale communities will be smaller, perhaps ranging in size from 2,000 to 6,000 acres. Why? First, assembling enough land nowadays is more difficult and expensive than it was in the 1960s. Higher initial land costs and related holding costs for longer periods destroy economic returns. Also, the changing and uncertain regulatory environment adds significant risks to a project over an extended period. So developers are opting either to purchase smaller land parcels or to negotiate phased acquisitions with purchase options based on performance, or joint venture agreements with the landowner participating in the risks and rewards.

Building The Woodlands would not have happened without federal help. In the 1970s, the federal government became involved in community development largely through a social program administered by the U.S. Department of Housing and Urban Development to help solve social and economic turmoil plaguing major cities at the time. Title VII of the Housing and Urban Development Act of 1970, passed during the Nixon Administration, provided loan guarantees of up to $50 million to support development of new communities that would agree to goals in affordable housing, environmental planning, and affirmative social programs. Thirteen new communities received federal loan guarantees. All but The Woodlands defaulted on those loans.

In the 1970s and 1980s, a number of master-planned communities were launched in the United States with the greatest concentration in Florida, Texas, Arizona, and California. Many were sponsored or funded by major corporations, such as Penn Central Railroad, Westinghouse, Mobil Oil, Exxon, Chevron, Phillip Morris, American General Insurance, and Weyerhaeuser. These giants of industry saw real estate as a way to diversify and enhance profitability. Most of their community development projects were tiny percentages of the corporation's invested capital and seldom warranted mention in their annual reports. Most of those corporations became disenchanted with their investments in master-planned communities and during the 1990s practically all were sold, usually at a discount. Many went to Wall Street investment funds, a few major pension funds, wealthy investors, or real estate investment trusts. Several publicly traded homebuilders have also broadened their market reach by acquiring or developing planned communities.

As we move deeper into the 21st century, we have a wealth of professional experience with master-planned communities and an emerging generation of owners and sponsors. We also have the challenge of reshaping our cities and applying reasonable smart growth principles to suburbia to protect the environment and quality of life. According to the U.S. Bureau of the Census, our population is expected to increase by almost 60 million people by 2025. Some would argue that population growth should be accommodated by urban infill development. That will be part of the answer. But others, such as Don Priest in an unpublished paper for the Urban Land Institute, correctly argue that expected population growth can't be met only by infill and that substantial suburban growth is inevitable. Given that circumstance, large-scale master-planned communities offer a better alternative to suburban sprawl. Those who argue for smart growth development policies should embrace large-scale master-planned communities as part of the solution. The Woodlands is a good example to explore.

But there is much more to the story of The Woodlands than the tale of a successful real estate venture. That's why I decided to write this book. I have unique insight into its growth and success, working for George Mitchell for decades and winding up as chief executive officer of The Woodlands Corporation, which developed the new town.

My experience taught me a lesson. Yes, any successful endeavor like The Woodlands requires capital, commitment, and knowledge. But most of all, it requires people. Some of those people worked for The Woodlands Corporation. Many more of those who were instrumental in its success came here to live and often work. They had no direct financial interest in The Woodlands, other than the personal value of their homes or businesses, but they invested their emotions in this new hometown. They saw The Woodlands as a place they wanted to put down roots and make this fledging real estate development a real hometown. And working together, developers and residents alike, we did just that.

Here are our stories.

Roger Galatas
The Woodlands, Texas
June 2004

---◆---

Part I

THE BEGINNING

The Woodlands, like all master-planned communities, needed large amounts of planning, money, and effort. But above all, it demanded vision. That vision came from one man, George Mitchell. As we shall see in these first few chapters, The Woodlands started as a good real estate investment, not as a desire to build a new kind of town. The plan for what was to become The Woodlands grew slowly, first in Mitchell's mind, and then through the work of numerous people.

The birth of The Woodlands would not have been possible without support from the federal government in the form of loan guarantees. It would not have succeeded without Mitchell's determination and willingness to put his considerable fortune, earned in the oil and gas business, behind his vision. The building of The Woodlands did not go smoothly in the early years. It faced every difficulty imaginable, from torrential rains to an international economic downturn brought on by the oil crisis of the 1970s.

Ultimately, the story of The Woodlands would have been a short one, but for the efforts of George Mitchell.

Chapter 1

THE MITCHELL STORY

———— ◆ ————

George Mitchell doesn't fit the stereotype of the Texas oilman. He looks like a kindly uncle. Age has stooped his tall frame. His hairline has retreated from his scalp. In public, he's quiet-spoken. Indeed, you sometimes must strain to hear him. But Mitchell does have strongly held views and in private is inclined to state them forcefully. And his former company, Mitchell Energy & Development Corporation, was known as a place where if you wanted to make your point in a business meeting you had better be prepared to shout along with everyone else.

Mitchell's life has taken many turns, but he has always been a visionary. He understands how things ought to be, and has a picture of how to get there. At the same time, he has recognized the critical need to involve others who possess the special talents he lacks. He is willing to pay for expertise and his recruiting decisions are swift. No lengthy interviews are necessary. While offering encouragement and rewards, Mitchell also does not hesitate to offer a generous but productive amount of advice and direction.

He is not a strategic planner in the formal sense. Mitchell was fond of saying, "The only thing more dangerous than a five-year financial projection is believing it is valid." Some might say that Mitchell's distrust of long-range planning led to the near collapse of both Mitchell Energy and The Woodlands Corporation. (The Woodlands real estate development company operated under several different names in its history, but for the purposes of this book, it will be called The Woodlands Corporation.) However, external factors, particularly high interest rates and chaotic energy prices in the 1970s and 1980s, were the real culprits. Mitchell understood the need for budgets and business plans, but he refused to let them stand in the way of unexpected opportunities.

Mitchell eschewed the usual American business focus on quarterly earnings. His eye was on long-term returns. A natural dealmaker, he delighted in driving hard bargains. It wasn't greed, but the love of the game. I've seen him negotiate long and hard to get the maximum return, and then donate much of that gain to charitable or civic causes. Conversations with Mitchell can be exciting adventures for those unaccustomed to his style. He gives everyone credit for knowing as much about any subject as he does. He tends to start in the middle and go forward at a rapid pace. Those on the receiving end of what's often a Mitchell monologue must listen carefully. He would, on occasion, call me at home. I would answer, say a couple of "OKs" along the way, and then "goodbye." My wife, Ann, would say, "That must have been Mr. Mitchell."

In fact, his nighttime phone calls were legendary. Mitchell could be counted on to attend the weekly staff meeting of The Woodlands Corporation, but his favorite method of communication was the telephone. Individual members of the various Mitchell enterprises could expect numerous calls, both at work and at home, in the evening and on weekends. On a good night, Mitchell would make ten to 15 calls. He would often tell several people to do the same, on the theory that if all were working on a problem, at least one would come up with a solution. Mitchell's employees soon learned to compare notes first thing each morning to make sure that the best-qualified person—rather than several uncoordinated efforts—would address the problem. Occasionally, Mitchell would call someone at home and forget whom he had called or what he wanted to talk about. Mitchell started one phone conversation with the question, "Who is this?" When told, he said, "Sorry, wrong number," and hung up. It's not that Mitchell was forgetful. His mind moves at such speed that it frequently outpaces his mouth.

Mitchell generally assumes telephones are made for talking, but on one occasion he listened. During a staff meeting at The Woodlands office in 1986, a call came in for Mitchell from his assistant, Linda Bomke. He took the call and listened without saying a word and then hung up. He returned to the conference table to say the Challenger had exploded. We all sat there in stunned silence and soon adjourned the meeting.

To really understand George Mitchell the businessman, it is important to know his personal history. The son of immigrant parents, he started with nothing and, through education, work, and vision, wound up one of the richest men in America. In 2003, *Forbes* put his net assets at $1.4 billion.

Mitchell was born in Galveston, Texas, on May 21, 1919, to Mike and Katina Mitchell. That wasn't the name Mitchell's father started with. He was born Savvas Paraskevopoulos in the small mountain village of Nestani near Tripolis in Peloponnesus, where he was "the youngest of four children and his legacy was about a quarter of an acre," George Mitchell said. "And he said, 'The hell with that.' In 1901, he emigrated to the United States through Ellis Island and soon got a job with the railroad."

It was in Utah while laying track that Savvas Paraskevopoulos became Mike Mitchell. George Mitchell over the years has told the story two ways. Since he is the sole source, I will give both of them. When Mitchell's father went to draw his first paycheck, his name also changed. The paymaster said he couldn't spell that Greek name.

Either Paraskevopoulos asked the paymaster his name, was told it was Mike Mitchell, and declared from then on that was also his name. Or, in the second version of the story, the paymaster changed the young man's name to his own.

Mike Mitchell worked for the railroads for four years, then moved to Houston, where he and a partner started a small shoeshine stand and dry cleaning shop. The two made a modest living. Later, the elder Mitchell moved to Galveston and opened the same type of business.

Mike Mitchell was a determined man. He knew what he wanted and went after it. Take his marriage. He saw a picture of a beautiful young woman from Greece in a Tarpon Springs, Florida–based Greek newspaper. So smitten was he that he immediately took a train to

Tarpon Springs, met the woman, who had come to America to marry someone else, and per-suaded her to marry him instead.

"He was really a very interesting person," Mitchell said of his father. "He had a lot of per-severance and he had lots of friends in Galveston. He could hardly speak English at all. He not only could not read or write English, he couldn't read or write Greek. He hadn't been to school a day in his life. But he had an unusual characteristic of getting along with people.

"He was a hell of a gambler," Mitchell said. "He loved playing poker. My momma always raised hell with him. We had no money. But he was a determined soul." Galveston at that time was still recovering from the Great Hurricane of 1900 that killed 5,000 people and dev-astated the town. Prior to that storm, the city had been the leading business center of Texas. It never regained that status, but instead turned mostly to tourism as an economic mainstay. But over the years, until the 1950s, Galveston was a tourist destination with a difference. While Texas was, and is, a generally conservative state, and then, as now, gambling, prostitu-tion, and other forms of vice were strenuously suppressed, Galveston had them all.

According to legend, they were under the control of the Maceo brothers, Sam and Rose—two barbers who gradually took over Galveston Island's vice operations. The brothers were connected to the national mob. They ran nightclubs and gambling halls and extended their protection, for a price, to the prostitution operations. Rose was the inside man and operator. Sam was the outside guy, the person who paid off those they needed to look the other way and to interact with the customers. Their most famous operation was the Balinese Room, a nightclub on piers, which stretched from the Galveston seawall into the Gulf of Mexico. It was connected to the land by a long walkway. It was said that the walkway was just long enough that the fastest Texas Ranger running down it during a raid could not arrive before all the drinking and gambling paraphernalia was tucked away. In many ways, Galveston was a great place to grow up in the pre–World War II years. The youngest of three sons and broth-er to a younger sister, George Mitchell made his summer money catching fish and selling them to local restaurants or to fishermen who had tried their luck and struck out. "Many a time I'd catch a red fish and sell it to a Houstonian for two dollars," Mitchell recalls. The man "would go to the car where his wife was and say, 'Look what I caught.' We'd laugh like hell, but we made good money."

The Mitchells were an unusual immigrant family because all four of the children went to college. His mother was the disciplinarian in the family. "She was very stern, but she was also very good. She died of a stroke when I was quite young. I was 13 and my sister Maria was 11." Shortly before her death, his father had been struck by a car and suffered severe leg injuries, so the decision was made to disperse the children among relatives. "I went to live with my mother's sister and her husband in Galveston. Maria went to live with another sister in Houston. Although my pop couldn't take care of us, we saw him all the time. That's the best we could do because Johnny and Christy had already gone off to school."

Christy, the eldest, went first to what was then Texas A&M College, where he majored in engineering. But after six months, Christy transferred to the University of Texas to study jour-nalism. Johnny also went to A&M but stayed, graduating with a chemical engineering degree in 1936.

Mitchell reports that his mother wanted him to be a doctor, and he had already been accepted into the premed program at what was then Rice Institute in Houston. Mitchell graduated from high school in 1935. His father thought he was too young to go to college at 16, so he spent the following year at Ball High in Galveston, where he took more advanced classes. (He attends reunions of both graduating classes.) In the summer of 1936, Mitchell went to Louisiana to work for his brother Johnny, who had started a small oil and gas production company there. The summer employment derailed Mitchell's mother's hopes for her son, the doctor.

"This is what I want to do," Mitchell remembers thinking after working in the oil fields that summer. "I wanted to be a petroleum engineer and geologist. Rice taught geology but not petroleum engineering. So I decided to go to A&M because it had the best reputation in the country—along with Oklahoma University—in petroleum engineering." Deciding to go to A&M and actually going were two different things. The country was still mired in the Great Depression. Mitchell's father made little money. "The first two years were pretty hard," Mitchell recalls. "I got a little bit from pop. I worked every summer in the oil fields with Johnny, so I was able to survive." Since Mitchell planned a double major of geology and petroleum engineering and saw no way to graduate in four years with a normal study load, he took 23 hours of classes each semester. He also played on the Aggie tennis team for four years. The biggest obstacle Mitchell faced each month was the $29 due for room and board. If the bill fell more than 45 days in arrears he would be kicked out.

When he faced expulsion for his unpaid bill, Mitchell would send a telegram to his father. "I'd say, 'Your son is among the top of the class, but I'm going to get thrown out of school because I can't pay my room and board.' So pop would take that telegram and go and see Sam Maceo. Sam would give him $100 and pop would send me $50 and keep $50."

To earn rent money during his first two years at A&M, Mitchell sold candy to fellow students from his dorm room. But he lived in an athletes' dorm. The football players would raid his candy store and not pay for what they consumed. In his junior year, however, he hit the jackpot. He made arrangements with a San Antonio printing firm to sell personalized stationery to other students, especially lovesick freshmen missing their high school sweethearts. "Those freshmen went crazy, I had a mate in every dormitory. I'd give them part of the commission and I'd keep part. My junior and senior years I was making $300 a month. In fact, when I graduated and went to work for Amoco as a petroleum engineering geologist in south Louisiana my pay was only $155 a month."

Mitchell graduated first in his class at A&M and was hired by Stanolind Oil and Gas Co., which later became Amoco. That stint lasted about 18 months, until the fall of 1941. Like every student at what was then an all-male, all-military school, Mitchell was commissioned an officer in the Army Reserve. He was called to active duty, sent to the Corps of Engineers, and spent World War II building ammunition plants, air fields, and a manufacturing plant for antiaircraft guns, all in Texas and Louisiana.

So how did Mitchell feel about his stateside duty while many of his generation were overseas fighting? Was he disappointed? "No," Mitchell replied. "Why the hell would I want to go out and get killed? I was a second lieutenant from A&M in the Corps of Engineers. Ten percent of my classmates were killed and another 10 percent wounded because the second lieutenants were cannon fodder. No question about it. And I knew it."

Wartime also brought Mitchell a wife, Cynthia Woods. One of twin girls, she was born in New York City, where her father worked in advertising. She came to Texas in 1939 to study at the University of Houston. On Thanksgiving Day 1941, Woods was riding on a train from Houston to College Station, Texas, when she met Lieutenant George Mitchell. They were married two years later, despite the fact that Mitchell wanted to wait until the war was over, afraid that he would leave his new bride a widow. But Cynthia Woods Mitchell prevailed, as she was to do many times in the future, including on the number of children the couple would have. Mitchell is an Episcopalian, Woods a Catholic. They have ten children.

In 1946, a year after the war ended, Mitchell got his discharge from the Army. He had been kept on active duty in order to wind up a number of construction contracts he was supervising. He was offered his old job at Amoco. Indeed, they were anxious to rehire him. But he declined. Others who had been able to stay out of the service during the war were now ahead of him, Mitchell notes. And more to the point, his long-term plan was never to work for someone else.

"I had an old professor named Harold Vance. He was head of the department of petroleum engineering [at A&M]. Harold's philosophy was if you want to work for an oil company you could drive a Chevrolet, be fine, and have a good life. But if you want to go around in a Cadillac, you better go out on your own."

When George was discharged from the Army, he made a deal with six investors. "I would work for them to look for oil and gas. They gave me $300 a month, enough to live on, because I was married and had one child and another on the way. Amoco wanted me back, but I said no. I'm going to be a consultant, even though I only had a year and a half of experience."

Mitchell lured his brother Johnny, who had spent World War II as a combat engineer in Europe and, following his discharge in 1945, had started a small oil exploration company in Galveston, to work with him in Houston. He also tried to get his brother Christy to join the new oil drilling company but was declined. Mitchell described Christy as something of a beachcomber. "I told him he could never make any money in Galveston," Mitchell said. "He replied, 'Any damned fool can make a million in Houston. It takes a real genius to make a living in Galveston.' "

George and Johnny Mitchell had another partner, Merlyn Christie, who was older, had some royalty income, and could survive on their new company's modest earnings. They called their company Oil Drilling. George was the inside man, doing geological work and looking for places to drill. They set up their offices in the Esperson Building in downtown Houston. Johnny, and to a lesser extent Christie, would make the deals. Most of that selling occurred in the ground-floor drugstore of the same building, where brokers gathered each day for coffee. In addition to his own company, George Mitchell also worked as an outside consultant to some of Houston's leading independent oilmen.

"We found a lot of oil and gas," Mitchell said. "We also drilled a lot of dry holes. If we made oil, we'd run to the bank and borrow a little money [to develop the well]. If it were a dry hole, we'd cry a lot. We used a theory that you don't go wildcatting—searching for oil where none had been discovered before—all the time. Out of every five wells, only one wildcat [would be drilled]. The rest ought to be semiproven [locations] where you could do a better job of analyzing the geology [and] have a better chance of winning. And we found a lot of oil and gas for all of [the investors]. They made a lot of money and we were making money."

Over the next few years, Mitchell remembers, as the company's capital increased, Oil Drilling started investing more of its own money in the wells it drilled. Within five years, the company was financing its own searches for oil and natural gas, finally buying out the investors in earlier deals. Then came the deal that sent Mitchell to the big time. And it was all because of a bookie in Chicago and a likable Texas oilman named John Mayo. Through Mayo, Mitchell met Louis Pulaski, a Houston businessman whom everyone addressed as "General." "He wasn't a general at all, but he was a hell of a gambler," Mitchell said. The nickname "general" came from a famous Polish general who had the same last name.

Pulaski and his brother had invested in a number of oil and gas wells drilled by Mitchell and his partners. Now he brought the deal that turned Mitchell's operation into one of the largest independent natural gas companies in the United States.

"He [Pulaski] called me up and told me, 'George, my Chicago bookie has a deal in north Texas. I want you to look at it.' " Mitchell was dubious, wondering how a bookie in Chicago could have a petroleum lease in north Texas that was worth anything. Still he called the bookie. "I started looking at it, and I was like, you know, that's pretty interesting. I think we ought to figure out how to maybe make this work."

Mitchell decided to buy the bookie's geological data about the north Texas field in the early 1950s, giving the bookie a small override on the eventual sale of the gas for bringing him the proposition.

Mitchell's company drilled a test well and sure enough there was natural gas there. Lots of it. But that wasn't the problem. The problem was that the gas was in what petroleum men call a "tight field," meaning that the gas was trapped by dense geological formations and would not flow naturally when tapped by drilling. But new engineering technology had just been developed to fracture the field, so Mitchell's company was able to break up the underground gas formation by pumping water into it and freeing the gas.

Mitchell started buying mineral leases from landowners in the area, mostly with borrowed money. Such leases give the landowner a small payment upfront, with the promise to share in the proceeds of oil or gas when the well is drilled. Knowing that other people in the industry would notice his efforts, Mitchell moved fast, picking up 400,000 acres within 90 days at an average cost of $3 an acre. But finding gas and getting it to someone who wanted to buy it was an entirely different matter. Natural gas in a domestic market must be delivered to its customers through a pipeline. Mitchell fought for two years before finally making a financially advantageous deal with Natural Gas Pipeline of America, which extended its line from the Texas Panhandle to Wise County to take the gas to the Chicago area.

"We have been furnishing Chicago with 10 percent of [its] gas supply for 45 years now. The same pipeline takes up the gas. We've ended up drilling about 2,000 wells in that area and they still have 4,000 to 5,000 locations to go. So it's been a big hit for our company, and very fascinating as to how we ran into it."

Meanwhile, Oil Drilling had gone through several transformations. In 1972, it went public as Mitchell Energy & Development Corporation. The reason for that move was simple, according to Mitchell: As a private corporation, every time the company took on debt, the partners had to personally guarantee the note. "Merlyn Christie had already gotten cold feet [over the note guarantees], so I had proceeded to buy him out because he didn't want any more debt."

At this point in his company's evolution, Mitchell said he faced a tough choice. Either sell out or go public. Through most of the various combinations and permutations of Mitchell's corporate enterprises there was B.F. "Budd" Clark. He came to work for what was then Christie, Mitchell & Mitchell on November 15, 1956. Clark had various titles with the Mitchell enterprises, but his primary task was to be the abominable "no" man to the optimistic Mitchell. Mitchell saw the opportunities. Clark was the inside man, the one who had to find the money to pursue those opportunities. While remaining close friends, the two men often clashed and those clashes were noisy.

Joyce Gay, who served as Mitchell's secretary for years and eventually became his top public relations executive, heard an earful over the years. "I learned a management style that has been to my detriment the rest of my life," Gay told Joe Kutchin, the firm's now-deceased retired public relations vice president, as part of a company oral history project conducted in 1996. "They used to joke and say it was management by decibel," she explained, "and they would scream in the offices, in the halls, everywhere. George and Budd would scream in the hall until Budd had arrived at the four-letter word and then George would yank them all back in the office and shut the door. At one time, they even put soundproof taping around the doors between my office and George's office so that the people outside couldn't hear them. I never thought it was vicious. It was just their style—they'd scream and yell.

"It was Budd and George the most," she recalled. "Then other people had to learn, including me, that if you didn't yell, you never got to say anything. They'd interrupt you in midsentence, and if you let that stop you, you'd never get to tell them what you wanted to tell them. I remember one time when [Mitchell and Clark] were on something really important. One of the lead attorneys with Vinson & Elkins [Mitchell Energy's outside law firm] came out and sat in my office and shut the door between George's office and mine. He said, 'I'm not going back in until they quit yelling.' It was a good five or ten minutes before the rest of them realized he wasn't there."

But Mitchell's temper, seldom displayed outside his office, was far overshadowed by his benevolence. He has given millions to charitable causes over the years. And he's also quick to help others. I can personally testify to that.

In 1993, the International Real Estate Federation gave its Award of Excellence to The Woodlands. That year the award ceremony was held in Jerusalem and George Mitchell suggested that my wife and I go to Israel to receive the award on behalf of The Woodlands Corporation. Ann was not feeling well before we left on our trip, so she visited our family doctor, who told her not to worry.

Four days into the trip, Ann's health continued to deteriorate. I went alone to the Real Estate Federation ceremony and received the award from Shimon Peres, then the foreign minister of Israel. He congratulated me and told the audience he was glad to have the opportunity to meet a representative of such an outstanding real estate development group, since his people had been involved in real estate acquisition and development for 5,000 years.

When I got back to the hotel, Ann was much worse and could not be roused. I called an ambulance and we went to the emergency room at Hadassah Medical Center. She was placed in intensive care and tests were run. I sat through the night in a straight chair in the hall. The next morning I was told that Ann had acute liver failure. She needed a transplant if she were going to survive. As luck or fate would have it, Dr. Eithan Galun, the doctor on duty, was a liver specialist who had trained at Johns Hopkins Hospital in the United States. He suggested that I get Ann to Paris or back to the United States for the transplant. I attempted to use the pay phone in the hall of the hospital, but the operator spoke no English and I don't speak Hebrew. An orderly came to my aid, securing an AT&T international operator who spoke English. I started calling people: my son and daughter, Ann's mother, The Woodlands Hospital, and finally, Clyde Black, the vice president for human resources at Mitchell Energy. He got the ball rolling. Black contacted a vice president at Continental Airlines who put him in touch with Swiss Air Ambulance Service in Zurich, Switzerland, which transports critically ill people. They would not depart Zurich before taking receipt of a $100,000 deposit. George Mitchell immediately authorized the funds. Black also contacted Dr. J. Ballentyne, the special medical director for Mitchell Energy and George's brother-in-law, who started the search for a transplant facility.

Swiss Air Ambulance received special permission to land at Ben Gurion Airport, which is near Tel Aviv. Swiss Air was scheduled to arrive there at 8 p.m. As we were leaving the intensive care unit, Ann was still unconscious on a gurney. Just before we left, the phone rang. It was Dr. Ballentyne in Houston. The liver transplant unit at Houston's Hermann Hospital had agreed to take her.

We left Hadassah in a well-traveled ambulance driven by a young man with a loaded .45 tucked in his belt. The trip back to Houston on Swiss Air took 18 hours with refueling stops in Zurich and Gander, Newfoundland. To keep my mind occupied in this flying intensive care unit, I practiced converting Fahrenheit to Celsius and shekels to dollars. We arrived in Houston at Hobby Airport the next morning and went directly by ambulance to Hermann. I met with Dr. R. Patrick Wood and Dr. Howard P. Monsour who confirmed the very serious nature of Ann's case. She was moved to the top of the waiting list for transplants. Around 4 p.m. the same day, Dr. Wood walked in with a smile and reported a donor organ was available in San Antonio. By midnight Ann was in the operating room. Within several days of her surgery, she regained consciousness. Ann had fallen into a coma in Israel and woke up nine days later in Houston to discover she had a new liver, having no advance knowledge she had liver problems. She came home three weeks later. Ann experienced a remarkable recovery and has led an active, productive life. It was all made possible by George Mitchell's caring nature.

As Mitchell's wealth mounted from Wise Field, he started looking for other opportunities. In the early 1960s, he dipped the company's toe into land development. The oil and gas business is cyclical, and buying land and developing it seemed a way to keep bringing in profits when the price of oil and gas dropped. He wasn't alone. Exxon, one of the largest oil companies in the world, became heavily involved in the real estate business during the same period, buying land and developing large communities in the Houston area.

Knowing of Mitchell Energy's diversification strategy, local brokers informed Mitchell Energy of a possible deal. The Grogan Cochran Lumber Company in Conroe, north of Houston, had about 50,000 acres. Three families owned the timber company. There were more than 90 heirs of the original founders. Over the years, the heirs had seen the timber company stymied by their own disagreements. "They couldn't even buy a pack of cigarettes they were so broke," Mitchell said. "But they had 50,000 acres of land. A lot of people had tried to put [the deal] together before I did."

R.A. "Mickey" Deison, mayor of Conroe at the time of the sale, knew the Grogan family well. The basic problem, he said, was a split between six of the Grogan descendents and their half-brother. The father left half his estate to his son from his second marriage, which set off a massive family feud. "If it were not for that fact," Deison believes, "they would probably not have sold the property and Mr. Mitchell would not have had the opportunity to make that purchase."

It took a year and a half and a lot of tough negotiating, but Mitchell bought the property for $125 an acre. "I figured that was what I could make from the minerals and the surface gravel on the land and the timber cutting," Mitchell said. Through loans, timber sales, and contracts for gravel, Mitchell bought the 50,000 acres with borrowed funds and with the sales paying off the note for the land purchase over time.

Much of the noncontiguous property was in western Montgomery County, north of Houston. About 2,800 acres became part of the future 27,000 acres that now make up The Woodlands. The timber company land was not Mitchell's first real estate venture. Earlier, his company purchased Pelican Island, a mostly undeveloped island with some industry adjacent to the largely residential Galveston Island. Someone else had a deal with the city of Galveston to develop Pelican Island, but it ran into difficulties and a lawsuit. Mitchell stepped in with an offer to settle the lawsuit by taking over development. Before doing so, he negotiated an agreement with Shell Oil Co. to sell them 100 acres of Pelican Island for an offshore oil-drilling base of operations. The Shell money provided the downpayment on the entire deal.

By this time, Mitchell Energy had also started a resort community on the western end of Galveston Island in an area not protected by the seawall that was built after the 1900 hurricane. It was named Pirates' Beach and Pirates' Cove with a nod to pirate Jean Lafitte, who made the island his base of operations from 1817 to 1821 before being driven out by the U.S. Navy. Mitchell had already seen two other resorts in the same area do well. He put together about 30 large parcels of land to develop Pirates' Beach on the gulf side of the barrier island area and Pirates' Cove on the bay side.

What really made the new developments fly was an agreement Mitchell made with the Galveston Country Club, the oldest such club in Texas, having opened in 1899. He acquired some of the land the country club owned in what is now Pirates' Cove and refurbished the facility for the club adjacent to Pirates' Cove, and his company managed the club for a number of years.

The Galveston real estate developments were certainly motivated by profit. But there was another reason Mitchell pursued them. Galveston residents who are BOI ("born on the island") have a fierce affection for and loyalty to their place of birth. It was these same motives that, years later, caused Mitchell to spends millions of his own money to renovate the Strand, Galveston's historic downtown area, and turn it into a center that attracts hundreds of thousands of tourists every year. Mitchell's redevelopment activities have earned him the respect of a majority of Galvestonians. And since no good deed goes unpunished, it has also earned the enmity of a minority of residents who charge Mitchell with trying to buy out the island.

Actually, Mitchell divided his real estate time and attention between The Woodlands and Galveston. Each Friday afternoon, he would travel to Galveston and spend a long weekend at his home at Pirates' Cove. He would return to The Woodlands or his Houston office by noon the following Monday. While on the island he would visit his many personal real estate projects, including the restoration of close to 20 historically significant buildings, in addition to several Mitchell Energy properties, including the San Luis Hotel and Condominium and the west end resorts. Saturday and Sunday mornings were devoted to meetings over breakfast with Galveston leaders to influence the political and civic structure of the island. Following these conversations, George would head to the San Luis Hotel where he would coach Ron Vuy, the hotel's general manager, as well as cooks, bellmen, wait staff, and any other employees. Vuy had the perfect personality to accommodate George's management style. But one Sunday night, I received a phone call at home from Ron and there was panic in his voice. He said Phydias, a parrot that lived in a cage in the lobby of the hotel, seemed to be in bad health. The bird was a gift to George from Dancie Ware, his friend and public relations adviser. The parrot had been affectionately given George's middle name and George was very fond of the bird—thus the reason for Ron's grave concern. Ron said Phydias had collapsed and was resting in a shoebox behind the registration desk. We agreed that Phydias should be given medical attention as soon as possible, but he died later than night. An autopsy was performed at a clinical lab in one of the university-based hospitals in the Texas Medical Center and the cause of death was ingestion of small steel filings apparently fed to Phydias by some evil visitor to the hotel. Later, Phydias II was acquired as a replacement, but I am not sure Vuy ever fully recovered his sense of confidence in parrot management.

With his early Galveston real estate developments off to a flying start, Mitchell turned to another opportunity in 1963. It would become The Woodlands. George Mitchell is the single most important factor in the success of The Woodlands. It was his vision, tenacity, and willingness to risk all the personal wealth he earned in the oil and gas business that made the difference. He purchased the land, assembled the development team, formulated the environmentally responsible development plan, and remained personally dedicated and involved in the community for half of his life.

After 30 years, Mitchell sold The Woodlands, but he remains wedded to its success. Or, as I have said to more than a few people, even though George sold the company in 1997 for millions of dollars, he still thinks he owns it.

Chapter 2

THE HUD EXPERIENCE

———— • ◆ • ————

In 1963, George Mitchell hired Jim McAlister as a financial doctor for Mitchell Energy. Little did McAlister know that he would end up as a key person in the conception of The Woodlands. He wasn't its father. That honor goes to George Mitchell. McAlister had left the company by the time The Woodlands was born, but he was there, providing care during the first vital months and years of the community's gestation.

McAlister went to work for George Mitchell & Associates, one of five names used by Mitchell's organization in its formative years. It started with Oil Drilling and wound up, after going public in 1972, as Mitchell Energy & Development Corporation. McAlister's title was assistant to the vice president, doing oil and gas evaluation and banking. By education, McAlister was well suited to the task. He had master's degrees in both petroleum engineering and finance. His main role was to bring financial discipline to the company such as setting up profit standards for investments and deciding how to spend the money on new ventures.

The company had no formal budget at the time. It had $250 million in assets, massive debt, and no formal method of evaluating potential acquisitions. Instead, McAlister recalls, "It was all done by George Mitchell. You have to remember that George has a lot of unusual qualities. Perception is one of them. But another one is a terrific capacity to recall. Therefore, George is comfortable flying by the seat of his pants. He carries files in his head that most people don't remember are in their file cabinets. The company was operating as a projection of George's personality. Well, we had to come out of that. We were growing. We had to have a budget and better-defined investment criteria."

McAlister was hired just about the time Mitchell purchased the Grogan Cochran land. So why did a reasonably successful oil and gas company buy 50,000 acres of real estate? "It was a heck of a buy," McAlister said in a 1995 interview with Joe Kutchin, Mitchell Energy's public relations man. "You're talking about $125 an acre. So George had one terrific acquisition. George is a man of vision, and he just saw it. I think it was his vision of the coming growth of Houston to the north. It happened to be in real estate and he seized the moment. That is the long and short of it."

Soon after the purchase, McAlister notes, Morris Thompson, a Mitchell vice president, made a deal with Georgia-Pacific to harvest the timber from the 50,000-acre tract. The contract called for thinning the timber, not clear-cutting. It was, McAlister said, "a real estate cut.

We were able to get $5 million for that cut, so now George is sitting with only $1 million invested in 50,000 acres of land, which makes quite an astute investment."

Other than cutting the timber and selling gravel on some sites, which incidentally brought in enough extra money to pay off the land, Mitchell had no specific plans for his new purchase. In several outlying areas, the company developed red flag subdivisions. These are primarily set in rural areas offering roads but no other amenities and are aimed at low- and moderate-income buyers. The name comes from the practice of selling land by the acre, and marking the boundaries of each lot with a red flag. But that still left a lot of land.

"The question," McAlister explains, "then became, what could we do?" An answer began to take shape. One possibility was to "develop a satellite city [to Houston], using one block [of land] close to Interstate 45 just north of the Harris County line. That tract was the core of what later became The Woodlands. Since the growth of Houston was going that way, the thought was to try to develop something up there to capture the growth. But we had not yet considered a concept of a totally integrated new community."

Around the same time, Mitchell's thinking about real estate had changed due to his experience with the Young President's Organization, a nationwide association of company CEOs who examine problems not only within their own companies but also of society as a whole. He took tours with the group to New York City and through the Watts section of Los Angeles. "I came to the conclusion that all our cities were in deep trouble," notes Mitchell, adding, "I said this is not a good way to urbanize America. Let's do something about it."

Mitchell first looked at a 2,500-acre site north of the city at the intersection of Interstate 45 North and Farm to Market Road 1960, which was closer to Houston than is the future site of The Woodlands. However, he let the option lapse when he was unable to buy enough adjoining property. He also tried to buy land in what is now the Kingwood community of Houston but was outbid for the property. Of course, he also had a profit motive. He had learned from the experience of Houston oilman R.E. "Bob" Smith, who was one of Mitchell's early investors in oil deals. Smith had made a fortune in oil and gas. He made another fortune by buying land along Westheimer Road on what was then the western edge of the city. The area is now perhaps best known for the Galleria shopping mall and mixed-use development. Westheimer Road itself is packed with commercial developments for miles.

What was to become The Woodlands was also in a prime spot. It was 27 miles north of downtown Houston. It was close to the main road to Dallas, Interstate 45, and convenient to a new airport—now named Bush Intercontinental—that opened in 1970. Mitchell began assembling more land. He just wasn't sure what to do with it. He added to the land around a small part of the Grogan Cochran tract near Interstate 45, eventually picking up another 17,000 acres. He knew the land was going to be extremely valuable somewhere down the line. And he was able to buy much of it relatively cheaply.

McAlister said they essentially had three choices with that land. They could sell it. (At one point Mitchell received an offer of $80 million for the land from another developer, according to Plato Pappas, an engineer with the Mitchell Energy.) They could partner with a company already in the land development business. Or they could develop it themselves. Of the last two options, however, each had its own problem. Developing the land meant finding someone to lend them the money. Land development isn't cheap. The larger the project, the more money needed, and they were looking at developing more than 17,000 acres. To secure financing for the project did not seem feasible, because, as usual, Mitchell's various enterprises were deeply in debt. This wasn't an aberration. It was Mitchell's philosophy. While many chief executives would get upset if debt grew too big, Mitchell was just the opposite. He believed in debt, believed that it was the only way he was going to grow. But that debt made it difficult to secure loans from banks or insurance companies to get the financing needed for the new community Mitchell envisioned. McAlister said that the company did approach a number of financing sources about loans, with the large block of land as security. Offers for financing did surface, but only with rather large hooks attached. Every offer required that George Mitchell be personally liable for the debt; if the project failed, he and his company would be wiped out. Another stumbling block, according to McAlister, was that all the potential financing sources reserved the right to cut off funding at any time. "They could leave you hung out and they could take back the project through their liens. And that was simply something that we could not live with."

McAlister also tried to find joint venture partners for the development. Mitchell would put up the land, and the partner would provide financing and own part of the project. "I remember one meeting," he recalls, when "we came in with absolutely the sorriest presentation that you ever saw. We just put together some information on the land with economic projections that weren't really thought out. We were trying to get them to. . . recognize the obvious value of the land, the potential of the site, and then step into it with us with financing." It soon became obvious that Mitchell and McAlister had to provide better information about the project if they were going to find a funding source.

In 1966, Mitchell told noted Houston architect Karl Kamrath about his plans for the satellite city. That conversation turned into an engagement for MacKie, Kamrath and Pickford Planning Development Associates. Within a few months, the firm presented Mitchell with a completed plan. It was for a 20,000-acre project and envisioned a total population of 50,000; Kamrath's plan was simply a concept with no market study or a look at finances. It was traditional Houston planning with a central shopping mall surrounded by homes and with light industrial zones on the fringes. While not adopted for the new development, the drawings did help Mitchell understand just how much land would be needed for a new town.

In the late 1960s, Mitchell hired Cerf Standford Ross, a Houston architect, to do some planning for the proposed development. He was paid $50,000 for his efforts. "He [Ross] had recently been involved in New Mexico and Arizona doing houses for [American] Indians," McAlister said. "That's what he did, and he did it with government grants. Cerf developed the first land plan for the development of what was to become The Woodlands, so we could go to Pic Realty and others who could finance the project. We were also working with First Mortgage Co. of Houston to develop other financing sources."

One day, McAlister said, Ross came into his office with information about a new federal program, Title VII, created under the Housing and Urban Development Act of 1970. It allowed the government to offer loan guarantees of up to $50 million for development of a new town. "Everybody we talked to about it said, 'Don't deal with the government,' so we were reluctant. Finally, there were no other alternatives. Cerf and I caught an airplane [for] my first trip to Washington, D.C.," McAlister said. At the time, HUD was still formulating just what they would require of those seeking federal loan guarantees, although they had already given preliminary approval to one proposed new town, which was proposed for a site in Flower Mound, Texas, in the Dallas–Fort Worth area.

To become eligible for a guarantee, HUD required developers to meet a broad range of social goals, most involving affirmative action in jobs and housing in the new towns. The agency had not yet developed any environmental criteria. As we shall see, the environmental planning by The Woodlands was virtually adopted by HUD for all other new towns. The federal agency was still uncertain about financial requirements for those who sought the loans.

It was during the early meetings with HUD that the name "Woodlands" first appeared. Mitchell has always contended that the name came from his wife. When he bought the Grogan Cochran tract he kept about 5,000 acres of it for his own use, building a weekend house for himself and Cynthia; their retreat was named The Woodlands. When it came time to name his new project, Cynthia suggested that they should call it The Woodlands and change the name of their wooded ranch. But The Woodlands name first surfaced in McAlister's office. He and Ross were scheduled to go to Washington to present preliminary plans in quest of a loan guarantee. The architect had been working through the night to get the plans ready. "We had a 7 a.m. plane to catch," McAlister recounts. "Ross called me at about 2 a.m. He was now ready to print. HUD had been very specific. They did not want a satellite community, so the name Satellite City [the working name for the project] had to go away. So we just bounced some names around and we came up with Woodland Village, printed it, and off we went to Washington." The plan Ross developed was quite different from the earlier one by Kamrath. It was also quite different from what was built. The Ross plan, still very much a preliminary one, was submitted to HUD in February 1970. In June, McAlister was told that HUD was interested in the proposal.

However, McAlister said, a HUD official told him that the plan as submitted was simply not going to pass muster. It needed a much greater degree of sophistication. HUD wanted more specifics about land planning, finances, and social goals from a planning team with nationally recognized credentials. In short, it was time for Mitchell to start spending some serious planning money if he wanted that government loan guarantee. He did.

McAlister says that despite the replacement, Ross deserves more than a mention in any account of The Woodlands. He was the person who made Mitchell aware of the possibility of obtaining federal loan guarantees. "Without that, there would be no Woodlands, because there was no other way that we would have ever been financed," McAlister said.

From a Houston architect friend, Glenn House, McAlister obtained a list of nationally recognized architects, engineers, and planners. They also talked to a number of Houston planners and architects. One of them was the well-known firm of Caudill, Rowlett, Scott (CRS), which did eventually do some of the planning for The Woodlands. However, Mitchell decided that the firm was not to be one of the primary planners. But one CRS employee, Robert J. Hartsfield, so impressed Mitchell that he immediately offered him a job as the in-house head of planning and design. There was only one problem.

McAlister explains: "George and I were leaving the next morning for California to interview a number of architectural firms and consultants from the Glenn House list. We needed
somebody to help us grade those architects. I couldn't do it. George couldn't do it. George
said [to Hartsfield], 'You're hired, but you need to be on the plane with us in the morning.' "

Hartsfield managed to do just that. McAlister notes, "Bob was a wonderful asset in select-
ing the team to plan the project." He also provided another huge contribution to the way The
Woodlands looks today. Hartsfield had a degree in urban planning and studied at the
University of Pennsylvania under Ian McHarg, a renowned ecologist and land planner.
Hartsfield urged Mitchell to read McHarg's book, *Design with Nature*. Mitchell did, and it
forever changed his thoughts about what the proposed project should be. He later hired
McHarg as the environmental consultant for The Woodlands—a choice that had profound
consequences.

After several weeks of screening, the consultants for the project were hired. To plan for the
economics and marketing, Mitchell, McAlister, and Hartsfield chose Gladstone Associates of
Washington, D.C. (Robert L. Gladstone had in the past been a consultant to the new town
of Columbia, Maryland.) William L. Pereira Associates of Los Angeles was named to handle
the master planning and design. (Pereira had done the planning and design for the new towns
of Irvine, California, and Dearborn, Michigan.) Richard P. Browne was the engineering consultant for Columbia, and he was added to the team. The first group meeting of these high-
powered consultants was at Mitchell's ranch on October 23, 1970. It was, as McAlister
remembers, a rather contentious one. There were disagreements about who was to do what.
And while the focus was on developing a plan that HUD would accept, there was more to be
learned, especially if building this proposed new town would be financially possible.

"We didn't know the financial answers ourselves," McAlister said. "We didn't know
whether it was an economic go or not, so we may not have needed HUD if it wasn't an economic venture. We still didn't have that answer. In other words, we don't know exactly where
we're going to end up, but we're going forward, which, knowing George, is not hard to understand because that's what he does. He's a very courageous man and he moves forward." Some
of what the Mitchell team needed to learn came from the experience of Jim Rouse and
Columbia. "Jim Rouse was very giving. We sat for hours with him and his staff. The principal point that we found from talking with all those new community people is that they all
had financial problems. They had this huge infrastructure cost. You couldn't sell enough lots
to pay the interest, let alone start paying principal, and therefore they had serious problems.
There were just too many front-end costs. So we had to make The Woodlands financially
viable. For sales purposes, you had to radiate out of a core in concentric circles to maintain
expenses and develop a sense of community for all those people who are there."

Still, McAlister said, the consultants hired by Mitchell were urged to think big. "Now this
was very important. We suggested that the team design to the fullest extent of their imagination. If you stifle someone before they start, they won't think it all the way through. Then you
throw away the unworkable ideas and end up with their best thoughts. McHarg called me
'Cash Flow' because everything had to go through the economic model." This was not always
a popular policy. During one meeting at Mitchell's ranch—George was not present—Pereira

threatened to quit unless he would be given the responsibility to decide what was and was not financially possible. But that wasn't going to happen. "The project," McAlister explains, "had to be economically viable, and it had to be able to exist independent of other Mitchell activities. The planning team was going to be graded at the end on economics. If it didn't make sense, it didn't work."

As we shall see, despite the best planning possible, things don't always work out. Or as new second lieutenants are often warned in the U.S. Army, the map is not the terrain.

Meanwhile, McAlister was lining up help in Washington. Senator Lloyd Bentsen, a Democrat from Texas, was a friend of McAlister's wife's family and his brother-in-law, Denman Moody, Jr., was on Bentsen's staff. Moody also helped to get Senator John Tower, Texas's Republican senator, on board the effort to obtain the HUD grant. Back in Houston, McAlister put together a team to digest the work of the outside project consultants and compile it all into what they hoped would be a winning submission.

The small in-house staff comprised Bob Wyrick, Bob Hartsfield, Charles Kelly, Louis Brasher, David Hendricks, Plato Pappas, and Larry Mahost. "Hartsfield did a lot of the drawings," says McAlister, "but he also did one [other] thing that was extremely important. He set up a critical path flow chart. He was able to put our work tasks in a prioritized time schedule and framework that allowed us to accomplish those things that we would not have done otherwise."

Still there was a huge amount of work to do, and very little time to do it. "The hours we worked were humongous," he adds. "In fact, my family throat doctor was in the building next door. We were tired. We would get sick. In the wintertime we would all have colds and congestion and his cure for your sore throat was gentian violet. They paint your throat with purple stuff and it hurts so bad tears come to your eyes. When we were sick everybody would go over there and get his shot and get his throat painted."

Hendricks, an economist by training who was hired by Mitchell in 1970 and first worked on the company's Galveston projects, was in charge of the social aspects of the planning. The HUD people Hendricks worked with were always more interested in social change than land development. Evidence of this prioritizing, he said, was a visit by a HUD lawyer to the site before The Woodlands proposal was submitted to the agency. Hendricks and Jim Veltman, an environmental planner from McHarg's firm, picked up Laura Crittenden, the lawyer, at the airport and drove to The Woodlands. "There was a grocery store on the way and there was a sign that offered, 'BOUNTY OWLES, 39 cents,' " Hendricks said. "She asked what they were. I said it was an owl found only in these parts and a lot of people like to eat them." Veltman chimed in, saying the owls lived in the bottomland hardwood forest along the flood plains. The local folks, he said, delighted in not only hunting them for their pot, but also to sell them to local stores. The lawyer asked if they were endangered. "I said just a couple more shotguns and they would be gone," Hendricks remembers.

"When I got the draft of the document from HUD [outlining requirements for getting the loan guarantee] it stated on page G-24 of the agreement that, 'The developer will protect bounty owls in the project.' So I called her and said remember about the bounty owls. I have to tell you this: What happened was the "T" fell off that sign. It was 'Bounty towels.' There's no such thing as a bounty owl. There was a long silence and then she said, 'You know what. Let's leave it in there. It will drive people crazy.' I give her credit for her sense of humor."

Years later, *The Villager*, The Woodlands' local newspaper, ran a center page spread on the bounty owl and how bird watchers from around the world were attending a conference in The Woodlands looking for the bounty owl. It was all tongue in cheek, but only to a few who knew the true story.

Eventually, the time came for the final presentation of The Woodlands' plan and application to HUD to obtain the loan guarantee. The whole working group on the loan application submission traveled to Washington, D.C., for the meeting. This time, George Mitchell accompanied them. Until then, he had met with agency officials on their home turf only once. The group met for dinner the night before at a Trader Vic's restaurant. As the group ate, Plato Pappas, the construction engineer on the planning project and a longtime Mitchell employee, told Mitchell something that has entered company lore. It's known as the "turkey story."

As Pappas recounts it, just a few days before the Washington, D.C., trip he had been doing some last-minute work on the engineering studies in the heavily wooded area that was to become part of The Woodlands. While there, he had seen two wild turkeys strutting through the area. Taking out the .22 caliber pistol he carried when out in the snake-filled woods, he killed one turkey and ate it for dinner.

"You killed a turkey?" Mitchell exploded. "I killed a turkey," Pappas replied. "That was my turkey," Mitchell said. "Those turkeys, I grew them from eggs. I took eggs from North Carolina and hatched them on my farm, and when they were good-sized turkeys, we let them loose here in The Woodlands and you killed one."

Pappas said, "George, how in the hell did I know that you had little pullets all over The Woodlands?" Mitchell almost fired the engineer right then and there.

Despite the uproar over the turkey story, the dinner included a discussion about the amount of loan guarantee they should seek from HUD. The agency had only recently granted its largest loan guarantee—$33 million for a new town in Flower Mound, Texas. McAlister wanted the maximum available guarantee, $50 million. Mitchell was not so sure. He was afraid that HUD officials might turn down a request of that size.

McAlister said he was convinced that they could get the maximum loan guarantee. He had compared the scope and finances of Flower Mound to those of The Woodlands. Based on that comparison, McAlister said, The Woodlands deserved the maximum guarantee. "We did a spreadsheet submittal to hand out so that people were able to see how HUD had funded the new communities. It was very obvious that we qualified for the higher number, that $33 million was correct for Flower Mound. But on that same basis, we would deserve something in the range of $50 million." Going into the meeting, Mitchell and McAlister had not resolved their disagreement. The amount of the loan guarantee they should ask for was still up in the air.

"The meeting with HUD was on March 31, 1971. Various members of Mitchell's project group presented facts on plans for saving the ecology of The Woodlands and shaping its social structure. McAlister went last, talking about the economics of the proposed new town: "I had to close and state our request. I said, 'And therefore, we respectfully request $50 million.' Total, total silence for the longest period. Mitchell begins to look around and looks at me with an expression that said, 'Uh-oh.' I was standing at the podium and the silence just went on. I didn't say one thing. If you know about sales, you know that the first person to speak loses. I just stood there and thought, 'God, I'm going to get fired and my life is over, it's done.' "

Finally, the HUD staffer in charge of the meeting spoke up, said it was a very fine presentation and the committee would take the request under advisement. Over the following months, there were additional questions from HUD and some more bargaining. Mitchell's group presented more details in August on the development plan. There was some wrangling between the agency and our group over the number of homes to be built for low- and moderate-income people, with both sides compromising. Mitchell countered with some talk about abandoning the HUD application and getting private financing, but no one on either side of the argument really believed he was serious. And on November 23, 1971, after HUD had accepted a revised financial plan from Mitchell, agency officials gave tentative approval for the $50 million loan guarantee.

With the HUD guarantee essentially in hand, McAlister said, it was then time for the final go or no-go on the project. Again, Mitchell faced three options similar to the ones when the whole HUD process started. One was to build a routine housing development, much like those found all over the country, the kind that are correctly described as suburban sprawl. He would merely need to build a major road and sell lots to developers. There would be the potential for very high profits with minimal risk. Or he could simply sell the land to others. Given the northward trend of housing developments from Houston, Mitchell would have made a nice profit, with considerably less financial risk.

"The third option was The Woodlands," McAlister said. "The internal rate of return on The Woodlands was less than 18 percent. It was a high-risk strategy, and risk has two factors. One is the probability of risk. The other is the severity of risk. The Woodlands had a greater probability of negative result than any of the other options. The worst-case scenario would have been the total loss of the Mitchell Energy & Development Corporation.

"George chose to do The Woodlands and his answer was a simple one. He'd been very fortunate, and he was putting something back into the pot. That's the way he is. My own view is that you can have great success and you can be a Donald Trump, but I don't think that's very much of a compliment to anybody. That's simply being rich and self-serving. George's monument, if he's building one, is reflected in something better for other people."

The success at HUD was to be McAlister's last task for Mitchell. He was, he said, uninterested in the construction that would soon get underway in The Woodlands. He left Mitchell Energy soon after the HUD loan guarantee was obtained to focus his career on land acquisitions for himself and others.

"Because of George, I made millions," McAlister said in an interview late in 2003. "I was a very young man when the project began to grow and [it] began to be recognized as a significant [venture] with great potential. Others in the company would have liked to take over the project. George. . .stood between them and me the entire time, and never once pulled away his support. And because of that, I would fight a bear in the parking lot for George Mitchell."

Chapter 3

LAND ACQUISITION

◆

With a loan guarantee from the Department of Housing and Urban Development assured, the work of completing the land purchases for The Woodlands got underway. Much of the land for the original 17,000 acres in the proposed development was already owned by Mitchell Energy, but more was needed. While the original 50,000-acre Grogan Cochran land acquisition was the genesis of the new town, a number of other land deals were necessary to make it large enough for the kind of development George Mitchell envisioned.

He had started to fill in the missing pieces in 1967. That was the year Charles Lively got the call from corporate headquarters in Houston. Mitchell wanted him to move to Houston from Bridgeport, Texas, but Lively didn't want to relocate. Lively had been in the Wise County town north of Fort Worth since 1954, working for Mitchell. Lively was a land man—the guy who persuaded farmers, ranchers, and other landowners to lease their mineral rights to Mitchell's energy company, which would then drill for natural gas. He and his wife were active in their church and had a lot of friends, and Lively liked both his job and his town.

It took a lot of convincing, but Lively moved to the Houston area for a month to see if he would like it. He never left. Before moving to Houston, Lively had not met George Mitchell. He was not told why Mitchell wanted the land. He just bought it for him. Mitchell knew why he wanted the land. He was putting together what was to become The Woodlands.

In fact, Mitchell had long been involved in the land business. His company had developed two beach resorts on Galveston Island, done industrial development on nearby Pelican Island, and partnered with a Houston homebuilder, Pacesetter Homes, on several subdivisions. As part of a company-sponsored oral history project published in the late 1990s, Mitchell explained his reasoning:

"There was a downturn in domestic energy, with the huge imports of oil in the 1960s. Our proration [the number of days per month the company was allowed by the Texas Railroad Commission, which regulates oil and gas production in the state, to pump from its wells] was down to eight days per month, so we thought, well maybe we could do something else, too."

In 1963, Mitchell purchased the Grogan Cochran tract. About 2,800 acres of that tract eventually became part of The Woodlands. At the time, Mitchell purchased the property only because it was a good buy. "I could pay for it out of the timber production, out of the gravel. I hadn't even thought about The Woodlands at that time. I knew the land was close to

Houston and it was beautiful land. The Grogans had bought it between 1903 and 1905, never paying more than $3 an acre. They didn't buy any wetlands. It was all high land. They weren't paying $3 an acre for a piece of swamp."

About the same time, Mitchell said, he tried to buy a large tract of land that later became part of another planned community in the Houston area called Kingwood, but that deal fell through. It was about that same period, however, that Mitchell's idea about land, housing, and the way people lived began to change. Much of that change came about because of Mitchell's involvement in the Young Presidents Organization (YPO). The group is composed of chief executive officers who are 44 years old or younger when they join. Their corporation must have a net worth of at least $10 million.

As part of its educational efforts, the YPO sponsored field trips to the Bedford-Stuyvesant area of Brooklyn and Watts in Los Angeles in the 1960s. "I was impressed with the fact that all our cities were in trouble," Mitchell says of his travels to inner-city America. "New York, Detroit, Washington, Cleveland—they were all being destroyed. The concentration of the disadvantaged and the flight to the suburbs of the middle-class whites were destroying our cities. How do you turn it around? I can't turn it around, but I can set an example. Let The Woodlands be designed to show the country you can do it better."

Before moving back to Houston, and despite his 13 years with various Mitchell enterprises, Lively had never met his boss. His contact had always been through Mitchell's brother, Johnny. And it started with a hot dog stand.

Lively grew up in Palestine, in east Texas, and graduated from high school midterm in January 1947. "When I graduated, a friend of mine who I played football with decided that we should go to Galveston and see if we could find a job down there during the summertime," Lively said in Mitchell Energy's oral history project. "I happened to be the brother of Maureen Pine, who married Alleyne Pine's brother, Ralph Pine." Alleyne eventually married Johnny Mitchell. "When they heard my friend and I were in Galveston, they said to go and visit Johnny, that he might have something for us to do."

He did. At that time, Lively said, Johnny was very much a figure in Galveston. He always wore short khaki pants, was very tan and outgoing, drove a maroon 1946 Ford, the same colors sported by his school, Texas A&M University, and was just getting started in the oil business. Johnny was also pals with the Maceo brothers, the operators of Galveston's vice industry.

"Johnny had these two little places out on the beach where he sold cold drinks, beer, hot dogs, and hamburgers." Johnny had named them, "Come and Get It," Lively said. "My friend and I went to work for him out there on the beach. We enjoyed it so much that summer that we came back the following summer and did the same thing. We just enjoyed meeting all the pretty girls in bathing suits." During the winters, Lively attended Henderson Junior College on a football scholarship. The Korean War ended Lively's education and summer fun. He enlisted in the Air Force.

In 1954, Lively was discharged from the Air Force and went back to Palestine. Johnny sent word to him to come to Houston, where he and his brother George were in the oil business. When he arrived at the Mitchells' office, Johnny Mitchell was tied up in a meeting and the receptionist told him to fill out a job application. Lively figured Johnny wanted him back selling hot dogs on the Galveston beach. Instead, despite his complete lack of experience, Johnny told Lively he wanted him to be a land man.

Then as now, land men are vital cogs in the oil and gas business. They are the guys—and in those days it was always men—who go out and make the deals with landowners to lease mineral rights beneath the surface. They must have the technical knowledge to figure out the confusing and arcane land records found in county courthouses—in Texas there are 254 counties. But their toughest task is convincing landowners that the deal on offer is a fair one. The most important attribute for a land man, Lively said, is his ability to communicate with other people and secure their trust, even though he's negotiating hard to get the best deal possible for his employer. Petroleum executives swear by good land men. Landowners on occasion have been known to swear at them. Lively spent six months in Houston learning how to access records. Then he was sent to Bridgeport in north Texas to help Mitchell sew up the natural gas fields that ultimately made him a rich man.

Or as another land man once said, "You can't be a good land man unless you know the territory. And you can't know the territory unless you've been in every beer joint." If you should happen to meet hundreds of land men, one thing you're most likely to find is a folksy nature. Land men have to be able to meet someone and become instant friends.

Lively found a tough situation in Bridgeport and surrounding Wise County. Lone Star Gas Co. dominated the region. It had the only pipeline capable of moving gas to large markets. Lone Star wanted to buy Mitchell's gas on its terms. Mitchell was determined to hold out until he could get a better deal. He did, eventually with Natural Gas Pipeline of America. But for two years, Mitchell drilled wells and found plenty of natural gas, but couldn't extract it. He had no way to sell the gas, given his dispute with Lone Star. During this period, the landowners saw no revenue from the wells on their property.

The Lone Star episode, however, was the exception to the rule. Most Mitchell interests were ultimately successful in holding on to the leases when landowners could not see revenues from them, Lively believes, because his employees became part of the local community. "We went to church with them, socialized with them. We became their friends, and as a result, we were very successful in being able to lease land and get some pretty good deals. . .so we could shut in the gas wells till a market was available.

"During that time, Christy, Mitchell & Mitchell [as the company was known then] held an open house in Bridgeport with a big picnic and barbecue. Johnny Mitchell was the public relations man for the company and he met with many of the local landowners. They really fell for Johnny. [They] liked the way Johnny talked, down to earth. We got a market for the gas, and signed a good contract with Natural Gas Pipeline of America."

Soon after the pipeline deal was made, Lively was summoned to Houston. In October 1967, he and his wife moved there on a one-month trial basis with the proviso that he could go back to Bridgeport if he didn't like his new location. Lively found that Mitchell wanted him to do more than deal mineral rights. Lively's new job would be to buy the land itself. That presented no problems, he said: "When you're working oil and gas or real estate, you're still dealing with land. Learning who owned the title to the minerals under real estate would be about the same as determining the owner of the land itself."

By the time Lively relocated to Houston, Mitchell had already bought the Grogan Cochran land that would form the nucleus of The Woodlands. (Part of that tract, now contained in one of the seven villages of The Woodlands, has a history going back to the Texas Revolution of 1836.)

"I thought I was just going to be here to fill in a few pieces, probably for the Grogan Cochran acquisition that was 50,000-plus acres. And sure enough, those were the first things I did. And I happened to meet up with people who owned some of what Mr. Mitchell considered to be very important acreage and adjacent to The Woodlands area," Lively recalls. He became friendly with these landowners, quickly learning that they would like to sell or trade land with Mitchell. "I sat down with them, found out exactly what they would consider doing. I worked out something they thought would make sense and then I came back to the Houston office."

When George Mitchell learned of Lively's report, he said he wanted Lively to come in and talk with him. "Well, I went in and met with him and gosh, he was treating me like some very important person. George says, 'I want a phone put in Charles Lively's car so if we need to we can communicate.' "

Mitchell next gave Lively a very difficult job, but one that proved vital to the future of The Woodlands. The original purchase of the Grogan Cochran land contained only about 2,800 acres in the area designated for the development of the new town. The original plan for The Woodlands called for 17,000 acres. It ultimately grew to 27,000 acres. Some of the land Mitchell needed to acquire was in large tracts. The Champion Paper Company owned one tract of 1,000 acres, for example, which became part of The Woodlands. Mitchell acquired that land by swapping it for property he owned in southern Montgomery County. Each parcel was appraised and Champion got 2.7 acres of land for every acre of land on The Woodlands site.

However, many of the 200 additional tracts of land and 100 tracts of mineral rights that Mitchell wanted for The Woodlands were quite small. "I found some of these little five-acre tracts that were part of something they called the Old McDonald Subdivision out here that they subdivided for the minerals," explains Lively. "It was a heck of a project trying to track down [the individual owners]. They might have died and left their heirs the land. Or they might have died intestate, without a will, and you would do [deed] searches until you were almost ready to give up. And finally you would get a lead. There was a lot more [to the process] than anyone realized, including George Mitchell."

The other problem Lively faced was that his boss didn't have a lot of money to buy land. One of the reasons Mitchell decided to go into the property development business was as a counterweight to the highly cyclical nature of the oil and gas business. He hoped that when oil prices were down, real estate would provide the cash flow. And vice versa. But both businesses also have a similar drawback. They require big upfront investments. And the payoff can be years in the future. (It was this problem that ultimately got Mitchell and his company into a tremendous cash bind.)

Lively also had to cope with rising expectations among landowners. They knew Mitchell was acquiring land. They were not sure why he was buying. Even Lively did not know the real reason until much later. As Mitchell bought more and more land, the adjacent landowners realized that something was up. And that something was increased land value. "The last parcels of land we got cost us a lot of money," Lively admits. "You know that's just the way things happen." Still, in most cases, Mitchell made no effort to disguise his identity in purchasing the land. Lively's greatest service in helping Mitchell assemble the land for The Woodlands was the way he made the purchases.

He went to Mitchell Energy's legal department and told them he wanted a simple option agreement to present to landowners wherein all option monies would apply to the price of the land. "I'd get six-month options, and where they wouldn't go that long, three-month options. And maybe I'd pay $100 down for the option to purchase the property and at a fixed price per acre. George had people downtown who would take the options on the acreage he was trying to acquire and go to different banking institutions to line up financing for the downpayment if I exercised the options. The deal usually required Mitchell to pay 10 percent down on the property—with that money coming from a bank loan—and the landowner would be paid the balance over ten years, or five years in the case of the five-acre tracts."

Regardless of the good deals the company made, the land purchases were still eating its cash. Mitchell had always believed in operating on someone else's money. The company was highly leveraged. The land purchases were only adding to the problem of high loan-to-asset ratios with steadily growing interest. Oil and natural gas production typically accounted for 80 percent of the company's revenues, even when The Woodlands became prosperous. But it seemed to the oil and gas guys that every time they looked around for money to expand their operations, land acquisitions had sucked up what was available.

"One day I went into [corporate headquarters at] One Shell Plaza, after the real estate division moved to The Woodlands and George was still downtown. Budd [B.F. "Budd" Clark, vice chairman of the Mitchell company] saw me with my briefcase and he said, 'Damn it, Lively, what are you going to do today? Are you going to buy downtown today?' I laughed and said, 'Budd, we're not involved in downtown at all.' And he said, 'Why don't you tell me that you're going on a trip around the world. We'd be a lot better off to send you on a trip around the world and hope you don't come back for two years.' "

Needless to say, with hundreds of options floating around, buying all that land got a little complicated. Lively said he submitted every option to the company's central records department, though he never really trusted the system. After all, this was well before companies started using computers. He kept a simple calendar on his desk. "If I had strictly relied on [the central records], we would have missed a few of them. Normally, when you have so many options, you would think that you're going to goof up on one of them and fail to timely exercise it or give notice. But not one did we ever miss."

The thorniest land purchase came not on property in The Woodlands but just outside of it, across Interstate 45. Almost all of The Woodlands is on the west side of the highway, which stretches from Houston to Dallas. And the west side was also the site of a proposed regional mall, a large project developed by Mitchell in partnership with Homart that would provide convenient shopping for residents not just of The Woodlands, but also much of north Houston and Montgomery County. Access to the mall site wasn't a problem for motorists driving southbound. They could get off and drive along the existing frontage road. Northbound traffic from Houston was another matter.

Richard P. Browne, an engineer and planner who has had an on-again, off-again relationship with The Woodlands for decades and was on the staff at that time, fought hard for an easy way for northbound shoppers to get to the proposed mall.

Browne knew that the Texas Department of Highways and Public Transportation would be willing to build a jug handle overpass into the shopping mall from land on the east side of the highway. But the department wouldn't buy the land. It was up to Mitchell to provide it.

There was a ten-acre site on the east side of Interstate 45, which would provide just enough land to build the overpass. Dean Couch, a local mortgage company owner, had the deed on the property Mitchell needed. But Mitchell and Couch had never gotten along very well.

At a meeting, Browne recalled, "I brought up the proposed land purchase and everybody at the meeting seemed shocked. There was an attitude that we had enough land. And I said, 'No, we'll never get a mall if we don't have those ten acres.' The response was, 'It belongs to Dean Couch. He'll never sell it to us.' "

Browne said he was told to forget about buying the ten acres. But at a meeting a month later, he again brought up the purchase. "And George Mitchell, to his credit, said, 'Wait a minute. Tell me again why we need it.' " Browne told the group that after looking at every potential shopping center site from the Houston city limits northward to the town of Conroe he found many better sites for a mall than the property in The Woodlands. Without that jug handle overpass to entice shoppers driving north on Interstate 45, there would never be a mall built in The Woodlands, he concluded. Mitchell gave Browne the go-ahead to try and acquire the necessary land.

Couch, like Mitchell, was a hard bargainer. "I thought it would be a mistake if Dean Couch felt that Mitchell wanted to buy that [land]," says Lively, who helped Browne on the Interstate 45 deal. He knew Mitchell wanted it and would likely pay any price for it. Lively asked a real estate broker friend to find a straw man buyer, one from outside the country. "We found a guy [in Mexico City] who had a lot of investments. He came up here and he was coached on what he was supposed to do in making the approach to Dean, that he wanted to buy it for an investment. And the bottom line is we wound up acquiring that piece of land in that manner. When it finally closed, Dean found out that we got it. I understand he threw a hissy fit about it. . .that he got tricked into something he didn't intend to do."

Couch may have been unhappy, but after the purchase went through, Lively said, there was great jubilation at Mitchell headquarters. Some of the planners threw a party for Lively. They gave him a gift, a very large bottle of whisky, with a jug handle on it. However, Dean Couch got his revenge. Later on, Mitchell wanted to expand The Woodlands to the south. There was a large tract of land there and it was up for sale. But Mitchell didn't move fast enough. Couch came in and bought the land and developed part of it on the fringes of The Woodlands.

Lively was not the only land man who bought property for The Woodlands. In 1977, Mitchell hired Tom Ledwell, because of his experience buying parcels for the Texas Parks and Wildlife Department, as well as at the state's highway department. Mitchell, himself, also did some of the negotiating, including one of the most vital pieces, the 4,000-acre Sutton-Mann tract. The land, co-owned by a Waco cotton broker and an east Texas banker, was rectangular with its shorter boundary on Interstate 45 and extending westward through what is now the heart of The Woodlands' Town Center. It included land now used as a right-of-way for the town's principal east-west thoroughfare, The Woodlands Parkway. That purchase was vital for the proposed development. Without the frontage on Interstate 45, much of the property would have had no access to the highway. Robert Mann, the east Texas banker, drove a hard bargain for the property. Mann wouldn't deal with anyone but the top guy, so Mitchell had to do the negotiating and that took three years. The portion of the land bordering Interstate 45 sold for 50 cents a square foot. Mann also insisted that he be given the right of first refusal if land was sold for a new bank in The Woodlands. Without the Sutton-Mann property, the development of The Woodlands principal commercial area, Town Center, would have been problematic.

G. David Bumgardner, who started work at Mitchell Energy as a mailroom employee at age 18 and after years of night school became a senior attorney, remembers the negotiations with Mann. "Mr. Mitchell went with us to meet Mann one Sunday afternoon at. . . Intercontinental Airport [in Houston], from which Mr. Mann was scheduled to depart shortly, a fact he kept reminding us of throughout the meeting. Several hours of intense negotiations ensued, during which Mann got so animated, he literally fell out of his chair. Mr. Mann finally gave Mr. Mitchell an ultimatum. Either make the deal the way he wanted it or he was walking out to get on his plane and leave. Mr. Mitchell said no, and Mann and his entourage stomped out of the room, only to return a few minutes later to sign the deal on terms acceptable to Mr. Mitchell."

Mitchell also was directly involved in buying 1,078 acres from the Roman Catholic Diocese of Galveston-Houston. The dickering for that land started in December 1967 and the final papers weren't signed until March 8, 1970. That purchase led to a disagreement years later. The diocese agreed to sell its tract before development started in The Woodlands, but they knew Mitchell planned to build some housing on it and they wanted to keep 67 acres for a future school and church.

Ledwell recalls that while they wanted the land, they didn't know where they wanted it. "So they said at the end of ten years, if they had not picked the spot, then it would automatically become the most northwesterly 67 acres in the block. At the end of ten years they had not made their election and so that's what it became. Unknown to anybody, including the Diocese and The Woodlands Corporation, the 67 acres were in the creek bottom of Panther Creek. When the church leaders found out just what their 67 acres contained, some of the members of the Diocese charged that Mitchell had cheated them, despite the fact they themselves had made the selection. Ultimately, the dispute was settled. The Woodlands wanted the 67 acres to improve drainage on Panther Creek. The disputed land was swapped for 67 acres elsewhere in The Woodlands. But Ledwell, a Catholic, who negotiated the deal, said that dispute "was sufficiently heated that I felt maybe I was going to have to join the Baptist Church."

The acquisition of land didn't stop when The Woodlands started, and it has never stopped. When the first construction started, The Woodlands contained 17,000 acres. Today, it's

27,000 acres. The Woodlands Corporation had a good reason to buy more land. They had established an excellent brand name. People wanted to live and work in The Woodlands. The more land they had, the more they could sell. But there were constraints to buying more property. Naturally, as The Woodlands prospered, the land around it became more valuable. The developer found itself paying an ever-higher price for land, which affected the profitability of the development. And there were those, seeing the success of The Woodlands, who figured they could make more money developing the land around it than they could by selling it to the primary developer. This change of strategy led to a series of poorly planned and visually unattractive projects near the community.

The last big land acquisition was for what eventually became the seventh village of The Woodlands. (It is the only undeveloped village in the community at the time of this book's publication.) It really came about almost by accident. The seventh village will be the only one in Harris County, the home county for the city of Houston. The land was originally bought to build a lake on Spring Creek, the boundary between Montgomery and Harris counties. Dick Browne convinced George Mitchell that the creek should be dammed to create a lake on the southern boundary of The Woodlands. The lake would enhance land values along the waterfront, not only in The Woodlands but also for surrounding land owned by others. In February 1978, Browne convened a meeting of adjacent property owners to try to convince them they should donate land for the lakebed. He wasn't successful. There were many small tracts owned by individuals who just didn't see how the lake would help them, especially because much of their land would be on the bottom of the lake.

"So we went back to George and told him we just couldn't spring this deal with donations," Ledwell said. "And Mitchell replied, 'Well, just see if you can buy the land.' We started on that project, expressly to build a lake. As the years went by, the cost to construct a lake got greater and the government's [environmental] regulations become more stringent. Eventually the lake project was abandoned. But by the time it was, we had acquired enough property [beyond the flood plain] that it made sense to take it a step forward and develop a village."

Over the years, out tracts—small parcels of land completely surrounded by The Woodlands—were also purchased. In 1982 there were approximately 900 acres of out tracts, but by early 2004 all but about 200 acres had been purchased by The Woodlands Corporation. "And we usually paid a very handsome price for those tracts."

While buying large tracts of land often involved tough negotiations, it was the small owners who often presented the greatest challenge. One small piece of property took Ledwell to San Antonio. The owner had bought the surface of the land but owned only one-sixteenth of the mineral rights. Under Texas law, the surface and mineral rights are often sold separately. In local courthouse records, Ledwell found the names of the owners of the mineral rights and that they lived in San Antonio, but no way to contact them. "I spent three days over there and tried everything. I couldn't find anything on them. Finally, I went to the public library and checked through city directories, year by year, over a period of 25 years. When they quit appearing in the city directory, I presumed they had died."

Ledwell went to the courthouse and found no probated wills, which might have listed the heirs. He checked the files of the two local newspapers and found no obituaries. Finally, he went to the Texas Department of Vital Statistics. Records of deaths are not open in Texas. But the clerk at the department did tell Ledwell the name of the funeral home that had buried the mineral owners. He called the funeral home and discovered that the mineral owners were African American. "The reason there were no obituaries was [the newspapers] didn't print obituaries for black people in those days. But the lady who owned the funeral home had been there for 40 years. She gave me the names of all the known heirs. They were scattered across Oklahoma. I sat down that night and called each and every one of them and cut a deal on the telephone. That sort of thing is an adventure."

A 90-acre tract purchased from a local bank presented Ledwell with another challenge. According to Ledwell, "It turned out the mineral [rights] owner was none other than the Jimmy Swaggert Ministries. The lady who inherited the minerals had donated them shortly before her demise. And so we sent Lynn Wingert, who used to work for Stewart Title Co., over to Baton Rouge to meet with representatives from Jimmy Swaggert Ministries. She said she got off the plane and there was a white Cadillac with longhorn steer horns mounted on the front and a little fat guy got out of the car with a white suit and a white Stetson and she said she thought Boss Hogg had come to pick her up. But she negotiated the purchase."

Lively, who retired in 1986, and Ledwell, who left the company in 2004, still look back with pleasure and affection on their work in making The Woodlands possible. Lively said he read in an airline magazine several years ago where Mitchell was talking about the success of The Woodlands. "He said, 'Well, number one, we have a good location and we've had excellent land planning. We've had outstanding acquisitions.' Then George told who did the original planning. . .and so on. Then they asked, 'Who did your land acquisitions? George replied, 'I did it. Me and one other man.' I took a copy of that [statement] and sent it back to George and I said, 'Who was this other man? He must have been a hell of a person.' Well, George certainly had more to do with it than anyone else. Without George, it would never have been done."

Chapter 4

PLANNING AND THE ENVIRONMENT

———— •◆• ————

W hen the first prospective residents moved to The Woodlands late in 1974, they found the beginnings of a new town that seemed very different from other real estate developments in the Houston area. Certainly the plan had the usual streets, thoroughfares, houses, and shopping areas. The difference was how all those elements fit together. The Woodlands' designers showed a respect for the environment and social interaction for residents not typical of suburban developments at the time.

When George Mitchell hired outside consultants to help his in-house team plan The Woodlands, he went after some of the top names in the country. The results of that effort were immediately apparent. In the long run, the design, construction, and attention to detail contributed to one of the most successful new towns in the nation, not only in sales but also in the continuing satisfaction of its inhabitants.

The most striking feature of The Woodlands came about because of the decision to preserve the forest and make the community's name more than just real estate hype. From the very first, planners set aside 25 percent of the total land area (the HUD project agreement required 23 percent) and declared it off-limits for building. These lakes, golf courses, forest preserves, parks, and natural wooded buffers between developments give The Woodlands a very different look than that of the typical suburban development.

Among Mitchell's first hires were the engineering consultant Richard P. Browne and William Pereira, a distinguished urban planner and architect from California. Browne originally built his business in Wayne, New Jersey, where he also served as mayor for a number of years. He headed up a team of engineers, planners, and architects he founded in the 1950s. Within a few years it had climbed to 186th on *Engineering News Record*'s top 500 consulting firms in the United States. In the early 1960s, Browne's firm was the engineer for a large regional shopping mall built by the Rouse Company of Baltimore, Maryland. "The Rouse Company was impressed with our performance and they invited me to come to Columbia, Maryland, where they had just acquired 11,000 acres to build a new town," Browne recalled in an interview for the Mitchell Energy & Development Corporation's oral history project. Jim Rouse, the founder of the company, hired Browne's firm to assist in the final planning, engineering, governmental approvals, construction, and management necessary to build the new town. Columbia opened 18 months later.

After that experience, Browne said, he decided he wanted to concentrate on new town planning. "From Columbia, Maryland, I went to St. Charles, another new town in Maryland, then [to] Flower Mound near Dallas. Later came Granada up in Rochester, New York. We were the prime consultants providing most of the technical planning, engineering, and feasibility studies," Browne said.

Browne was and is a different kind of urban planner. "I told Jim Rouse that if [Columbia] was just going to be a collection of subdivisions, I wasn't interested." Browne's philosophy about how a new town should be built was heavily influenced by Robert Ardrey's book *African Genesis*. "I read that and became entranced by the information on genetic propensities that remain inherent in us today. As a result of the evolutionary forces on our lifestyle over several million years, we still carry a lot of genetic traits that shape our behavior and response even today." Another book by the same author, *The Territorial Imperative*, outlined the human relationship to space and crowding, Browne said. "I was really impressed with what this knowledge could add to the design of built environments. I came to call this the fifth dimension of community planning." By the time Browne met Mitchell he had moved his planning business to Columbia and, along with others connected to the Rouse Company, was holding a series of new town seminars to share his experience with other people who might want to build new communities. "George Mitchell, I believe, came to one of those seminars in which I was usually a speaker. We went to dinner and he said he had assembled some land north of Houston and would like to talk about it more." Later, at another seminar held in the new town of Reston, Virginia, the two men met again. "That was an interesting day for me. George invited me to play tennis. It was a long, hard set, which George won. He then retained my firm. We came to Houston to do the engineering feasibility on drainage and transportation for The Woodlands and then to sit in with [environmental planner] Ian McHarg and others to start to brainstorm on how to develop the new town.

"George used to say, 'I have the best from the East and the best from the West [Bill Pereira].' He put the two of us together to argue through what the town should be. I always have felt proud that [Browne's team] won the battle. Pereira wanted to do a linear commercial urban center like a main street that would go from east to west and the residential development villages would be behind and off that main street.

"He used FM 1960, a conventionally developed residential and commercial area south of The Woodlands, as a model. I opted for continuation of the Columbia concept, which called for a number of self-contained villages off a hierarchy of town roads that would both provide access to the villages and separate them one from another."

"Pereira was following the traditional Texas development pattern like FM 1960. And he was saying, 'That's what Texas is used to, that's what Texans would like, and that's what they expect.' " Browne argued for village centers surrounded by a variety of housing in a series of self-contained communities where people wouldn't "feel lost in a sea of suburban sprawl."

While not diminishing the role of Browne, Pereira and many other accomplished urban planners, landscape architects, and ecologists described elsewhere in this book made significant contributions to the overall quality of planning and design of The Woodlands. With a project of this magnitude and duration, the final plan for the new community actually evolved over the life of the development period. Planning was a process of the dynamic tension arising out of the discussions and disputes among talented professionals. Bill Pereira was a talented and highly respected planner and architect with notable credentials. He died in 1985, so we were unable to interview him about his view of the early planning process.

Just how did that planning theory work out in practice? Let Robert Heineman explain.

Heineman is an unusual urban planner. Planning professionals often lead nomadic lives. Planners move as jobs are completed and new opportunities arise in different parts of the country. Heineman has been at The Woodlands as a planner since 1971, spending almost his entire career in one place. He also has the distinction of having once been fired by The Woodlands Corporation and not knowing it for several years.

Heineman has another unique claim. Over the years, The Woodlands has hired many individuals and planning firms. Of all those hired as part of the original team, either as consultants or on staff, Heineman was the only one still employed by the company as of the writing of this book.

He wasn't supposed to be. Heineman, a graduate of both Rice University and Harvard, took a summer job in Washington, D.C., in 1967 and rented a house from a student at George Washington University named Bill Clinton. He first came to work on The Woodlands' planning team in 1971, three years before the community opened. In 1973, the development corporation was facing tough times, thanks to an unstable national economy and internal management changes. Soaring gasoline prices, brought on by the Oil Producing and Exporting Countries (OPEC) decision to boycott western economies, had brought both suburban residential and commercial sales of land to a standstill. As part of the original team of planners, Heineman was also a victim of the "old-guy syndrome." Mitchell had brought in a team of executives from other master-planned communities to help build and sell The Woodlands. The new guys brought in their own people. Due to the economic downturn, layoffs were inevitable.

"There were three junior people in planning at that time," Heineman recalled. "There was me, there was James Marshall, who was a six-foot-seven-inch architect, and Scott Mitchell, the son of the owner of the company. You can imagine I did not attract as much attention [as they did]. As the story goes, everyone in the company knew that I was going to be laid off that Friday. Everyone, except me. The pink slip never came." Several executives in the company had interceded and saved Heineman's job.

As Heineman and others have pointed out, The Woodlands is not just a planned community. It is a master-planned community. There are many of them nationwide, and more than a handful in the Houston area. Of course, all real estate developments—residential, commercial, or industrial—are planned in one way or another. What's different about The Woodlands is the comprehensive way it was planned. While The Woodlands' planning effort differs little from the kind of painstaking work seen in similar master-planned communities around the nation, it was very unusual for Houston at the time. One might even call it the "Un-Houston."

Another of the original consultants hired by George Mitchell was famed ecologist, landscape architect, and urban planner Ian McHarg, who was also chairman of the University of Pennsylvania Department of Landscape and Regional Planning. Retained early in the planning process, he had a huge impact on Mitchell's vision for The Woodlands. His book *Design With Nature* was considered by many as the best blueprint around for designing new communities with the least impact on the natural landscape. McHarg was, to put it lightly, not beloved among real estate developers. In his book, he railed against developers who put profit before nature. In person, the Scottish-born McHarg, with his tweed jackets and bushy mustache, could be intimidating. He was known for his pronouncements on the perfidy of man against nature. An example can be found in his seminal book:

"Let us abandon the self-mutilation which has been our way and give expression to the potential harmony of man-nature. The world is abundant; we require only a deference born of understanding to fulfill man's promise. Man is that uniquely conscious creature who can perceive and express. He must become the steward of the biosphere. To do this he must design with nature."

Despite his views, or perhaps because of them, Mitchell liked McHarg and that was what counted. The same could not be said of all the members of The Woodlands team. They had looked, with some trepidation, at other parts of his book where he described land merchants like themselves as people whose ethos "sustains the slumlord and the land rapist, the polluters of rivers and the atmosphere." They, and especially Mitchell, saw that heeding McHarg would offer pluses as well as minuses. They believed that preservation of the forest and underbrush that covered much of The Woodlands site would serve as a tremendous selling point. They also realized that the relatively flat terrain of The Woodlands, if not developed correctly, would subject future residents to a persistent Houston problem: That flat land combined with heavy rains, especially during hurricanes and tropical storms, often results in extensive flooding. Keeping the trees and avoiding that flooding would turn out to be an important selling point in the future. The forest and its green floor would provide both a beautiful setting for the community and a natural flood barrier.

McHarg certainly agreed. In a 1975 article in *Landscape Architecture* on the master plan for The Woodlands, he said that the ecological studies he did for Mitchell "were contracted less with a profound conviction of their necessity than as a concession to public environmental consciousness."

Mitchell's interest in protecting the environment did not start with The Woodlands. His viewpoint about protecting the environment is instinctive, a trait often found in farmers, ranchers, and owners of large landholdings. Taking care of critters and their environment is just the right thing to do. A story related to me by Terry Hershey and Hanna Ginsburg underscores George's longstanding interest in environmental issues before The Woodlands got underway. In the late 1960s, Mitchell served as president of the Buffalo Bayou Preservation Association and Hershey and Ginsburg served on its board. By way of background, Buffalo Bayou is a stream that flows from west to east through the city of Houston. Its downstream portion, east of downtown, has been dredged and enlarged to create the Houston Ship Channel, one of the nation's busiest seaports. Upstream and west of downtown, Buffalo

Bayou had been left in its natural state as a beautiful, wooded stream meandering through residential neighborhoods. It occasionally overflowed its banks during torrential rains common to the region. The common practice of the U.S. Corps of Engineers in those days—and sometimes even today—was to design a flood control plan to clear, straighten, excavate, and construct a concrete lining for Buffalo Bayou, much to the dismay of homeowners whose homes backed up to the beautiful wooded stream.

George Mitchell and the Buffalo Bayou Preservation Association set out to thwart the Corps's plan. They met with and gained the support of their congressman, George Bush, who then represented the congressional district covering west Houston. Bush took their cause to the Corps Commander and asked that plans to improve Buffalo Bayou be scuttled. According to Hershey and Ginsburg, the Corps representative asked young Congressman Bush if he really did not want the Corps to spend money in his district to prevent flooding and Bush's reply was: not on this project. Ginsburg also said she called Mitchell's attention to the work of Ian McHarg, whom she had seen on a public television program. Later, George met Bob Hartsfield, which led to his formal introduction of McHarg.

McHarg appointed Jim Veltman, a graduate of McHarg's master's degree program at the University of Pennsylvania, as team captain for the environmental studies to be performed for The Woodlands. It was Veltman, with his strong ecological and architectural background, who was responsible for the site evaluation and played a key role in integrating environmental concepts into a workable master plan. Veltman recalls the first meeting he had with Mitchell in McHarg's office. According to Veltman, Mitchell started the conversation by saying, "I have named my project The Woodlands and there had better be some woodlands when we get done." The key for the environmental consultants was to determine how to save trees for Mitchell's sake. For McHarg, the stakes were much higher. He wanted to use the project to show how ecological information could be used in the planning process.

McHarg, Veltman, and others on their staff set out to do a complete ecological assessment of the original 17,000 acres of land that then made up the proposed new town. They performed an ecological inventory of wildlife and the climate conditions under which they lived. They looked at the kinds of limitations on development the land imposed. They forecasted the potential impact of development on the site's flora and fauna, topography, soil conditions, and streams. And they advised Mitchell on where to place different types of projects—houses, commercial space, and other developments—to minimize their impact on environmental assets. When the ecological studies were complete and the report was submitted in 1971, Mitchell recognized that it would be beneficial for the project to have someone who understood the ecological implications of the site to be on the development team. Veltman became Director of Environmental Management for The Woodlands.

George T. Morgan, Jr., and John O. King in their book, *The Woodlands, New Community Development, 1964–1983* (Texas A&M Press, 1987), outlined seven goals McHarg established for The Woodlands master plan:

- Minimum disruption of the hydrological regimen of the ground plane's surface and subsurface.

- Preservation of 25 percent of the woodland environment.
- Establishment of a natural drainage system in the floodplains, swales, ponds, and soil capable of absorbing rain.
- Preservation of vegetation noted for species diversity, stability, and uniqueness.
- Protection of wildlife habitats and movement corridors so that wildlife living on the site might remain.
- Minimization of capital costs of development.
- Avoidance of hazards to life or health of residents.

McHarg was most proud of the plan to use natural drainage in The Woodlands. When builders cover water-absorbing soil with houses, roads, sidewalks, and driveways there is less of it to soak up what falls from the sky. Developers build curbs, gutters, and sewers along streets to guide rainwater away from houses. To achieve this flow, the streets are graded lower than the surrounding yards. The result is that motorists both in Houston and its suburbs with heavy precipitation frequently complain about flooded streets. In effect, the lowered streets act as holding or retention ponds to contain the rainwater until the storm sewers can accept it. Better to have water in the streets for a limited time than in the houses. McHarg's plan did away with that costly infrastructure. At The Woodlands, streets and yards were to be at the same level. Drainage ditches were to be built on one or both sides of the road to funnel the water away from houses. Naturally low points in yards were left that way. They would serve as mini–retention ponds to hold rainwater when the ditches filled. Natural drainage is employed throughout the entire development.

In a January 12, 1975, story in the *Washington Post* by correspondent Tom Curtis on The Woodlands, McHarg talked to the reporter about the drainage system at The Woodlands: "This was one thing we did which was enormously profitable. It saved them $14 million for a storm sewage system." McHarg commented on the need to reconcile environmental conservation with economic imperative. "It would be very nice if the forest remained a forest. But if it remained a forest it could not be a new town." And sometimes the balance was not to his liking. McHarg conceived of a network of pedestrian paths in The Woodlands that were to be covered with wood chips. Instead, when built, they were paved with concrete. Despite McHarg's harsh words for the concrete paths—he called them "incredibly expensive and entirely inappropriate"—the pathways are The Woodlands' most popular amenity. The only complaint was when we elected to use asphalt instead of concrete on one pathway to make it more comfortable for jogging. Some residents thought we were compromising quality by not using concrete. I'm not sure what the reaction would have been to wood chips. Still, McHarg told the *Post*'s Curtis that, in The Woodlands, "builders found that they could love profits and trees at the same time."

As we shall see, the wood chip–covered paths were not the only part of McHarg's plan determined by Mitchell and his development team to be less practical than expected. Still, most of the initial environmental agenda remains in the present development. The triumph of McHarg's contribution was how it was used to plan the streets, roads, and housing sites in

The Woodlands. In developing lots for homes, the developers follow an oft-used suburban pattern. Many of those lots are in culs-de-sac containing a few houses instead of long, straight streets. Homeowners love culs-de-sac. There is no through-traffic. They and their children can walk, bicycle, or play in the streets confident that speeding cars won't be using them as short-cuts to someplace else. By and large, transportation experts aren't so enthusiastic. Extensive use of culs-de-sac slows down traffic and makes neighborhoods hard to navigate. Indeed, a running joke among law enforcement patrols is that crooks will get lost—and caught—before fleeing the area with stolen goods. Before my new urbanist friends take offense, let me report that residential neighborhoods in each village are connected to shopping and schools by an extensive pathway system to encourage pedestrian traffic. The plan also includes some neo-traditional neighborhoods with front porches, rear alleys, and sidewalks. Master-planned communities can accommodate different scales of development, resulting in a variety of neighborhoods that share common amenities and are connected by a sense of community.

The Woodlands' developers also planned from the first to build all streets using concrete instead of asphalt, which is a less expensive material. In the long run, however, concrete streets cost less to maintain. But the lower cost of maintenance would not benefit The Woodlands Corporation. A year after the streets were dedicated as public rights-of-way, Montgomery County took over maintenance. The decision to use concrete was a thoughtful marketing decision. The then largely rural Montgomery County had seen several subdivisions built with poorly constructed blacktop streets and roads. The Woodlands was going to be sold as first class all the way. Constructing concrete streets, even in areas where traffic was light, was a way to indicate that quality.

But it's on its major thoroughfares that The Woodlands presents a completely different pattern of planning and development. To understand just why it is different, let's look at the usual way such streets are treated. Just a few miles south of The Woodlands is an area known as FM 1960. The name comes not from the year but that it is bisected by Farm to Market Road 1960, roads originally conceived by the state do just that—getting farmers out of the mud and giving them a way to move their crops to the city. When Houston, like many met-ropolitan areas, saw its population explode in the 1950s and 1960s, the FM 1960 area, like The Woodlands after it, became a prime housing site with upscale developments and lots of retailers catering to the new residents.

There were no architectural or land use controls on the retailing explosion. When a retail-er or developer would build a shopping center it would simply cut multiple driveways into FM 1960. Traffic slows and what was planned as a way to move farm vehicles long distances efficiently became, in essence, a local shopping street.

Robert Heineman, Mitchell's in-house urban planner, took a different approach with The Woodlands Parkway, which is a major artery for access to The Woodlands from Interstate 45 North. A commuter coming from work in downtown Houston who lives at the far west end of our community exits onto the parkway to get home. But instead of traffic-choked streets, the motorist finds a relatively smooth ride with speed limits set at 45 miles per hour. The dif-ference? The way the street was designed and built. Shopping doesn't line the parkway. On each side, you see nothing but tall trees. Retail developments were limited to either dedicated shopping districts or small neighborhood centers buffered by greenbelts of native vegetation. Not only does traffic move more quickly, but also the frazzled commuter traveling home from a hard day on the job sees those calming trees and a natural landscape instead of huge signs and thousands of parked cars.

Landscaped thoroughfares come at a higher price for the developer, but they're a smart investment. There's the cost of the land for medians and greenbelts. And there's the cost of building a network of access streets to the shopping, business, and commercial areas. Probably the most significant cost of such amenities is the loss of building lots with street frontage. Land along major thoroughfares has always commanded top dollar from merchants who lust after the pocketbooks of passersby. Tucking your store in the woods means shoppers have to find you. They don't just happen upon you. That's especially true in The Woodlands, where the same planning ethos affected the placement of neighborhood shopping centers. They aren't located directly on the street. Instead, there is a screen of woods and underbrush between them and the road. Each is in a commercial enclave, much like a residential neighborhood might be. Heineman said the developers could have abandoned the principle during the hard times The Woodlands faced during the oil crisis of the 1970s. To increase profits, the corporation could have turned The Woodlands Parkway into a strip of commercial developments. It didn't.

Most retailers were not happy about the way they were denied prime street frontage for their operations. They resisted the relatively secluded areas The Woodlands mandated for shops, set back behind a dense strip of trees and understory.

"They didn't like it," Heineman said of merchant reaction to The Woodlands plan. "First of all, they had to purchase more land than they were used to buying." Someone has to pay for the screen of trees and brush, so it's folded into the cost of the retail site. Then there's the lack of visibility. According to Heineman, the best example of the struggle to redefine land use conventions can be found with the The Woodlands' experience with McDonald's.

The hamburger chain had a site on Interstate 45 near The Woodlands. As the community grew, however, the franchisee wanted an additional site in the development itself. But it had to be in a buffered commercial area, cutting visibility. Even worse, The Woodlands' sign regulations forbid the four-story-tall Golden Arches sported by nearly all other stores in the hamburger chain. It took several years for the local McDonald's owner to agree to open a store tailored to The Woodlands' regulations, Heineman recalls. Within six months of opening, the store became one of the highest-grossing McDonald's in the Houston area. "Once that happened, it just opened the floodgates for [other] retail development in The Woodlands," Heineman said.

What worked in The Woodlands might not work elsewhere. "There's somewhat of a captive market in The Woodlands, especially in the interior areas. You don't necessarily need four gas stations on four corners." The developer had control of land use by virtue of its extensive property holdings, giving it the ability to avoid unnecessary duplication of commercial locations.

The environmental information Ian McHarg provided was extremely useful in building roads, streets, and shopping areas. In other situations, it proved less so, Heineman states.

"Basically," Heineman said, "[McHarg's] process consisted of evaluating environmental factors such as soils and vegetation, then layering the results together to form a composite map of constraints and opportunities. This map might be used to determine locations for various land uses. A permeable soil was one that had high recharge capacity. During heavy rains, the water would recharge into the soil. On that soil we would ideally locate a low-density, low-coverage product—estate lots, for example, where the parcels are larger, leaving plenty of exposed soil to soak up the rain. On impermeable soil with little recharge you might locate a high-density use, such as a shopping center.

"One problem," said Heineman, "was that the soils, other than those in the floodplain, had only moderate recharge and capacity. They had about one to two inches of recharge. Vegetation? Well, The Woodlands site had been logged for years, so much of the vegetation was not as different, not as varied, as the early McHarg report might had led you to believe. For example, there was presumably a fantastic growth of huge oak trees near the Sawmill Park area on the maps. Unfortunately, a field trip failed to reveal the grove of trees.

"The end result was that you really could not locate land use using only soils and vegetation as determinants in The Woodlands because they were not varied enough. It made more sense to locate land uses based on other factors such the location of the major thoroughfares rather than by environmental data. Rather than using environmental constraints for macro planning, it was used much more at the micro level. After the location of a particular use had been determined, significant vegetation was surveyed, and the design of the project attempted to respond to this. And there's also the argument regarding the relative value of trees. Is a pine tree valued higher than a hardwood tree? Or what about mature trees versus young trees? If older, more mature trees are more likely to die than younger trees, which is better for preservation? So there was a constant dialogue regarding the ranking and importance of the various environmental factors."

McHarg's natural drainage plan, which was supposed to save the developer $14 million, didn't survive unscathed either. Originally, McHarg suggested building 50 or so small dams to retain drainage during heavy rains. But the topography of The Woodlands did not necessarily offer the proper soil conditions for the natural drainage system envisioned by McHarg. The alternative was to look for one, two, or three large areas in The Woodlands where the topography and location were optimal. You could build a dam, detain a lot of water, and have a small number of strategically located reservoirs rather than 50.

McHarg's mandate to ban curbs, gutters, and storm sewers from residential neighborhoods was also dropped after being used in the early villages. The Woodlands is made up of seven planned residential villages, and within each village there are a number of neighborhoods. The first village built was Grogan's Mill, named after the sawmill operation that was on the property when it was part of the Grogan Cochran Lumber Company. It, and about half of the second village to be constructed, was built according to McHarg's guidelines. And there is no flooding from rainwater. Unfortunately, not everyone was happy with the plan, including many of the people who bought homes in the villages.

McHarg was in favor of retaining drainage on lots. If there was a low spot in the backyard it stayed. That worked well until families moved in and kids wanted to play in the yard. To make matters worse, the low spots bred mosquitoes. In summary, some of the ideas on water detention looked good on paper, but they did not function as well in reality.

"Another consumer problem," pointed out Heineman, "was neighborhood roadside drainage. Initially, in Grogan's Mill the roadside drainage was open. In large estate areas, that works." On smaller lots, however, "a third of the frontage along the streets is carved up by culverts, [making] a real visual and marketing problem. The homebuyer preferred the more attractive curb and gutter streets." Conversely, the major collector streets have roadside ditches to carry the drainage. From the standpoint of maintaining traffic flow during heavy rainfall, that's excellent because the road is built up rather than depressed as in a curb and gutter street. The roadside ditches carry heavy rainfall better than the curb-and-gutter street.

As a result of the changes, subsequent villages in The Woodlands have neighborhood streets built with curbs, gutters, storm sewers, and depressed streets. The other villages do have a look different from that of the original Grogan's Mill. Just how different, and how it pleases the eye, depends on individual taste. Heineman, for one, is of the opinion that The Woodlands developers probably should have changed the drainage for the residential areas one village sooner.

The greatest success following the original environmental plan, Heineman believes, was in preserving 25 percent of the natural environment found in The Woodlands before development. The challenge, he adds, isn't just over the trees. Most homeowners love trees. The struggle comes from preserving the underbrush that covers the ground in a natural forest, what Heineman calls the "understory." When The Woodlands Corporation sells land to commercial developers, it puts a covenant in the deed requiring that the understory within selected areas be left intact. That covenant is not always heeded.

Recently, Heineman said, a service station in The Woodlands changed managers. The new manager decided he could get more visibility for his operation—and improve sales—if he removed the understory. So he directed his maintenance crew to do just that. The development company cited the station for violating the covenant; the station's lawyer looked at the covenant and agreed. His client replanted the understory.

It's a tough job to supervise the natural environment of such a large development, Heineman said. There are several people on The Woodlands' staff who do nothing but monitor tree preservation and retention, landscaping, and reforestation. The biggest advantage of The Woodlands' environmental agenda has been its appeal in the marketplace. Commercial users and homebuilders alike want to be there. They are mindful of the rules because they don't want to be banned from further work in the development. It seems that over the years people have bought into the notion that those rules benefit the overall community.

Still, says Heineman, "If you aren't completely vigilant, if you allow one business owner to violate the rules, every business in The Woodlands will become aware of that one incident and say, 'If he can, why can't I?' So you have to be consistent on enforcement, or you risk losing your control."

Land sold for residential use has a different set of covenants. Homebuilders are required to preserve areas of natural vegetation on each home site. Typically, 25 percent of each frontyard is preserved. Homeowners agree not to cut any trees over four inches in diameter or remove the understory from frontyard preserves. And they are asked to do no cutting for six months, to see if they can live with the different look of their yards. It does not always work. Many of our homeowners appear to be much like those elsewhere. They move to the suburbs and want to start a grass farm. After acquiring their house, new residents are quick to dedicate a weekend to brush removal.

Generally, those who enforce the covenants have found that if they can get homeowners to leave the natural vegetation in place for a period of time, they usually buy into the concept. It sure saves the time and the expense of mowing grass and creates a more pleasant street scene.

Not all the planning was perfect. Planners, like anyone else, can err. The most elaborate war plan, for example, seldom survives the first shot of the battle. But most of the mistakes made by The Woodlands planners turned out to be minor in nature. One of them, all agree, was the location and design of the first neighborhood shopping center in the Village of Grogan's Mill, which was to become home to 13,350 people. It should have been built closer to the major thoroughfares to give it greater accessibility. Its construction also was a bit unusual. It was called The Wharf, since it fronted on a manmade lake. Instead of the usual configuration with stores facing a parking lot, it was a small, enclosed mall. It turned out to be too small. The Woodlands' developer labored to get a grocery store for The Wharf. It would be the first one in The Woodlands. They faced a chicken/egg problem. People who thought about buying a home in The Woodlands were put off by the fact they would have to drive out of the community to buy groceries. Yet no grocery store wanted to build a store in the early days with few customers nearby. It was a triumph when they persuaded the operator of an upscale local chain, Jamail's, to take a space in The Wharf. However, the original configuration of the shopping center and the smallness of its retail spaces created some problems. Jamail's had about 25,000 square feet. Most supermarkets today are twice that size. In the end, The Woodlands Corporation admitted defeat with The Wharf. Jamail's pulled out, the existing shopping center was converted to a conference center for a major energy company, and a much larger, and more conventional shopping center was built adjacent to it.

The Woodlands Corporation also made a mistake when it initiated the development of the Village of Panther Creek, Heineman said. The mistake was not recognizing upfront that they needed to produce a selection of housing types in a broad price range from the beginning of development in each new village. The Woodlands Corporation had committed to the U.S. Department of Housing and Urban Development that they would construct housing for a wide variety of families, from upscale estates down to rent-subsidized apartments. The initial residential offerings in Panther Creek included only lower-priced homes and apartments, including some that were rent subsidized with federal aid.

Panther Creek initially "achieved a little bit of a low-end stigma," Heineman notes. If developers are committed to building homes for the cross section of people who are going to live and work in a particular area, Heineman says, they ideally need to build a mix of single-family homes, apartments, and condominiums concurrently. If they focus on single-family homes first, he adds, they will find another problem. The people who live in those homes will be upset when higher-density housing is added later.

Then there have been instances in which the original plans for The Woodlands have changed dramatically, not so much because they were wrong but because subsequent events made the original ones unrealistic. One such change involved land set aside for business and industrial purposes. From the beginning, George Mitchell's plan for The Woodlands was to make it a real town, not just a bedroom community. He wanted people to live and work in The Woodlands. And he has been successful. The original plan set aside 5,000 acres for what was called the "business crescent." This is the area closest to Interstate 45. Town Center was set aside for retail and office buildings and auxiliary enterprises like hotels, restaurants, and entertainment. There was, for example, the Research Forest, an area designed to house businesses and technology companies that Mitchell hoped would take advantage of The Woodlands' proximity to the thriving complex of hospitals and medical schools in the Texas Medical Center of Houston. And there was the Trade Center. It is the only part of The Woodlands on the east side of Interstate 45. It was thought that the rail-served trade center would be an ideal site for light industrial and distribution businesses. Heineman said that the Trade Center simply did not develop at the pace expected. There were other locations in the Houston area that had equal or better access to markets.

Recently, The Woodlands Corporation successfully changed much of the Trade Center land to residential use, attaching it to the Village of College Park. Unlike the other six villages of The Woodlands, College Park is separated into two pieces, one on either side of Interstate 45. The housing component includes attractive, affordable offerings for both retirees and young families that are clustered around a community college campus, shopping, and a hospital.

Looking back over the years The Woodlands has been around, Heineman sees failures as well as successes in its planning. "In hindsight, we spent a lot of time back then in wasted motion and effort. Whether you could have gotten through that period without going through that, I couldn't say given the newness of it all. What we were proposing was completely new for the Houston market, from the hierarchical road system to saving trees to the natural drainage system. There were so many things that were different that some of the trial-and-error process was necessary at that point."

There is no question that George Mitchell's oft-spoken comment that he was attempting, in building The Woodlands, to provide an example for other developers to follow has been heeded. D. Scott Middleton, a land use and conservation consultant in Washington, D.C., and a former student of McHarg, summed up the pluses of the planning process in the June 1997 issue of *Urban Land*, a publication of the Urban Land Institute. His comments are especially valuable because they come from an outsider.

"The Woodlands can be a model for other planned communities and an alternative model for growth, and other developers in the Houston market are beginning to emulate its approach," he wrote. "The Houston region has more master-planned communities than any other major metropolitan area in the United States. Together, Houston's planned communities account for 25 to 45 percent of the new home sales" in the Houston area.

Middleton continues: "The Woodlands was the first new community to prepare a voluntary environmental impact statement, in 1973, before any such studies [were] required. In his

1997 autobiography, *A Quest for Life*, McHarg identifies the plan for The Woodlands 'as one of his proudest accomplishments' and credits Mitchell for being 'a powerful advocate for ecology and ecological planning.' Environmental stewardship is a key component of [The Woodlands Corporation] prescribed mission. The resulting appreciation in land values is an important business goal. . . . Lessons learned from their experience can help increase collective knowledge about how to design with nature in a way that is both environmentally responsible and profitable."

Part II

———— •◆• ————

COMMITMENT
TO DEVELOP

T he long wait was finally over. By 1972, the land for The Woodlands was assembled, all 17,460 acres. Final approval of the development plan by the Department of Housing and Urban Development had come through and the project agreement was signed August 12, 1972. On September 6, 1972, the $50 million in The Woodlands Corporation debentures guaranteed by HUD were sold to the public; proceeds from the sale were deposited in a fund with Chase Manhattan Bank as trustee. Now all George Mitchell had to do was build The Woodlands. It proved to be much more difficult, and expensive, than anyone had anticipated. In the end, the cost of building this new town would require Mitchell to pledge his personal fortune to keep The Woodlands Corporation solvent.

Chapter 5

A CHALLENGING START

—◆·◆·—

When George Mitchell took the first steps toward building his new town, he relied on a few members of his own staff, plus the expertise of outside consultants. But after receiving the loan guarantee from HUD, assembling the necessary land, and completing the initial planning, he needed people with hands-on experience to transform The Woodlands from a plan to a place. No one was available locally. He reached out to experienced executives from other new town developments, especially from the Rouse Company and its new town of Columbia, Maryland.

Mitchell was impressed with the talent he found in Columbia and at the Irvine Ranch in California, and sought to establish a team with similar characteristics. He made overtures to experienced members of his outside consultants on his planning team and to key executives who helped to realize Columbia, settling on J. Leonard "Len" Ivins, a vice president of the Rouse Company and director of development for Columbia.

Mitchell made Ivins a senior vice president in charge of real estate for Mitchell Energy & Development Corporation, president of The Woodlands Development Corporation, and a member of the board of Mitchell Energy. In effect, Ivins was in charge of getting The Woodlands up and running as a business concern. He reported directly to Mitchell.

Ivins came on board in December 1971 and immediately started hiring colleagues from Columbia to help run the operation. They included Ralph Everhart, who was named senior manager in charge of land development; Robert Grace, vice president and director of land development; Jack Price, the project manager for utilities; and Ben F. Worley, the development director of what was to become The Woodlands Community Association. In July, another Rouse alumnus, Salvatore T. Calleri, was hired as senior vice president of finance for Mitchell Energy. He had previously been the chief financial officer of Howard Research and Development, a subsidiary of the Rouse Company. To long-term employees of Mitchell, these new hires soon became known as the "Columbia Boys." Mitchell hired so many people from Columbia that Rouse had a lawyer call Mitchell and threaten a lawsuit if he did not stop.

In September 1972, construction started on Grogan's Mill, the first village in The Woodlands. A number of decisions made at the time caused a financial crisis two years later; one that came close to sinking not only the real estate project but also its parent company.

Ivins relied on his experience at Columbia in his new job at The Woodlands. He had seen how spending upfront for amenities at Columbia had brought in early sales from dazzled potential homeowners. He set out to duplicate that effort outside Houston. Columbia had enjoyed a spectacular early success until the full impact of the economic recession of early 1975 brought the Maryland town near ruin. That same recession, along with other factors, would affect The Woodlands, too. To be fair, Ivins, who was at Columbia from 1965 to 1971, experienced only the positive side of spending big upfront to lure homebuyers. By the time the crash arrived at Rouse's development, Ivins was already working at The Woodlands.

He persuaded Mitchell Energy's board of directors to spend huge amounts on construction of amenities beyond that necessary to prepare lots for sale at The Woodlands. That was in addition to the spending on infrastructure called for under the loan agreement with HUD. The projects initiated by Ivins included a 335-acre commercial, conference, and leisure center that contained extensive shopping, commercial, office, and recreation facilities including a large sports center, the 200-room Woodlands Inn, an 18-hole golf course, an information center for prospective buyers, and a 15-acre lake. The expanded construction also required building major thoroughfares to connect to interchanges at Interstate 45.

"There was a decision made to open The Woodlands with an enormous impact," said Michael Richmond. He was a certified public accountant in Maryland whose clients included the Rouse Company. He was hired in 1972 to serve as the financial controller for The Woodlands Corporation, where he eventually rose to the position of president. "We had borrowed approximately $12.5 million to build the conference center and the swim center, the retail, the golf course, and all that. With overruns, I don't remember the exact number, but it might have been $30 million. Part of that was self-infliction. And part of it was just that they probably underestimated the capital cost of opening up a project of this magnitude."

David Hendricks, one of the original four who put together the HUD proposal for Mitchell, was by this time an assistant general manager for the project. According to Hendricks, Ivins was not the tightest of managers. "He felt his job was to create this great new town. His attitude was we had to preservice the project. We can't sell lots by putting up signs saying this was the site of a future golf course or a tennis complex. We had to have them in place. That was the Columbia concept."

Hendricks also said there was one amenity that did not get built. "At the time, my wife and I rode horses, so I was really interested in building an elaborate equestrian center. But George was a tennis player. So you know which one won out. We opened with a nice tennis facility."

Plato Pappas, a longtime employee of Mitchell Energy who supervised construction at The Woodlands, summed up Mitchell's thoughts on that huge increase in staff and the spending by Ivins and the Columbia Boys. Riding into the office together one day, Pappas asked Mitchell how he could afford to pay all the construction contractors and hire a huge staff of project administrators and managers at the same time: "I said, 'How can we afford this, George?' He says, 'Plato, have you ever built a new town?' 'No, George, I have not.' 'Neither have I,' he said. 'We don't have anybody in the company who knows how to build a new town. I figured this [extra expense] might go up to three-quarters of a million dollars and I asked myself whether I can afford the expense. And I can. This is going to be a good lesson,' he said. 'But it's going to be an expensive lesson.' That's how he justified it." The lesson, it turned out, would be much more expensive than Mitchell had thought.

Despite the government loan guarantees, Mitchell did not have much money to spend. Using the HUD guarantee, he had borrowed $50 million but received only $48 million. The other $2 million went for fees and closing costs. Immediately $23 million of that went to pay off the various mortgages and lien holders on the land. That was a requirement of the HUD guarantee. If The Woodlands went broke, the government agency wanted clear title to the land so it might recoup some of the millions it would be forced to pay to holders of the debentures. An additional $3.6 million went to pay predevelopment costs incurred by The Woodlands Corporation. That left $22 million, plus $5.5 million invested by Mitchell Energy & Development Corporation, to help build The Woodlands. And here we run across one of the truths of big-time land development. A lot of money will be spent before the developer sees much, if any, coming back in land sales. For The Woodlands, that $27 million for infrastructure costs would soon be gone.

Then there was the weather. Normally, The Woodlands can expect 49 inches of rain a year. In 1972 and through the early part of the next year, 96 inches of rain fell on the area. In balmy southeast Texas, where freezing temperatures are a rarity, it also snowed. Twice. The two largest problems, however, were money and the lack of controls on how the money was spent. Given the circumstances, both were probably unavoidable.

"Len Ivins was the main one [hired] from Columbia and he brought in four or five others," George Mitchell recalled years later. "Len was an extremely bright guy, but extremely hard to handle. I think he brought in some good people, which I needed, because we didn't have anybody in this part of the country who had that type of experience."

Robert Heineman, who had been working on planning for The Woodlands before the arrival of the group from Maryland, believed that the Columbia Boys "really wanted to surround themselves with their friends, compadres they knew from Columbia. And I think from a planning standpoint they probably wanted to bring in a planner from Columbia." Others, however, were not so circumspect about the Columbia Boys. They often used the word arrogant when referring to them. Jim McAlister, who left Mitchell after being in charge of obtaining the HUD guarantee, said, "They came in with the attitude that they were here because we couldn't do it." The Columbia Boys' attitude also caused problems with officials from Montgomery County, who resented being treated like hicks. Mickey Deison, then mayor of Conroe, said his relationship with Ivins "was really bad. I had such feelings about it, I called Jim McAlister one day and told him that I thought there were things George needed to know about what Len was doing. Jim set up a meeting. [Mitchell] was very noncommittal [at the meeting]. But Len didn't last long after that."

The partying ways of the Columbia Boys, usually charged to the company's account, was another source of resentment among Mitchell's old hands. Pappas said, "I do not know what controls they had placed upon them. However, I understand some of their expenses were quite heavy."

L. David Bumgardner, then an attorney with Mitchell Energy, also remembers the excessive entertainment costs: "I think Len lived by the creed, 'Life is uncertain. Eat dessert first.' "

Bumgardner said he once complained about Ivins to Budd Clark, the number-two man at Mitchell Energy. "It's probably safe to say that Budd was not enamored with the Ivins management style. Nonetheless, Budd remained philosophical and gave me probably the most sage advice I ever received. After listening to one of my complaints, he calmly told me not to worry about it. I asked if things were going to change and Budd said no, I would get used to it."

Hendricks, though not one of the Columbia Boys, soon became close to them. "Ivins reported to Budd Clark," Hendricks recalled. "Once Budd just had a hissy fit over Ivins's expense account. George's response: 'Budd, that's the cost of having him here. I'm willing to pay for it, so shut up.' "

Ivins quickly found a way, however, to get around Clark's wrath about his expense account. "One of my jobs," Hendricks said, "was to carry credit cards around and pick up the check whenever Ivins went out. Len approved my expense account and Budd approved his. Len liked to drink good wine and eat good food. You did your work and then you went out afterward and you talked about work. But while you talked you ate dinner and drank wine. Our days were not eight to five."

The early days of free-spending managers, the expense of amenities designed to attract new homeowners, and the high cost of infrastructure resulted in cash flow problems. In fact, very soon after construction started, The Woodlands Corporation started having problems paying bills. The company was running out of money. Worse, it lacked effective cost controls.

When the staff "had to meet a deadline, all hell broke loose to get it done," Richmond said. "We finally opened The Woodlands in 1974, in October, but we did not have very good control over how much we had really spent. The bills started rocketing in and all of a sudden we hit the liquidity crunch. We had set up what we called a vendor-control list, just to keep track of what was owed. The company had limited funds, so every Friday we would try to figure out who we were going to pay, who we weren't, who we could negotiate with."

Throughout that period, The Woodlands Corporation followed a policy of trying to pay small contractors first, while holding off big ones. "The biggest one was Austin Bridge, which built The Woodlands Parkway," Richmond said. "They had in effect lent us three million dollars and [got paid] over time."

Pappas was not a confidante of the Columbia Boys and did not share in their partying ways. He also disliked their management style. But he gives them high marks for getting the job done. "They knew how vulnerable the project could be because of the heavy financial burden that any project of that size can have in the initial stages until you have a marketable product," Pappas said in an interview. "They were tough. I'm no expert in finance or new towns, [but] were it not for that constant push, I don't think The Woodlands would have opened in two years. It was expensive, no question about it."

Richmond agreed with Pappas. "When you look back on it, could things have been done better? Probably. But the magnitude of the opening—including the signing of the Houston Open golf tournament on a golf course that was barely finished—really differentiated The Woodlands in the market and made it a big player. Could it have been done more economically? Probably. Interstate 45 was four lanes then and really just like a farm-to-market road, so we were out in the middle of nowhere trying to create a more urban than suburban type environment. It was challenging to bring recognition to a large piece of land. Part of [the problem] was that we were undercapitalized. But we survived."

The Woodlands' finances were further strained as Ivins went on a hiring spree during his tenure. The Woodlands Corporation staff ballooned to 365. Of that number, 65 of them earned more than $30,000 a year, or $128,000 in 2003 dollars. One consequence of the expanded staff was that at times it was difficult to find out who was in charge. Because of this chaotic management structure, people were often working at cross-purposes. At one time, Pappas said, he sat down and counted 15 different engineering companies working in The Woodlands. "Some were doing design work, some of them field engineering work. It was not manageable."

The large number of outside consultants and engineers also resulted in snafus and wasted assets. One day during the heavy rains, for example, Pappas went to check on the construction of a sewage treatment plant. First the crew had to remove rainwater from the area. Then it rained again, and the task had to be repeated. The project was important because it was to service an area set aside for the largest homebuilder working in The Woodlands. The only person on the site was a man sitting in a pickup truck that was parked on top of an embankment. The man in the truck identified himself as an engineer who was there to supervise the work. But there was no one working there. "I saw this happen more than once," Pappas said.

Despite the problems—the chaos in management, the heavy rains and snow—Pappas constantly downplayed the difficulties he faced in the two years from the start of construction in 1972 until The Woodlands officially opened in 1974.

In truth, there were plenty of problems that came close to causing The Woodlands to be stillborn. The bottom line was its developer didn't have enough money to do all the things it wanted to do. And perhaps the money it did have was spent on the wrong things. At least it seemed that way in 1974.

A dispute with HUD delayed the sale of residential lots, lowering The Woodlands Corporation's early revenue potential. The corporation had submitted proposed deed covenants or restrictions on residential land to HUD in January 1973. Officials at HUD objected to one of the terms that required residents to pay a fee to The Woodlands Community Association to finance recreational amenities. A year passed before the dispute was settled. Until HUD approved the covenants in January 1974, The Woodlands could not sell land, which meant that sorely needed money was not coming in. The Woodlands was also supposed to receive supplementary grants from HUD for planning and installation of sewer, water, and drainage systems. But the federal government, hit by soaring general deficits and preoccupied with an upcoming presidential election, clamped down on spending and the grants were never issued.

Despite such setbacks, construction continued at The Woodlands but was falling behind. The original official opening date for the new town was earmarked for March 1974. It was postponed until August. The Woodlands finally officially opened on October 19 of the same year. On January 1, 1975, the first family moved into a new townhome. Within days, ten more attached houses were occupied. On April 1, The Woodlands Corporation set up shop in the first office building. By early August, the second office building was completed, along with a 50-unit apartment project, and construction had started on the first 21 single-family residences.

When The Woodlands finally did open, one party wasn't enough. The opening stretched over three weekends in October. There was a parade of antique cars from Houston to The Woodlands. Specially designed flags were unfurled. Speeches were made by both George Mitchell and U.S. Representative Charles Wilson, the Democratic congressman whose district included The Woodlands. A rather different set of celebrities and events were staged in an effort to attract crowds to the opening. Actor Buster Crabbe spoke and showed episodes of his old-time movie serial, *Flash Gordon*. There was an archery exhibition by international stars. William Shatner, star of the *Star Trek* television series, appeared. Country and western, mariachi, and Dixieland bands played. In all, 22,000 people showed up to look at this new suburban development. There were smiles all around. But those smiles didn't remain much beyond the last months of 1974.

On opening day, The Woodlands was in deep financial trouble, as was the country, which was in a recession. President Richard Nixon, no fan of the federal new town program, directed that all further grants be suspended. For The Woodlands, that meant an expected $33 million never came. Mitchell actually debated suing the federal government for breach of contract but decided against it.

The recession had also dried up many conventional sources of mortgage money. The Woodlands Corporation couldn't sell lots to builders if the builders' potential customers couldn't get loans to buy homes.

Adding to such woes was the cost of Ivins's building program. The peak cash requirements for The Woodlands ballooned from $61 million to $98 million. The Woodlands Corporation was $37 million short.

All those problems might have been overcome, except for a 1973 event thousands of miles away. Troops from Egypt and Syria invaded Israel in what come to be known as the Yom Kippur War. Israel managed to defeat the invaders, but soon after the war's end, the Organization of Petroleum Exporting Countries (OPEC) cut off oil shipments to the west. OPEC demanded, and got, much higher prices for its exports. With long lines at the gas pump and prices skyrocketing, few people were interested in buying a new home in The Woodlands. The 27 miles from downtown Houston to the new town seemed a long way to go. Those still looking for homes, and not put off by the higher mortgage rates, had plenty of choices. There were numerous empty houses and apartments much nearer downtown Houston. As a result, the expected boom in home sales at The Woodlands simply did not materialize.

The figures show what happened. The economic projections for The Woodlands said 1,450 homes would be built in 1973 and an additional 825 units built in 1974. Only 62 homes had been constructed by the end of the year. There were 479,000 square feet of office space built but only an 81 percent occupancy rate. The Woodlands Corporation had built 100,000 square feet of industrial space. None of it was rented.

The Woodlands received $15 million in additional equity from Mitchell Energy as a stopgap. HUD, whose permission was needed, delayed even that equity advance. It took the agency months to approve the measure. The Woodlands wasn't the only new town in desperate shape. Since the inception of Title VII, HUD had guaranteed loans for 13 new towns. All were near bankruptcy. Otto G. Stolz, general manager of HUD's Office of New Community Development, announced a moratorium on all new town grants, admitting that the entire program was in economic and political disarray.

Mitchell made it his business to bring financial stability to The Woodlands. During the 1972–1974 period he had largely been hands off, deferring to Len Ivins on operational decisions. Now at the start of 1975, he stepped in, reducing the staff of The Woodlands Corporation from 365 to 160. The entire Department of Institutional Development was sent packing. This department was supposed to build social institutions in The Woodlands, part of the plan to make the new town more than just a housing development. As we shall see later on in the book, this potentially devastating move was mitigated by the volunteer efforts of our residents.

Among those laid off were Ivins and many of the Columbia Boys.

Hendricks, who was also banished in the layoffs, said the staff reductions were not mean-spirited. It was just something that had to happen due to financial constraints. The Woodlands had huge costs and no revenue. For Hendricks, the landing was soft. His brothers, Randy and Allen, were sports agents who represented some of the top professional athletes. He went to work for them.

In Mitchell's view, it was not the construction cost overruns that almost sank The Woodlands. "Yeah, we had cost overruns. In a project of that magnitude, you're going to have cost overruns. However, the overruns weren't that serious. But what was serious was that we used all our HUD money to pay off the land."

Fortunately for Mitchell and The Woodlands, the same energy shortages and skyrocketing costs that caused sales to plummet at The Woodlands also brought increased profits for Mitchell's oil and natural gas business. Budd Clark said the price of oil jumped from $2.50 a barrel to $12 a barrel. "The banks didn't realize it. The employees didn't realize it. The directors didn't realize it. The real estate people didn't know it because of their problems. What's with George? He isn't upset. I didn't realize what he had done. He had taken our reserves and just multiplied by the higher price in his mind. No problem on value. The only real problem was there was no cash." Even with much higher assets, Mitchell Energy still needed cash to continue work on the new town. Or as Hendricks said, "The Arabs saved The Woodlands. If we had not had that oil embargo, we might not have survived."

"So we had to struggle with the banks on that, but we worked it out," Mitchell said. To satisfy Chase Manhattan Bank, a major lender to Mitchell Energy and its real estate operation, Mitchell took extraordinary steps in structuring his debt obligation. Mitchell pledged his personal stake in Mitchell Energy & Development Corporation to secure corporate obligations to HUD. Chase actually sent a banker to Houston to sit in the Mitchell offices and vet any expenditure on The Woodlands. It was only after Mitchell substituted a letter of credit issued by Manufacturers Hanover that HUD released his stock and he was able to regain full control of The Woodlands operation.

As a stopgap measure, Mitchell brought in Leland Carter as acting head of The Woodlands. Carter was a lawyer and engineer who ran Southwestern Gas Pipeline Company, a Mitchell Energy subsidiary in Dallas. He got a New York investor to inject funds into Mitchell's drilling activity in north Texas. Later, he served as president of Mitchell Energy & Development Corporation, with operating responsibility for both energy and real estate. Mitchell served as chairman. Carter saw The Woodlands as a drain on Mitchell Energy's oil and gas activities and made no bones about his desire to see the experiment come to an end.

In June 1975, Richard Browne said he told Carter, "You know, I think we can make this work and I'm going to move to The Woodlands and help do that." Browne said that Carter replied, "You're crazy. I'm going to put a chain across the entrance road and shut this down. George doesn't agree, but I think that's what should be done."

Within a couple of weeks, Browne recalled, Carter was no longer head of The Woodlands. "George won, as I knew he would," Browne said. "I stayed on and we did our best to make this a special place."

But there was more to Carter's leaving than the dispute over The Woodlands. Carter was one of the few people who had an employment agreement with Mitchell and it contained a provision that tied his compensation to improved profits of Mitchell Energy. With the OPEC oil embargo and related price increases, Mitchell's profits increased dramatically through events not related to Carter's performance.

Apparently George tried to renegotiate the employment agreement with Carter to take into account the windfall compensation, but Carter refused to renegotiate, which led to his departure from the company.

Len Rogers, a Canadian-born certified public accountant who had extensive experience in community development in California, replaced Ivins. In a 1984 interview with George Morgan and John King, coauthors of The Woodlands book published by Texas A&M, Rogers said when he arrived in late 1975 development in the new town was at a standstill.

Business started picking up in 1975, but it was not nearly as much as the optimistic forecasts had envisioned. The original plan for The Woodlands called for completion in 20 years. Thirty years later it is still being built. During 1975, 251 single-family homes were built and construction started on 90 more. By year's end, the town had a population of 900. In 1976, new home sales increased again but still came in below target. The year also saw the leasing of substantial office, commercial, and industrial space to several companies including Continental Oil Co., Peerless Engineering Company, and Texaco, Inc.

Mitchell believes The Woodlands turned the corner to sustained profitability within four or five years of its opening, that is 1978 or 1979. From that point, the town went on to be at or near the top in growth in the greater Houston area.

Chapter 6

THE TURNAROUND BEGINS

───◆◆───

At the dawn of the 1980s, things began to look up for The Woodlands. In part, better management fueled the change. After the convulsions of construction, the problems of welding together a team composed of people from many different backgrounds, and massive layoffs, management at The Woodlands learned what needed to be done and how to do it. Primarily, however, the road to prosperity was a function of the economy. As the rising tide lifted all boats, The Woodlands rose with them. Early and substantial spending on infrastructure and amenities was beginning to pay off for George Mitchell and his new town.

I came to The Woodlands on February 1, 1979, at an opportune time, just as the new town started to turn around and recover from its crash in the early 1970s. I would like to think my skills had something to do with its subsequent prosperity, but honesty forces me to admit I greatly benefited from the luck of timing. My initial role was to start a new residential development division for the company. The new division was not top heavy with staff; there were just three people—Ted Nelson, Barbara Nash, and myself. Our job was to expand the residential business and to integrate planning, engineering, and marketing efforts with community development objectives.

I didn't know much about The Woodlands. The first time I had ever heard of it was when my son, now a lawyer, was a youngster playing on a T-ball team. We were at a practice on the athletic field of Lamar Elementary, which is now part of The Woodlands but then was just a new school near Interstate 45. In the woods behind the school a bulldozer was working. I asked someone what was happening and was told, "Well, this rich oilman is going to build a city back there." I thought it must be a joke, but asked the oilman's name. George Mitchell, I was told. I guess that was probably in 1973. Little did I know that in fact there was a George Mitchell, a city would be built, and I would be associated with it. Six years later, I joined the company.

I grew up in Benton, a small town in northern Louisiana. I graduated from Louisiana Tech with a degree in geology and went to work for Humble Oil & Refining Company, which later became Exxon. I worked just two days before leaving the company to join the Air Force, where I remained for three years. In my first year, the Air Force sent me back to college. I went to Oklahoma State University to study meteorology in the graduate school and for the next two years was a weather forecaster. Most of those two years was spent at Homestead Air Force base in Florida, south of Miami, where the weather was exactly the same most days—except for the occasional hurricane and we didn't have one while I was there. I had one of the highest success ratios of any forecaster in the U.S. Air Force for one year, simply because I could forecast the same thing every day.

After leaving the Air Force, I came back to Humble Oil & Refining Company. In the time I was gone I had gotten a $20 a month raise, so I was making $420 a month. I worked as a geologist and geophysicist for Humble. I married Ann Webb in Hattiesburg, Mississippi, while I was working in the Humble office there. And my wife and I moved almost every year, which was part of the training program. We finally got transferred to corporate headquarters in Houston. We had two children by that time, Susan and Bob, and had lived in five different cities. We thought it would be nice not to have to move so often. I discovered that Exxon had a land development subsidiary called Friendswood Development Company that only worked in the Houston area. If I could get into that, I thought, we could stop moving every year. I campaigned for a transfer and got it.

I didn't know anything about land development, so there was a lot of on-the-job training. To learn the business side, I took night classes in accounting, finance, and tax at the University of Houston. I worked with a group in Friendswood that was developing a mixed-use project in the city of Houston called Woodlake. The property included an old par-three golf course. Our job was to convert this golf course into an upscale commercial and residential community. My first development assignment was to coordinate the construction of Gessner Road that connected across Buffalo Bayou. It connected Memorial to Westheimer much to the chagrin and dismay of the people who lived on the Memorial side of Buffalo Bayou. I moved into the marketing part of the business and helped acquire some land that was later developed into another project in the Houston area. In 1974, I went to work at Kingwood, a master-planned community northeast of Houston that Friendswood was developing jointly with the famed King Ranch, the largest ranch in the United States. It had opened in 1972 and I worked three years in Kingwood, in charge of its residential division.

One day, I got a call from a headhunter who asked if I'd be interested in going to work for The Woodlands. It was intriguing to me because The Woodlands was in Montgomery County and we lived in Montgomery County. It seemed to be a good opportunity and I took the job.

My knowledge of the company was limited. Someone asked me why I was leaving the secure confines of the Exxon Corporation after having been there for a number of years. They suggested that The Woodlands Corporation might be in financial jeopardy and I was really taking a risk, which frankly was the first I had thought about that. I had two kids and a wife and we were all happy and secure in the protective arms of Exxon and I had walked away from all that and joined something I didn't know that much about.

My first meeting with George Mitchell was after I had agreed to come to work for the company. He and Ed Lee, the president of The Woodlands Corporation at that time, met at least weekly to discuss business and development activity. And the week I came to work I was invited to that meeting. It was the most confusing meeting I have ever attended. Both Lee and Mitchell talked nonstop. Neither one listened to the other. I sat there wondering whether I made a terrible career decision. Things turned out okay, but that was the first exposure I had to The Woodlands Corporation. There were frequent meetings between George Mitchell and Ed Lee and they were all the same. Ed would try to make a point, George would try to make a point, and they would make different points at the same time. It was out of those chaotic— I can't think of a more accurate word—but challenging staff meetings that I first learned about the company and formed some early opinions.

The Woodlands itself was at a rather awkward stage of development. There were financial challenges, operational challenges, and management challenges within the company itself. There was conflict between the company's energy and real estate operations as to how the capital funds should be allocated.

There also were about 5,000 residents in the community when I arrived and sales in the range of 300 to 400 lots a year. But the process of community development wasn't working well. There were delays in installing amenities, in providing the infrastructure that people expected. There was just a lot of uncertainty. When I started work at The Woodlands Corporation, I had to make a cultural adjustment. Exxon was very structured. There was a high degree of trust. Most people who worked for Exxon intended to work there their full career, so they made decisions based on a very long-term view of relationships within the company. It had financial stability. It was very efficient. It recruited good people. It continues to do those things today.

The Woodlands Corporation and Mitchell Energy were far less structured and a number of people who knew George went to work for him on a personal basis before it was a public company and continued to play important roles after the public company was formed. There were a lot of personal relationships between individuals within the energy company particularly. Most of the people in real estate were recruited from the outside. They had neither a historical perspective, nor connections with people at the energy company. For the most part, energy was one entity and real estate was another. To compound this already complex relationship between the two, this was also a time of rapid growth and expansion for energy. Mitchell was in the process of adding a pipeline business, gas processing plants, and a drilling operation to his exploration and production company. There was competition for capital and for executive time. Employees didn't mix much in the early years. Over time the companies became more integrated. Financial planning and capital allocations were done in a more orderly way. It became a more businesslike enterprise.

The Woodlands was still recovering from the turmoil of its opening. Its original president, J. Leonard Ivins, had been let go. The next person, Len Rogers, was given the title of general manager and served in that position for several years. But Mitchell really wanted to recruit somebody from the developer of the successful master-planned community of Irvine, California, because of his respect for their accomplishments. I think he wanted to recruit Ray Watson, president of the Irvine Company. Of course, Watson would not be terribly interested in moving to The Woodlands to join a startup project after having built the Irvine Company. But he had an assistant, Ed Lee, who was recruited as the second president of

The Woodlands Corporation. He started to organize the real estate operations based on his experience in Irvine. Unfortunately, he passed away at an early age in 1986. I succeeded him in that role.

When I arrived at The Woodlands in 1979, things were improving but the hangover from earlier problems persisted. The Woodlands opened in October 1974; by 1976, $50 million available through a HUD loan guarantee was gone. The money had been burned through pretty quickly with the construction of the conference center, the first golf courses, some initial housing, and major infrastructure. And the economy was cratering. The energy crisis came along. Crude oil prices went up, which helped the energy company, but also drove up the price of gasoline and commuting costs became a problem and concern. We were in a period dubbed "stagflation." Interest rates ballooned to 20 percent and holding costs, the Achilles' heel of master-planned communities, increased dramatically. In 1980, the increase in the annual cost of living index hit almost 16 percent. Wearing a sweater, President Jimmy Carter gave a nationally broadcast speech from the White House, where the thermostat had been turned down to the low 60s.

Another fundamental problem was administrative organization, or lack of it. The aggressive startup followed by a tumultuous and rapid reduction of staff within the original development team affected those who were left. These were talented people committed to George Mitchell's vision for The Woodlands. Most stayed with the company and contributed for many years. We were still in the formative stages of the real estate company, but from that chaotic beginning emerged an experienced nucleus of professional friends.

An early task for the residential division was to improve our relationship with the community associations and residents. I had a lot of meetings with homeowners trying to alleviate their anxiety about things that hadn't been done yet, but would be done. And we had to deal with homebuilders who were frustrated over the untimely delivery of lots. We had an outstanding employee named Bob Williams who sold new homes and homes for resale. And Bob would hear the concerns of homebuyers because he was dealing with them face to face. When they had a problem after the purchase they would call Bob to try to solve it. He didn't have anybody to turn to in the company. And there was no system for resolving problems that were small at the beginning but could quickly become larger if not handled properly. Bob and I got to be friends. He and I would meet with residents in their kitchens and have coffee. They would invite their neighbors in and we would talk about schedules for installing streetlights and building parks and things of that nature. We tried to build credibility by addressing issues, even if we could not fix them immediately. In this way, we made friends who became supporters of the company.

One thing that made it easier, then and now, to deal with those problems was the fact that most of the people who worked for The Woodlands Corporation also lived in The Woodlands. We were not absentee owners. If there was a problem, we shared it.

When I arrived, the basic plan for The Woodlands was well along. A lot of engineering design work had been done: infrastructure planning for water, sewer, wastewater treatment, stormwater retention, and preservation of open space, parks, and pathways. The environmental concepts had been adopted. There were details to be ironed out and modifications from time to time, but the general plan was pretty much intact and adhered to, which was an advantage.

But more planning was necessary as we continued to buy acreage. We were somewhere around 18,000 acres in 1979. We bought land as it became available. We saw in the early stages of The Woodlands that we were creating a brand name. We could take advantage of that and apply it to other lands that were immediately adjacent to the town, eventually controlling 27,000 acres.

The Woodlands continued its expansion despite financial challenges. That was due to George Mitchell. The most successful ingredient of The Woodlands overall was its continuous ownership by Mitchell for some 25 years and his vision, tenacity, and wealth to see it through. His son Scott Mitchell, who was a homebuilder here, told me that George had told some members of his family that he was going to carry out the vision of The Woodlands and he was going to commit his own personal wealth to make sure that happened. He made that announcement so his family would know about it. I never heard a word of regret from him about undertaking The Woodlands. The only statement of regret I remember from George was the day he sold the company.

But it was more than Mitchell, more than the people working for him, who ultimately made The Woodlands successful. There were a number of dedicated pioneers, residents who moved to the new town in the early days. They had bought into George Mitchell's vision and they were staunch supporters. They recognized the potential and they were willing to tolerate some of the discomfort. Not that everyone agreed with all the decisions that were made by The Woodlands Corporation. They were quick to tell us when we made the wrong decision, and were ready to back up their thoughts with actions.

Here's just one story about how those pioneers felt about the place they chose to live. It concerns Pat Moritz, now a real estate agent in The Woodlands.

"We arrived in the summer of 1981 because we came from overseas and our last stop was in Mexico," Moritz remembers. "And we bought our house [sight] unseen. Just did it over the telephone, because we thought anything in The Woodlands would be wonderful. I'm still in the same townhouse."

Her husband was reading the newspaper one morning, she said, and learned that an Exxon gas station was going to be built right across the street from her home. "We had come from all around the world through hell and high water to get to a nice place and we certainly didn't want a gas station behind our house. We feared they were going to just make it a bald corner, and cut down the trees. I just got upset about it and I thought that that's not right. So we put little signs—actually, we just had little pieces of paper—and we handed it out to people on Monday morning and said, 'Do you realize they're going to put a gas station on this beautiful forested corner?' No one realized it. And a lot of people were upset about it, and before Wednesday that week we had about 200 people [who] were really, really genuinely concerned and upset and displeased. People said you can't stop progress. Well, we were promised a forest."

On the morning the bulldozers arrived, Pat Moritz and others were there. The story has grown over the years, how Moritz chained herself to a tree or sat down in front of the bulldozer. That didn't happen, but she probably would have. Some trees were bulldozed. But the developers did listen. "They did have Exxon and The Woodlands planning department come," Moritz said. "They did sit with us and they handled it very, very well. They changed the plan. They reforested [the site]. Those trees are now 30 feet to 40 feet tall. I'm a [real estate agent] and that's one of the reasons that I believe in The Woodlands and sell here."

The Woodlands Corporation did learn something from that experience. Of course, we thought we were doing a great service for the residents. It was the first gas station in The Woodlands. That was during one of the great gasoline shortages. It was hard to get any oil company to even build a new station.

In the midst of the Moritz protest, George Mitchell got involved. He got in touch with Randy Meyer, who was president of Exxon at that time. They talked about the service station and whether or not to build it and how it should look, including the signage and the setbacks. Their decision was to build the station and screen it with trees and vegetation to satisfy the residents. The episode helped to set a pattern for commercial development and better communications in The Woodlands.

Moritz says she uses the saga of the gas station today in talking to people thinking about buying in The Woodlands. "It's my best sales promotion. I use it to this day. [The Woodlands Corporation] listened. And that's what gained my respect. So they had no further problems from me." And Pat is still a good customer at the Exxon station.

As we moved forward with development, Houston's economy was really booming in the early 1980s and The Woodlands moved in concert with increasing activity. New home sales rose to 800 annually. Capital was available for growth, and grow we did. We formed a home-building company, Hometown Builders, and participated in the construction of more than 1,000 apartments, including Village Square, Holly Creek, and Parkside. Hometown Builders also constructed affordable condominiums, townhouses, and patio homes. The company constructed several speculative office buildings and a major neighborhood retail center in the Village of Panther Creek, in addition to providing support for development of The Woodlands Hospital. The third residential village, the Village of Cochran's Crossing, opened in 1983.

The following year, however, there were signs of trouble in the Houston economy. Rising interest rates were slowing home sales. Plunging crude oil prices dragged down energy companies, a mainstay of Houston's economy. By the end of 1987, Houston had lost 200,000 jobs and the unemployment rate was above 10 percent. Citywide, the office vacancy rate was 32 percent. Foreclosures reached record levels. New home sales and starts declined by more than 70 percent.

This sinking economy devastated the real estate industry. We had to shrink The Woodlands Corporation to reflect the times. We discontinued Hometown Builders and also terminated a number of employees—some of them close personal friends. That was not a pleasant chore by any definition.

In the uncertainty generated by growing unemployment, falling housing values, and increasing foreclosures, the five major master-planned communities then in the Houston area, including The Woodlands, remained relatively strong. They were buffeted far less by the economic free fall that plagued much of the city's housing market. Homeowners became more conscious than ever of protecting the value of their housing investment. As the economy deteriorated, the master-planned communities increased their market share to 50 percent of all housing starts in the Houston region. People were no longer just buying homes. They were buying community and the protection it offered. Foreclosure rates were lower in master-planned communities and values declined less. Homebuilders tended to prefer master-planned communities for the same reasons.

Commitment to job growth and economic development in The Woodlands began to pay off during this regional economic downturn. While Houston's employment declined 4 percent between 1980 and 1986, employment in The Woodlands rose 49 percent to more than 6,300 jobs. More than one-third of its residents worked here at the time.

Like the rest of Houston, we had to work our way back to prebust levels. By 1990, residential lot sales had recovered to an annual rate of 900 and operating earnings rebounded to approximately $20 million. In the period from 1990 through 1997, The Woodlands Corporation saw tremendous expansion of retail, office, and institutional development in addition to residential growth. It was during this time that the regional mall was opened, a power center containing big-box stores like Target was developed, the community college opened, new public and private schools were built, and restaurants and entertainment venues opened. Major corporations moved in. In short, The Woodlands became a regional destination for jobs, shopping, entertainment, and education.

Chapter 7

SUCCESS EMERGES, SLOWLY

———◆——

The Woodlands continued to experience tough financial times in the late 1970s and through most of the 1980s. For that matter, the national economy saw a battering throughout that era. Interest rates soared into the teens. Mortgages of 12 to 15 percent were business as usual. Those high rates priced out many homebuyers. Higher mortgage rates make homes less affordable as a greater percentage of the monthly house payment must go to pay for interest. And high prices at the pump meant potential homebuyers thought carefully about the cost of commuting—not a pleasant prospect when you are trying to sell homes 27 miles from downtown Houston.

Then in the mid-1980s the price of oil dropped. It was a boon for the rest of the country but a bust for Houston. All through the period of soaring energy prices Houston had boomed. Houston's prominence in the energy industry originally came from the huge deposits of oil and natural gas found in the state. But over the years as those reserves were depleted, Houston took on a difference face. It can logically be compared with Hollywood, where, at one time, almost all American films were made. Then the business changed. American filmmakers began making movies all over the world. But they still came to Hollywood. It became the place where the deals were made to finance the picture and contracts to distribute it were signed. The same thing happened in Houston in the energy business. All through the oil boom of the late 1970s and halfway through the 1980s, Houston was on a roll. Thousands of Sunday copies of the then-dominant *Houston Chronicle* were shipped to Detroit each week. Why? Because the paper was fat with "help wanted" advertisements and people in Detroit were looking for jobs. It was the time when the American auto industry had been whipsawed by its dearth of fuel-efficient cars during an energy crisis and the superior quality of imports, particularly those from Japan. So the people on the assembly lines, and many others in the industrial Northeast, were flocking to Houston. Houstonians generally welcomed them, although there were some signs of strain on both sides. Some of the newcomers expressed suspicions about that welcome. People were so nice to them, many remarked. What were those nice folks really after? On the other side, you could see more than a few bumper stickers proclaiming, "Don't tell me how you used to do it up north!"

The good times crashed along with the price of oil in the mid-1980s. Houstonians thought that the $30 a barrel price for crude oil would soon reach $50, or even $100. Instead, it went to $12. Thousands of homes and office buildings speculatively constructed for all those people and businesses flocking into town now sat empty. Houston added a new term to the language: "see-through buildings." Here were skyscrapers built during the boom but never rented or finished inside with interior partitions. You could look through a window on one side and see out the window on the other.

The Woodlands prospered somewhat from the boom, although the high price of gasoline limited the number of people willing to making the commute. Conversely, when the bust came, our community suffered, but not as much as others. Housing prices in the Houston area plunged. It wasn't until the early 1990s, said Michael Richmond, by then The Woodlands' chief financial officer, that the new town started to see a positive cash flow. The big reason for that turnaround, Richmond said, was "because the volume of sales grew faster than the infrastructure requirement. I mean, we were working off this massive infrastructure in place, which included brand-name everything. We had all the wheels going. We had all the product lines in place; we had all the markets available. If I were to pick a year, it would be when the mall opened [in 1994] because that was the symbolic thing that expanded and broadened our base."

But all through the bad times, The Woodlands Corporation kept plugging along, using every ploy possible to keep sales going.

Steve McPhetridge came to work for The Woodlands Corporation in 1976. He was marketing director for a homebuilder in southern California when he got a call from a headhunter who said that a new master-planned community was being built. "I didn't know a lot about master-planned communities, but when I drove down Woodlands Parkway, I thought, 'This is pretty neat.' "

He was hired to direct the sale of new homes, and later became responsible for selling commercial property in The Woodlands. As we shall see, the two are closely related. McPhetridge soon developed a close relationship with George Mitchell based a mutual love of tennis. McPhetridge is a good tennis player and Mitchell, the captain of his college tennis team, continued to play in his later years. But like a lot of canny players, as he aged he switched to doubles and sought out a partner who could make up for what age had taken from him. The tall and athletic McPhetridge fit the bill. Of course, they played whenever Mitchell was ready for a game. "One of the secretaries would call up and say, 'George would like to play tennis at 4:30,' " McPhetridge recalled. "It wasn't, 'Do you have any time?' It was, 'Yes, ma'am, I was planning to do that anyway.' One hot August day, George and I were playing two other guys and my arm was getting tired and I was serving. I said to myself, 'I'm going to rip this one to see if I can break everything loose. I hit George right in the back of the head. He dropped to his knees like he had been shot and the first thought that I had was, 'God, I've got to sell my stock. He's dead.' He got up, didn't turn around, and just said, 'Second.' "

When McPhetridge arrived in April 1976, there were fewer than 1,000 people living in The Woodlands. There was no grocery store. There was no gasoline station. There was one road in and one road out. There were two restaurants in the area—the privately owned

Hyden's, which later burned down, and The Glass Menagerie, which was located in a conference center owned by the developer. In McPhetridge's opinion, with the amount of money The Woodlands Corporation lost on its restaurant, it was a pity that the wrong one burned. But it did serve a purpose—an upscale restaurant that was available to corporate types and their families.

So what was McPhetridge selling? "Lifestyle. The people who moved here in the beginning had a little bit of a pioneer spirit and that was really neat. That was reinforced by the fact that you weren't one of 20,000 people. You were one family out of a very manageable number." He points out that, wherever you went in The Woodlands—to the Swim and Athletic Center, the country club, the schools—you knew virtually everybody. "It was a very safe environment. It was removed from all the ills of the urban city and it was out in the woods, so you had the squirrels, the chipmunks, the deer. It was a very ideal setting if you could get past the lack of convenience, shopping, and the commute to work."

Market research conducted by The Woodlands Corporation has long shown that half of the people who buy homes in the town learned about it from a current resident. One reason for that loyalty was the relationship between the residents and the developer, personified by George Mitchell. "Everybody [who lived in The Woodlands] thought of him as the patron saint, and to a large degree he was," McPhetridge said. "The people who didn't like that, didn't move here, so it was kind of a Darwinism working. But the people who did move here had that very strong feeling of love for George, respect for the money, and [for] the effort that he put into it. If something went wrong for some reason, us poor mullets who were working here were the ones who just really didn't ever understand George's vision to begin with. So they never really attached anything to George. It was always us poor peons down in the trenches."

One way The Woodlands Corporation stimulated sales in the bad times was something called the nest-egg program for market-rate apartments. As McPhetridge explains, "We had apartments that were vacant, so we allowed some people to rent an apartment with half the rent going into a nest-egg program to become the downpayment for the purchase of a home. That turned out well. We also gave incentives to employees of Woodlands-based companies who didn't live in The Woodlands, thinking that if we could help them get over the hurdle, they would make their commute shorter if they had the choice. We gave them a discount on a country club membership or a little bit of help with a downpayment."

One problem in the early days of The Woodlands involved real estate agents, those people who sell the majority of homes to buyers. "In a lot of new-home markets around the country, some cities have a strong Realtor base and others don't. And sometimes new home developers will cooperate with outside brokers and sometimes they won't, and we've vacillated back and forth," McPhetridge said. "At the beginning of The Woodlands there wasn't a strong inner-city Realtor base that would ever bring anybody up here. They didn't want to waste the time, the money, the gas, and once they got here they didn't know the product, so that just didn't happen. So really, the only Realtors in the beginning were locally based. If they have a client who is also locally based, certainly with all the advertising we were doing, they're going to come see us. Why did we need a Realtor to bring them along and pay them a commission? Sometimes if the builder thought the Realtor was important, the builder would pay the commission. Sometimes we, the company central sales office, would pay a standard fee less than the 3 percent that a selling broker would normally get.

"As The Woodlands became more established, there were more Realtors who legitimately would bring their customer, as opposed to tagging along with a customer who was already coming here," McPhetridge said. Gradually the change came, and now 80 to 85 percent of new home sales involve an outside Realtor. As The Woodlands became established, Realtors from all areas of Houston were willing to make the drive north with a client. Realtors are now an important component in our residential marketing program.

Over the years, The Woodlands developed an important niche in the relocation market. Today, about half of the new residents move from within the Houston area. In the early days, McPhetridge said, "Probably better than half came from out of town. At the time, in the 1970s and 1980s, the oil companies had a two- or three-year rotational cycle for a lot of their people. They would go to California or overseas or wherever, and when they came back to Houston, it used to be that they would all move to Kingwood," referring to a rival master-planned community northeast of Houston. "We gradually pulled a little bit more off each year. Early on, most of the people coming were from one coast or the other. They enjoyed a master-planned community, and knew what one was."

The relocation business ebbs and flows, according to the national economy, McPhetridge said. "But even in the national economic downturns, oil companies tend to shed regional offices in Tulsa or Oklahoma City or Denver and pull some of those people back into Houston. We have always had somewhere between 40 and 60 percent [of residential buyers] move here from outside Houston."

Another market for homes, which has grown over the years, is sales to residents of The Woodlands. McPhetridge explains this particular niche: "Early on, we didn't have much of a population base in The Woodlands to sell new homes to existing residents, but that grew over time. I would venture to say that [today] 25 to 30 percent of new home sales in The Woodlands are [local] people who are moving up, down, sideways, empty nesters, whatever the case may be. And there's another big segment of the new homes sales that are folks who have lived here before, got transferred wherever, and came back. The number of people who are second-time buyers in The Woodlands is strong."

One advantage The Woodlands has over most other master-planned communities in the Houston area has been its commitment to creating jobs as well as homes. The Woodlands Corporation has nurtured that advantage not only by luring companies—and their present decision makers—but also by identifying and courting future corporate leaders, especially people working at lower levels in energy companies who already lived in The Woodlands.

"As people grew up in the company that they worked for, we began to have more and more decision makers here who had that same proprietary feel for The Woodlands. And whether they were able to move a division of a company, or they were influential with one of their peers in another company, we ended up having some fairly good success with those kinds of people," McPhetridge said. That internal lobbying was especially useful when The Woodlands snagged the relocation of one of Houston's most venerable manufacturing companies, Hughes

Tool. It was—and is—a company founded upon a superior oil-drilling bit originally developed by the father of Howard Hughes.

The Hughes Tool move to The Woodlands made a tremendous difference, not just due to the jobs it brought to the community, but also because it sent a message that this new town was acceptable to a major corporation. "Hughes Tool was like a lot of commercial deals. You race around and raise a lot of dust, but you really sit by the phone and wait for it to ring," McPhetridge said. "We got a call and somebody said Hughes Tool may be interested and so we started talking to them. There were two major things that caused their move: One was a terribly large, inefficient, and aging physical plant down on the east side of Houston. They had a million square feet down there and you thought if the rust ever went away, the whole thing would collapse. And the second was the workforce issue." Hughes was in the process of trying to completely modernize the manufacture of drill bits and they had problems because of an aging physical plant and a need to upgrade their trained workers.

The company decided the only way to turn itself around was to start over. "So they looked outside of their local environment and decided the suburbs were a good place to hire the kinds of people they wanted. North was good for them because there was a lot of blue-collar labor . . . driving from Montgomery County down to Houston. If they could provide them a drive that was a third as long and get them closer to home, they would have a leg up on hiring them. It gave them the opportunity to tell the worker bees we're going to The Woodlands and we want you and if you weren't one of them, you retired. So they got a new upgraded workforce, a very modern physical plant, and they did it in a very white-collar environment that they thought would have tremendous future value for their state-of-the-art physical plant. And all that's worked out."

Moving a major manufacturing facility to what is not only a suburban area, but also one that prided itself on its environmental sensitivity, could have presented problems. It did not. "It is hidden behind the trees, which is a great cure-all for industrial architecture. They sit back in the forest and nobody knows they are there. From a planning standpoint within The Woodlands, we placed them relatively close to a major road to [give the company access] to the freeway, so we didn't have trucks winding their way past the shopping areas or through the residential areas. [We] were able to tuck them back in an area that still to this day you drive by and don't know it's back there. It's all very internally oriented and a very clean manufacturing plant controlled by the latest technology."

Hughes brought 400 jobs to The Woodlands. Many of those workers lived in Houston and had no way to conveniently or economically commute to our town, so the developer helped Hughes organize a shuttle that ran in opposite directions to the usual commuting traffic, reducing the amount of time employees sat in their cars. That was one of the elements that helped Hughes make the decision to move to The Woodlands.

"It was interesting to me when we closed the transaction," McPhetridge said. "Hughes Tool is a major company and at closing only one person showed up, [the chief executive officer] Andy Szescila. He had a check in his coat pocket for the purchase price of the land. He hadn't signed it yet. The people on our team and our lawyers all gathered around the table and it was just Andy by himself. He negotiated the final details of the transaction, signed the check, signed the closing statement, got up, and left. It was just as simple as anything in the world.

"Andy told me that the reason he left Houston, in part, was the company had been in Houston 88 years and no one from the city or county had come by to ask if they could help him do anything (Hughes funded its own fire department and security service). It was not until he had announced he was leaving that anybody from the city or county showed up and then it was only to complain that he was leaving. Actually, Hughes also looked at a site in Fort Worth. They looked broader than The Woodlands. The Greater Houston Partnership, the umbrella organization of business leaders, became a bit concerned that we were stealing companies out of Houston. Our defense was that we really kept them in the Houston region because they were looking at sites much further away."

The other influential corporate relocation to The Woodlands was by Anadarko Petroleum Co., one of the top international players in the oil and gas business. "Anadarko was a different experience altogether. Their lease at Greenspoint [a mixed-use development closer to Houston and near the city's major airport] was going to be up in three years," McPhetridge notes. "I went down and called on them—just kind of a cold call. I knew Don Willis, their director of corporate service. And he [told me that] Bob Allison, the chairman and CEO [of Anadarko], said that, 'If we move, it's going to be in the Greenspoint area because he lived [near there].' " But that was not the end of the story. "I called him a couple of days later and asked if he would mind if we just gave him a proposal, more to placate [my boss] Roger than anything. So we got Gensler Architects and D.E. Harvey Builders to do a design and pricing exercise. We had a neat-looking rendering of a building that is just strikingly close to what they ended up with. So we walked back in and said, you know, we appreciate you guys wanting to stay [put], but here is what it may look like if you move to The Woodlands. One thing led to another and they finally moved up here. [Anadarko is] a very good corporate citizen, and they built what turned out to be the building that we had planned on all along.

"Since the original decision, Anadarko has purchased a second building and moved approximately 2,000 jobs to The Woodlands."

One thing McPhetridge promised Anadarko wound up costing The Woodlands Corporation $2 million. The oil company wanted a full-service corporate hotel nearby for business visitors and they wanted its construction tied to their contract. The Woodlands Corporation had talked for years about building such a hotel and leasing it to an operator.

So The Woodlands Corporation agreed to build the hotel. A completion date for the hotel was set, but Anadarko insisted on a penalty fee should the project be delayed or fall through.

The hotel wasn't built on time. "By that time," McPhetridge notes, "Crescent and Morgan Stanley had bought The Woodlands. Crescent apparently didn't quite understand what that commitment meant, so they put a halt to the planning of the hotel. We would have had plenty of time to do it had we not taken a nine-month hiatus. The hotel was built, but not before The Woodlands Corporation had to ante up a $2 million penalty to Anadarko."

The relocation of Anadarko to The Woodlands is another example of the loyalty felt by those who live in the new town. "Don Willis at Anadarko lives in The Woodlands. His wife is a schoolteacher here. His daughter grew up, went to Texas A&M University, and is now a teacher at Galatas Elementary School in The Woodlands. It's that proprietary feeling that gives us such a leg up," McPhetridge believes. If you don't do the parks right and the schools right and homes right and the whole environment right, the lifestyle that we talked about, then you don't get the fruits of that labor." McPhetridge has since left The Woodlands Corporation to go into business for himself, but still lives here.

It was during that same era that The Woodlands Corporation ended its relationship with the U.S. Department of Housing and Urban Development, the guarantor of the $50 million loan that paid for initial financing of the new town. That guarantee had been vital for The Woodlands. Doubtless Mitchell would have done something with the land. But it is far more likely a conventional suburban development would exist where The Woodlands does today.

Over the years, relations between HUD and The Woodlands Corporation waxed and waned. At several points, HUD had threatened the new town developers with various sanctions, usually over administrative procedures and in one case, an allegation of self-dealing because of work done in The Woodlands by a Mitchell-related company. All those disputes were later settled. On the other side, The Woodlands' developer frequently complained that HUD had promised grants for additional infrastructure for The Woodlands, but reneged on its pledges.

Joel Deretchin, who spent the first part of his career with The Woodlands Corporation as a liaison with HUD, notes that legislation setting up the new town program had promised grants and funding for projects that would normally be done by a public entity like a city or county. "Under the New Communities Program, the developer and the community association were eligible to receive the funding. HUD also promised that it would be a conduit for funding by other federal agencies, like the Environmental Protection Agency, for sewage treatment. They were long on promise and short on performance. It took several years for HUD to get the funding for the community development block grants and then when they got it, it lasted only about three years before that funding was curtailed. It was not just us. Twelve other developers made significant financial commitments to do these projects with the understanding that the infrastructure would be publicly funded, only to find out that after a few years [the funding] terminated. For a few years, [The Woodlands] got money from HUD for parks, pathways, streets, and low- and moderate-income housing. But that stopped and the burden fell upon the developer to fund facilities that would normally be funded by the public. It put a tremendous economic burden on the project. We got our first sewage treatment plant funded by the EPA, within that brief window when things were working. Then after that, a subsequent treatment plant had to be developed and funded by other means.

"I think HUD's interest in the program waned pretty fast because the other communities in the program failed at a very early stage in their development. Most of the projects came on line in 1974 and 1975, during a recession. Most of the others didn't have the deep pockets to carry the projects through the recession. But for the grace and commitment of George Mitchell and Mitchell Energy & Development Corporation, The Woodlands would not have weathered that recession either. So HUD lost its appetite very, very fast for the whole program. It had to honor its guarantees and essentially foreclosed on most of the other projects.

"And there was The Woodlands all by itself. The only successful project, the only one continuing and asking for these grant funds. The New Communities Administration [of HUD] didn't have any clout within the department or with Congress to continue the funding. By 1982, they had decided to get out of the new communities business. The funding had dried up. It was such a hassle to do business with [them]." Deretchin added, "We were happy to have HUD terminate the program, terminate our involvement since we weren't getting the benefits that we had hoped for [that would] let us go on as a fully independent project."

The Woodlands Corporation and HUD decided to terminate the loan guarantee. As part of the termination, the developer agreed to continue its effort to provide low-income housing and an affirmative action program in both housing and employment. HUD also stated that they had every confidence that the developer would continue to develop the project in compliance with the original goals of the program. The corporation was relieved of most of its obligations under the loan guarantee. So it was a divorce. Debt financing was provided to The Woodlands through its parent company, Mitchell Energy.

One interesting side note: The original loan guarantee had been collateralized by the land, but to keep the development going during the hard times of the late 1970s, George Mitchell had also pledged a portion of his stock in Mitchell Energy & Development Corporation to guarantee repayment of the $50 million loan secured by HUD's guarantee. As part of the termination agreement with HUD, Mitchell's stock was freed up and that was a benefit to him.

So why and how did The Woodlands succeed when all the other new towns established under HUD loan guarantees foundered? Deretchin believes there are three principal reasons.

"You have to remember that the program was promulgated by the U.S. Congress and administered in a political context. There were people allowed into the program not because they had the experience, not because they knew what they were doing, not because they had a good plan, but because their congressman got them into the program." One new town developer was a church, another a veteran civil rights leader. All had good intentions. What they didn't have was experience in community development. What they did have was a congressman or senator who got them into the program.

"Second, many of these projects were located in places that were not and were never going to be well situated to their marketplace. They were out of the way. They were in places people didn't want to live. The Woodlands may have suffered from that [problem] in the early years to some extent, but [proximity] to the international airport and Interstate 45 made the north side [of Houston] a credible place to consider living.

"And then the last thing—and I think this is very important—is that other developers either were not committed to putting the resources in when the project started to fail or didn't have the funds. When I was a consultant to HUD [before going to work for The Woodlands], I got around to a number of these projects to do workout scenarios for them. When their developers saw the thing failing, they said, 'I'm out of here.' They didn't have money in the project and they walked away from it. What distinguished Mr. Mitchell's commitment was that he had more invested than any other developer that I'm aware of. Plus, he had his stock pledged, so he wasn't able to walk away from it. He convinced his board of directors that this was something they should stick with and they did."

Part III

---◆---

BUILDING
INSTITUTIONS

Building civic, social, and educational institutions within master-planned communities is a bedrock activity that distinguishes them from the laissez-faire expansion of typical suburban developments. It is how a sense of community is forged, requiring an evolving compact among the developer, residents, and agencies with institutional experience. At the early stages of a community's life, the developer must play a more dominant role in the formation of institutions. As the community matures, residents' involvement expands as they step in to assume the critical role of directing institutional growth and management.

Building institutions within a master-planned community means dealing with a series of transitions. You start with a concept that you believe will succeed when there is a critical mass of people, residents, or customers. You also know that critical mass will not materialize unless there is evidence that the concept will become reality. The challenge is to balance resources and market expectations during the transition period from startup to completion without stubbing your financial toe. Each case has unique requirements, but working out a system for delivering service through institutions is a critical success factor in community development.

Rules, customs, expectations, and financial resources vary from region to region, state to state, and jurisdiction to jurisdiction. However, there are consistent human needs regardless of community location. These include good schools, public safety, open space and environmental sensitivity, places of worship, participation in government, transportation services, health care, well-maintained roads, and the celebration of festive events. These are the "software" components of development that elevate the community's quality of life.

Institutional development was a key to advancing quality of life in The Woodlands. Following is a look at the various methods both the developer and residents of the community used to build viable institutions.

Chapter 8

INTERFAITH

———— • ◆ • ————

Don Gebert left the job he loved in Philadelphia to help build a brand new community called The Woodlands. A Lutheran minister, Gebert did not come as an employee of The Woodlands Corporation. He was supposed to help the company's Institutional Planning Committee, which was providing expertise to build social infrastructure for the new town. Specifically, he was to be the link between the committee, a quasi-independent agency, and the religious community. Gebert loaded his wife and five children into the family car, and with a moving van trailing behind them, arrived at The Woodlands Information Center in early 1975. Waiting out front was Charles Kelly, the head of the planning committee. Kelly told Gebert that all of the committee members had been laid off—the result of a severe cash flow problem at The Woodlands Corporation. Gebert recalled Kelly telling him he might as well turn around and go back to Philadelphia. Happy New Year.

First, Gebert said, he cried. Then he got busy, and stayed that way for the next ten years. He catalyzed the volunteer effort that has been so important to The Woodlands. People like Gebert—and over the years there have been thousands—had a sense of what needed to done. And they did it. Most developers of planned communities like The Woodlands would have put in place infrastructure that would help these things get done. When Gebert arrived, The Woodlands Corporation couldn't do it because of financial constraints. Later on, The Woodlands did get more involved in community building. But it was the pioneers like Gebert who built a social infrastructure when doing so looked hopeless.

When Gebert arrived there was simply no social structure in this new town. There were no houses of worship, no community centers, no senior citizen groups, no child care.

Gebert did not start out to be a minister. "I went to the Wharton School at the University of Pennsylvania to be trained in business because my father and my grandfather [each served as] chief operating officer of Lee's Carpets, the biggest division of Burlington Industries, which is the biggest textile company in the world. And that was supposed to be my job." But Gebert found he was much more interested in helping people than running a large corporation. He went to his pastor and told him he wanted to be a minister. He was told to tell his father of his decision. Gebert did, recalling his father was less than enthusiastic about his son's plans. "And my pastor said, 'Finish the Wharton School first, because we don't have many pastors in the church that have the administrative and business side and we need that really badly.' So I did. Then I went to seminary and became a pastor. . .in the Evangelical Lutheran Church in America."

Gebert's journey to Texas started without his knowledge. Before The Woodlands opened, George Mitchell assembled a meeting of the leaders of many of the religious bodies in the Houston area, including Catholic, Jewish, and Protestant. "He brought them together in one room," Gebert said, "and told them he was developing The Woodlands. He told them he knew how to do the hardware, but he needed somebody to do the software. That is, he needed somebody to plant the religious community and all the human services in this new town."

The religious leaders that day formed a corporation separate from The Woodlands called The Woodlands Religious Community Incorporated. It's now called Interfaith.

"Mr. Mitchell was a devoutly religious man," Gebert noted, "and felt that the human aspects of The Woodlands were very important, that making money was important, but making people happy also was the right thing to do. His [Episcopal] priest, Dick Wheatcroft, became the first president of The Woodlands Religious Community Inc. That organization then proceeded to look for somebody to be its staff person here in The Woodlands. They went through all the national offices of the denominations looking for people. By the time I was contacted, they already had 66 candidates for the job."

Gebert wasn't looking for a job. "I had what some people said was the best job in Philadelphia. I was associate director of the Philadelphia Foundation, which had $150 million, and my job was to give the money away to organizations that were in need and make the connections between the haves and the have-nots in Philadelphia. It was the 1970s, right after Dr. Martin Luther King had died, and there was a lot of turmoil in the inner city. I worked hooking up the inner city with the banks and the business leaders of the community to try to improve the quality of life in Philadelphia."

Someone called Gebert and asked if he might be interested in this new community called The Woodlands. Gebert's knowledge of Texas mainly came from western movies. He thought Texas was all desert and sagebrush. "When they told me this place was going to be called The Woodlands I laughed and said, 'What have you got, three trees?' " Gebert, like many people, wasn't aware that Houston has a semitropical climate, which averages 49 inches of rain a year, and lots of trees.

Because Gebert was not that interested in the job, he wrote a ten-page summary of his ideas, "knowing that this organization would probably be run by the Southern Baptists and they would reject me immediately and I wouldn't have to worry about it anymore. It was all liberal ideas of how the church should get involved with people and how the garbage collection is more important than whether you got a cross on top of your building or not. Really kind of radical stuff I would say. Well lo and behold, I got a phone call, saying, 'Come down here and interview. You're a breath of fresh air.' " Gebert was hired in December 1974. The Woodlands had been officially opened just one month at that time. There were about 50 residents. When he arrived in March, the number of residents had doubled, to about 100.

What made Gebert move to Texas? "Well, first of all my brother, who was in charge of one of the big real estate investment companies, Franklin Realty, had all the contacts. He looked up George Mitchell in Dunn & Bradstreet, and he did a bunch of checking and said this guy Mitchell's for real. If you really want to have an adventure, go on down there and work with

George. So, I said okay, you know, I'm going to do that. Never been to Texas, but I'm an adventurer. My wife said, 'Let's go for it.' So we did."

On his arrival came the news from Charles Kelly. Gebert called Dick Wheatcroft, the president of the Interfaith Woodlands Religious Community board, and said, "Look, I've been told to go back home." Wheatcroft said, "Don't you dare. We've got to find a way to do this." To get the ball rolling, Wheatcroft arranged a lunch meeting between Mitchell and Gebert.

The two men immediately disagreed. Mitchell wanted to copy the system employed in Columbia, Maryland, which has three religious centers that host all religious services. All the denominations own a part of each building. Gebert didn't think much of the Columbia model: "Well, I was scared to death, but I had to open my mouth because I had visited Columbia and [believed] it had the lowest percentage of people attending church of any city in the United States, and I knew what the reason was. They were asked to share with other denominations things they didn't want to share. [There was an effort] to erase the lines between the Baptists and the Lutherans and the Presbyterians, and I knew that in the 1970s in Texas that wasn't going to work. So I opened my mouth and said, 'Mr. Mitchell, we can't do it that way.' He said, 'What?' I said, 'Sir, forgive me, but here's what we need to do. We need to get the churches in here. We need to provide incubator space for them, but we also need to provide land for them to have their own buildings, rather than putting them all in one interfaith center. And we need to have enticements like big discounts on land next to schools and parks, so that they don't have to buy a lot of land. You could save a lot of money by not selling them a lot of land since you're selling it to them at a discount, and we could get them to commit to work together with each other long term through this organization we have, The Woodlands Religious Community Inc.'

"He sat there for about two minutes without saying a word. I thought this was the end of me. I was going back to Pennsylvania. He said, 'Let's try it your way.' And that's why we have this model—a totally different model from any of the other new towns in the United States. But it's a model that we knew would work and it did work."

Now, all Gebert had to do was develop an organization on a mere $40,000 a year—a sum provided by the member organizations of Interfaith—and even worse, with only 100 residents to help him. "How do you start churches? So, I'm the victim of accidental genius, and trust me it is accidental and it is ingenious. I decided there's only one thing to do, and that is to visit every household in The Woodlands and to set up my office in a place where I can catch everybody as they move in. I'll take three-by-five cards and carry them with me, and I will write down all the pertinent information on every family; as clergy, I could even find out who needs Alcoholics Anonymous. I told people I was a clergy person, but didn't tell them of what denomination. And they opened up to me. I visited the 100 families that were here and set up my office at the old information center. Interfaith was there because this place really is a jungle. You can't find your way around, so every moving van had to come to the center to find out how to get to the [right] house. I bought a little one-and-a-half horse-power auto cycle, with top speed about 14 miles an hour with a tail wind, and used it to follow the moving vans. I spent the first six months doing nothing but following moving vans around this town. And I visited people day and night as they moved in and found out I had a gold mine because I had more information than the developer did on the people who were here.

"I got a call from Mr. Mitchell's secretary saying, 'Don, we need you to come in and talk about sharing that information you have on the people because we have to report to HUD on our ethnicity, on our income levels, on everything, and we don't have the data; you have it.' So my second stroke of accidental genius was to go and sit down with Mr. Mitchell and say, 'I am happy to share [statistical] information with you, but I need something [in exchange].' I said I needed funding for [additional staff] to visit these new people as they move in. I visited the first 1,200 families all by myself. It was an exhausting job. I never saw my wife and kids. Besides trying to put together the Interfaith organization, I was spending all my time visiting people. Mr. Mitchell agreed, but asked if I would do one thing for him—set up an information referral service with a special phone number that all residents can call when they have problems. [The Woodlands Corporation was] getting nothing but phone calls from residents with problems. I was the people organization, he said. Let the people call me. I agreed. I went to the United Way office in Conroe and said, Would you give us a little bit of funding to set up an information referral service?' "

Some of the questions that referral center received were about churches and religion, Gebert said. But most were things more along the lines of, "Where is the nearest dry cleaner?" "Is there a movie theater close by?" "Where is a restaurant?"

There were other happy accidents that became very important to the growth of Interfaith. In the summer of 1975, Gebert talked with Ruth Adams, one of the first residents of The Woodlands: "I said, 'Ruth, it would be great if we could pass around a couple of sheets of paper that have everybody's name, address, telephone number, and birth dates of children, and [that were] coded by their neighborhood.' [The idea being that] somebody who moves in here with a three-year-old kid can find the other people who live in the same neighborhood who have a three-year-old kid. And we can help senior citizens find each other. I [may have] promoted more senior citizen romances than anybody in the history of the whole United States. Anyway, Ruth said, 'I can type that up for you, [but] I'm in a wheelchair. I can't go anywhere. We'll get your friend, Jack O'Sullivan, who has this little mimeograph machine to run it off, and you, Don, you've got your auto cycle, [so] you deliver it to everybody.' The first resident directory was four pages long, had 197 people in it, and was coded by neighborhood—had everything in it but the religious preference. We didn't publicize that to each other.

"We started a Grogan's Mill Village Association, which was the first village association. And we also put out a four-page newsletter so that people would know what was going on. Well, that became a very popular thing and we started putting out that little four-page newsletter every month, and then every week. That's what became *The Villager*, which is our newspaper now."

The next big battle Gebert faced was over child care. "It was advertised at the [The Woodlands] Information center with a great big picture, 'Child care for everyone,' but there was no child care. So about half a dozen ladies called me and asked if we could do anything about this. And I said, 'Yeah, you want to be on the committee?' Whenever anybody volunteered to do anything in this community, they became committee chair, or at least [a member of] the steering committee for the group. So we formed a child care committee. We went to Len Rogers, who was then running [The Woodlands Corporation], and said, 'We'll start the child care center, we'll pay all the expenses, we'll do everything, just give us some free space to start it in.' He said, 'I'm not giving you any free space to start a child care center. You guys need to make money out of this and the developer needs to make some money off of it.' I said, 'Len, you've been advertising for two years now that there was child care here in The Woodlands, there isn't any, and people are upset.' He said, 'Nothing I can do about it, Don.'

"Well, a week later, on a Monday morning, Len walked into his office. . .and there were 12 ladies sitting [there] with their infants crying and babbling and making noise. Some of them were [even] sitting on his desk—the only sit-in that ever happened in The Woodlands. Len went around the back of his desk, picked up the telephone, and called me, saying 'Don, what in the you-know-what are you doing?' I said, 'I'm working at my desk, Len. What are you doing?' He said, 'You've got my office filled with children.' I said, 'Len, what are you talking about?' He said, 'What do you want?' And I said, 'You know what we want and we're willing to do all the work ourselves. Just give us some space.' He said, 'Okay, you got it.' And I heard a huge cheer over the telephone coming from the other end."

With a child care center up and running and an information and referral service in place, Gebert turned his attention to his primary task at Interfaith, which was to establish religious institutions in the community. "We were just waiting for the time when we had enough people of each denomination. The denominations loved us because we ended up being able to have them start instant churches without [investing] the $50,000 or $100,000 to develop a church, because we knew who the Methodists, the Baptists, the Episcopalians, the Catholics were.

"The first thing we did was really interesting. We started Sunday night vesper services. That's what I called them because that's the term for evening and it's a religious term so I thought it sounded good. One Sunday we'd have a Catholic priest give a 15-minute speech on what was unique about Catholicism and then we'd have a Catholic service. We'd have a Methodist preacher the next time, a Lutheran the time [after]. I'd have a rabbi [hold a service]. We covered the whole works. And it was wonderful. When we had 500 residents in The Woodlands, 200 of them would come on a Sunday night for the vesper service at our little Interfaith office in the Information Center."

The first church established in The Woodlands was the Southern Baptist. "The exciting thing about the Baptists," Gebert says, "was. . .that Charles Lee Williamson, who was the mission director for the Baptist General Convention of Texas, was on our board of directors. [Williamson] said, 'We can do stuff here that we can't do in the rest of the Southern Baptist Church because I'll just tell them it's an experiment.' In 1976. . .they started a building program. . .and built a separate side chapel area so that other denominations could use it for incubator space. The Disciples' [of Christ] congregation started there. Our Lutheran congregation started there, the Interfaith Child Development Center moved there, the Nazarene congregation started there, all because Interfaith did not yet have our own incubator space. The Baptists did that for us and they became the leading light in getting Interfaith going."

Cooperation of religious denominations came from unexpected places, like the Church of Latter-Day Saints. The Mormons came to Gebert seeking to build a church in The Woodlands. "This is the most mind-boggling story of all because the Mormons had never before joined a cooperative ministry," Gebert explained. "Mr. Mitchell gave me permission to say to them, 'You cannot have land in The Woodlands unless you join Interfaith, and to join Interfaith you've got to pay that $5,000 a year that the other denominations paid for their first three years here. It's going to cost you $15,000. We will sell you land at a 60 percent discount like we do for the rest of the churches, and you can be part of Interfaith.' " It took some convincing of Mormon leaders in Salt Lake City, but the deal was made.

"We're up to 38 churches in The Woodlands now," noted Gebert. But his accomplishments were even broader than that. "Mr. Mitchell's planning department was great about putting these church sites next to parkland and schools where we could share parking and outdoor areas. But we didn't have enough space to incubate the denominations, and we were in the one school district, Conroe Independent School District, that in those days would not allow their schools to be used for church. I gathered a bunch of community, business, and religious leaders, and development corporation people, and said, 'Look, we need to build an Interfaith Center.' [We needed it] for incubator space, our child development center, and administrative space because now our programs [and staff] were starting to grow."

In order to build the center, Interfaith needed $330,000. The year was 1979. Gebert decided to sell bonds. Mitchell agreed to donate the land for the center. The money was for the structure. Over 400 families bought bonds and at that time there were only 600 families in The Woodlands. "The thing that really kicked it off was Mike Richmond, the controller of The Woodlands Corporation. Somebody suggested to me if you get Mike Richmond to buy a bond, everybody would buy a bond. I went to Mike and he said, 'You've got to be kidding me. What's the collateral?' I said, 'The collateral's that dirt road back there where we're going to. . .open a child care center. . .and fill it within three months. And we're going to have money to pay back these bonds.' He said, 'Gebert, you're out of your mind. But. . .if it will help you, I ought to come up with a thousand bucks and buy four $250 bonds.' So I said, 'Well you're only allowed to buy these bonds if you let me publicize the fact that you did.' He said, 'What am I getting out of this?' I said, 'The good Lord will take care of you.' So he did it. And the moment everybody heard about that, everybody bought these bonds. We made every bond payment on schedule. And every bond was paid off by 1993. We built the Interfaith Center, incubated the churches, and built that wonderful child care center."

In addition to the challenges of establishing congregations and raising funds for various projects, Gebert faced another kind of problem—he called it "the New Town Syndrome." He reports, "The divorce rate in The Woodlands was unbelievably high. The reason was people came here from other places with very high expectations. This place looks like it is paradise and would solve all your human problems. So people moved out here thinking that walking hand-in-hand down the bike path and lying around in a hammock was going to solve their problems. And when they got here, they came to the one place that had none of the systems developed that they needed to fulfill their life." To combat the syndrome, "We started a whole bunch of human service programs. We started a senior citizens' program, which [became an]

SAM ASHE SCHOOL (SO. OF F.M. 242 & I-45)

Long before The Woodlands appeared on the scene, a portion of the land it now occupies was owned by the Grogan Cochran Lumber Company, which operated the Tamina Sawmill. The Sam Ashe School (shown) served mill workers' children from 1917 to 1927.
Courtesy of Jim and Wanda Cochran

A timber train carries logs to a mill owned by the Grogan Cochran Lumber Company, circa 1925.
Courtesy of Jim and Wanda Cochran

George Mitchell, founder of Mitchell Energy & Development Corporation and founding developer of The Woodlands, posing in his dress uniform and boots while a student cadet in his senior year at Texas A&M. He graduated in 1939.
Courtesy of The Woodlands Operating Company, LP

George Mitchell (left) ran his first company—a petroleum exploration firm called Oil Drilling—with his brother, Johnny Mitchell (right), Merlyn Christie (middle).
Courtesy of The Woodlands Operating Company, LP

William L. Pereira, a nationally recognized architect and urban planner, brought credibility and experience to The Woodlands planning process through his previous involvement in the development of Irvine Ranch, a successful master-planned community in California.
Courtesy of The Woodlands Operating Company, LP/Ted Washington

Ian McHarg, chairman of the University of Pennsylvania Department of Landscape and Regional Planning and author of the seminal book *Design With Nature*, was selected as environmental consultant for George Mitchell's planning team. McHarg was influential in making the preservation of natural resources a priority in the development plan for The Woodlands.
Courtesy of The Woodlands Operating Company, LP/Ted Washington

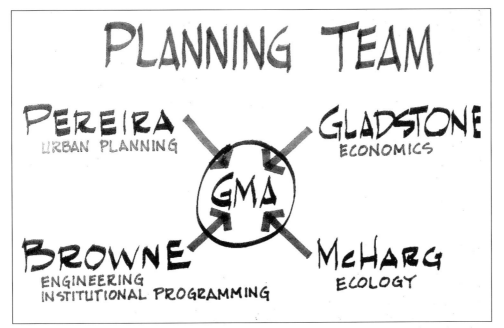

HUD insisted that George Mitchell commission a professional team with recognized credentials and experience in master-planned communities in order for it to seriously consider his application for loan guarantees. The chart above shows the team members of coordinating entity George Mitchell Associates (GMA), an early corporate name. The planning team assembled for The Woodlands' master plan included economics consultant Robert L. Gladstone, environmental consultant Ian McHarg, engineer Richard P. Browne, and urban planner William L. Pereira.
Courtesy of The Woodlands Operating Company, LP

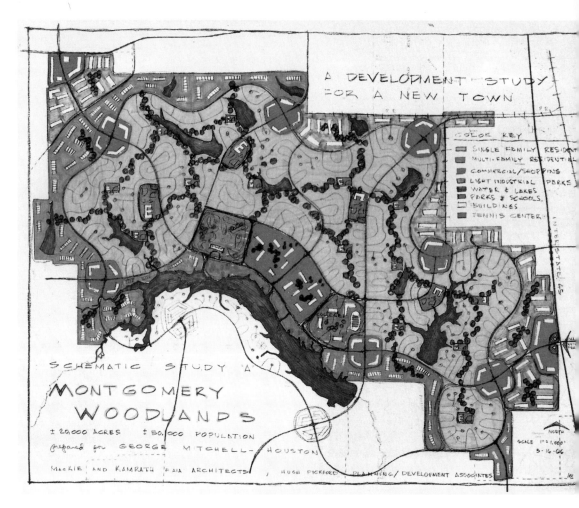

A DEVELOPMENT STUDY FOR A NEW TOWN

COLOR KEY
SINGLE FAMILY RESIDENT
MULTI-FAMILY RESIDENTIAL
COMMERCIAL/SHOPPING
LIGHT INDUSTRIAL PARKS
WATER & LAKES
PARKS & SCHOOLS
BUILDINGS
TENNIS CENTER

SCHEMATIC STUDY A

MONTGOMERY
WOODLANDS

± 20,000 ACRES   ± 50,000 POPULATION

prepared for GEORGE MITCHELL - HOUSTON

MacKIE AND KAMRATH FAIA ARCHITECTS / HUGH PICKFORD PLANNING/DEVELOPMENT ASSOCIATES

NORTH
SCALE 1" = 1,000'
3-16-66

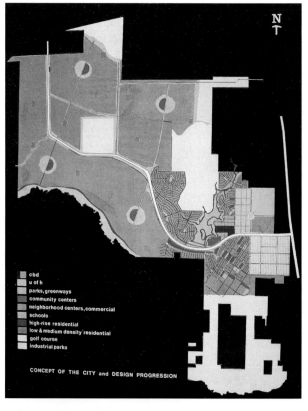

N

cbd
u of h
parks, greenways
community centers
neighborhood centers, commercial
schools
high-rise residential
low & medium density residential
golf course
industrial parks

CONCEPT OF THE CITY and DESIGN PROGRESSION

...series of plans shows the evolution of the process
...ed to the current general plan for The Woodlands.
...nitial plan (opposite, top) was conceived by Karl
...rath of MacKie, Kamrath and Pickford Planning
...lopment Associates in 1966 to help George Mitchell
...rstand how much land would be required for a new
.... The second plan (opposite, bottom), prepared by
...Stanford Ross, a Houston architecture firm, was
...oped as part of the preliminary application for a HUD
...guarantee in 1970. The third general plan (right,
...—developed by a team that included architect and
...n planner William L. Pereira, engineer and planner
...ard P. Browne, environmental consultant Ian McHarg,
...urban planner Robert J. Hartsfield—addressed and
...mented conditions set by the HUD agreement cover-
...he original 17,455 acres of the project. The current
...ral plan (right, bottom), which covers 27,000 acres,
...nds and refines earlier plans to address new market
...rtunities.
...sy of The Woodlands Operating Company, LP

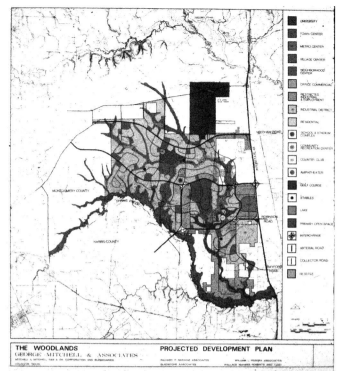

THE WOODLANDS — PROJECTED DEVELOPMENT PLAN
GEORGE MITCHELL & ASSOCIATES

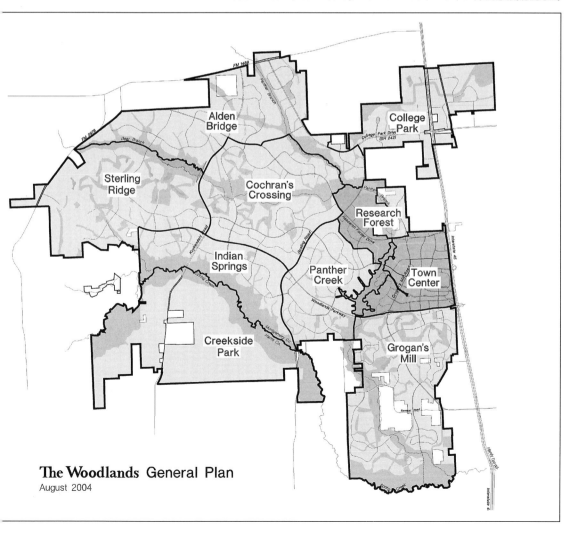

The Woodlands General Plan
August 2004

The Woodlands' grand opening on October 19, 1974, was attended
the development team and local dignitaries, including Jim Rush, th
developer's director of marketing; George Mitchell; Lynn Coker, cou
judge of Montgomery County; and Cynthia Woods Mitchell.
Courtesy of The Woodlands Operating Company, LP

An early advertisement shows the starting price of a new home at
The Woodlands. The ad attempts to create a sense of urgency—
"visit this weekend for best lot selection"—despite the fact that
there were more than 17,000 acres yet to be developed.
Courtesy of The Woodlands Operating Company, LP

GRAND OPENING #4

The Woodlands presents four new
Homewood model homes from $49,9

Visit this weekend for best lot selection

In all, 22,000 people dressed in their 1970s casual best turned out f
The Woodlands' grand opening.
Courtesy of The Woodlands Operating Company, LP

The Woodlands Corporation, a division of Mitchell Energy & Development Corporation, hired Plato Pappas (left), vice president for engineering, and Vern Robbins (right), senior vice president for land development, shown here circa 1973, to coordinate infrastructure design and construction during the formative years of The Woodlands' development.
Courtesy of The Woodlands Operating Company, LP

Completed in late 1974, the Wharf and Conference Center, including its golf facilities, served as the early signature feature of The Woodlands, establishing the new community's identity in the region.
Courtesy of The Woodlands Operating Company, LP

The Woodlands Swim and Athletic Center, one of the first amenities in the new community, is an Olympic-quality aquatic training center.
Courtesy of The Woodlands Operating Company, LP/Ted Washington

In July 1983, the formal opening of Cochran's Crossing, the third residential village built in The Woodlands, was attended by Roger Galatas, Bill Cochran, Rev. Don Gebert, Ed Lee, Montgomery County Commissioner Weldon Locke, George Mitchell, and Montgomery County Judge Jimmy Edwards.
Courtesy of The Woodlands Operating Company, LP/Ted Washington

Urban planning firm Terradevaco Inc.'s general plan for the initial development phase of Grogan's Mill, The Woodlands' first residential village, which opened in 1974. The plan shows the curvilinear streets, extensive greenbelts, and pedestrian paths that characterized the new community.
Courtesy of The Woodlands Operating Company, LP

**Grogan's Mill Village
First Phase General Plan**

This plan for Alden Bridge, the fifth residential village to be developed in The Woodlands, features a retail center, walkable neighborhoods and greenbelts.
Courtesy of The Woodlands Operating Company, LP

s in The Woodlands are designed and constructed to complement and blend into their natural setting and to take advantage of adjacent
ties, including golf courses, lakes, and open space. Natural vegetation on homesites is protected by covenants and enforcement of
ʳuction standards.
ᵤrtesy of The Woodlands Operating Company, LP/Ted Washington
Zane Segal

The Woodlands' original entrance sign (above) sat in a sea of bluebonnets, the official Texas flower. The sign stayed in place until 2001, when a new entry sign (right) was installed on The Woodlands Parkway. The long stone wall, signage, and land-scaping, designed by David Smith of SLA Studio Land, is complemented by artist Curtis Zabel's bronze statues of whitetail deer.
Courtesy of The Woodlands Operating Company, LP/Ted Washington

The second hospital in The Woodlands, St. Luke's Woodlands Community Medical Center, opened in 2003. It is a full-service, 84-bed facility with an emergency room.
Courtesy of The Woodlands Operating Company, LP/Ted Washington

In 1973, torrential rainstorms repeatedly disrupted construction of critical infrastructure such as The Woodlands Parkway (top), a situation that delayed the opening of The Woodlands. A 1995 photograph of The Woodlands Parkway (bottom) shows how greenbelts serve as buffers between vehicular traffic and adjacent development.
Courtesy of The Woodlands Operating Company, LP/Ted Washington

e Woodlands, a 200-acre freshwater lake, excavated in 1984 (top) and filled with ter in 1985 (bottom). With public parks and erfront access, it functions as a recreational visual amenity for the entire community, ough swimming is not allowed and boating mited to motorboats and skulls to prevent sy gasoline-powered craft from disturbing leisurely setting. The eight-foot-deep lake tocked with fish and serves as a habitat for erfowl. Residential neighborhoods front the stern and eastern shores, while major office npuses are located on the northern reaches he lake.
tesy of The Woodlands Operating Company, LP/Ted hington

Roger and Ann Galatas are photographed walking c
pathway in The Woodlands shortly after he was na▮
president of The Woodlands Corporation in 1986.
Ray Sakers Photography, Inc.

Arnold Palmer; Ed Seay, chief
operating officer of the Palmer
Course Design Company; and
Ed Lee, then president of The
Woodlands Corporation, were on
hand for the announcement of
the selection of Palmer as archi-
tect of the new course in the
Village of Cochran's Crossing,
in the early 1980s.
*Courtesy of The Woodlands Operating
Company, LP/Ted Washington*

This 14th hole fairway at the Tournament Players Course is typical of the high-quality design, construction, and maintenance of the seven signature courses in The Woodlands, which were designed by golfing legends including Joe Lee, Von Hagge–Devlin, Arnold Palmer, Jack Nicklaus, Gary Player, and Tom Fazio.
Courtesy of The Woodlands Operating Company, LP/Ted Washington

Earl Elliott was honored by both the PGA Tour and the United States Golf Association for his work as a volunteer announcer on the No. 1 tee during the PGA tour events in The Woodlands from 1983 until 2001.
Courtesy of the Houston Golf Association

Lightning caused by a passing squall line provided a dramatic, celebratory backdrop for the inaugural concert at the Cynthia Woods Mitchell Pavilion by the Houston Symphony on April 27, 1990.
Courtesy of The Woodlands Operating Company, LP/Ted Washington

They laughed when George Mitchell poured oil and gas money into a model community. But Mitchell saw a real estate hedge for his energy company and . . .

Nobody's laughing now

Mitchell Energy & Development Corp. Chairman George Mitchell
"With real estate, in a good location you've got a 40-year return."

WHEN HOUSTON OILMAN George Mitchell officially opened his new 23,000-acre community, The Woodlands, seven years ago, a lot of people thought he was heading for disaster. Why would such a successful wildcatter take the cash flow from his booming Mitchell Energy & Development Corp. and pour it into real estate just when rising energy prices were making the oil and gas business a license to print money? In fact, as Mitchell remembers it, at one low point in 1974 the bankers "refused to honor their verbal agreement to lend me $10 million" in new financing for his Woodlands project north of Houston.

Nobody thinks George Mitchell is out of his mind these days. While cash flow from these operations will turn positive only in the coming year, the appreciation in land value has been enormous. Mitchell bought the land at an average of $1,688 an acre, then spent about $25,000 an acre more to develop it. Today, the average Woodlands acre sells for $62,000, with the choicest going for up to $152,000. The Woodlands is only 22% developed today. When fully developed, even if the land never appreciated further, it could go on the market at $1 billion.

Mitchell, 61, a paper billionaire on his holdings of 62% of the outstanding stock of Mitchell Energy, says he knew all along the project was a good business investment. He recalls how he conceived the project in the 1960s, when the oil and gas business was less certain than it is at present. It's not a matter of a quick, high return, he says, but of a long-lived, cash-producing asset. "The return on investment in energy, since the boycott of 1973, might be as much as 30% aftertax, vs. only 10% or 12% for real estate. But that's not the point. The average life of a well is only seven or eight years. Then you have to redo it. With real estate, the initial investment is it. In a good location you've got a 40-year return and an appreciating asset."

Why didn't shrewd Houstonians and bankers and FORBES in a critical 1977 article see the promise of The Woodlands years ago? Two reasons. Mitchell Energy was in technical default in 1975 on some of its borrowings for the project. But there also was George Mitchell himself. He seemed a little too visionary for his own good. A Greek immigrant's son who bused tables and carried out laundry to work his way through Texas A&M's renowned petroleum engineering school, Mitchell brought social concern as well as geological knowledge into the business he founded in 1946. Mitchell and the company spend $200,000 every other year underwriting symposia on sustainable growth. George Mitchell has always talked of The Woodlands as a social ideal as well as a profitable investment.

The project is one of 13 model new

FORBES, MARCH 2, 1981

This *Forbes* article from March 1981 offered a measure of justification for George Mitchell's decision to put Mitchell Energy & Development Corporation funds into a model community. Mitchell saw real estate as a hedge for his energy company, but financial and planning challenges at The Woodlands in the 1970s, including the OPEC embargo, posed a serious threat to the project's success. By the 1980s, with an improving national economy, the new community's prospects were brighter.
[Text] reprinted by permission of Forbes Magazine ©2004 Forbes, Inc.
Photo: John Grossman

George Mitchell and Cynthia Woods Mitchell attended a tenth anniversary party for The Woodlands. Ian McHarg, the environmental consultant on Mitchell's original planning team, was also in attendance and was recognized for his ecological contributions to the development plan.
Courtesy of The Woodlands Operating Company, LP/Ted Washington

More than 50,000 people visited The Woodlands Mall during its grand opening in October 1994.
Courtesy of The Woodlands Operating Company, LP/Ted Washington

McDonald's refused to open a location in The Woodlands without the typical 40-foot golden arches, which would have violated the community's development guidelines. Following three years of negotiations, McDonald's local franchise owner convinced his company to open a location in The Woodlands marked only by a sign 3.5 feet high.
Courtesy of The Woodlands Operating Company, LP/Ted Washington

Israeli statesman Shimon Peres presented the International Federation of Real Estate's 1993 Award of Excellence to Roger Galatas, who accepted the honor on behalf of The Woodlands Corporation in a ceremony in Jerusalem.
Courtesy of The Woodlands Operating Company, LP

The Mitchell Energy & Development Corporation headquarters building in Town Center, The Woodlands' mixed-use commercial district, was constructed in 1980.
Courtesy of The Woodlands Operating Company, LP/Ted Washington

This view of Lake Robbins Bridge, which spans the Waterway in Town Center, with the 30-story Anadarko Petroleum Company building behind it, has become the signature image of The Woodlands for those traveling on I-45, the adjacent interstate highway. The tower and several smaller office facilities house Anadarko's 2,000 Woodlands employees.
Courtesy of The Woodlands Operating Company, LP/Ted Washington

George Mitchell makes a donation to the University Center, established in 1998 in The Woodlands by local educational institutions so that community college graduates could earn bachelors' degrees. Also shown are Dr. John Pickelman (left), chancellor of North Harris Montgomery Community College, and Elmer Beckendorf (right), the college's chairman.
Courtesy of The Woodlands Operating Company, LP/Ted Washington

ed on a 100-acre campus acquired from The Woodlands Corporation, North Harris Montgomery Community College's student enroll- now exceeds 4,000. Continuing education and technology training programs have played an important role in business development b creation in The Woodlands community.
sy of The Woodlands Operating Company, LP/Ted Washington

The first technology facility in the Research Forest opened in 1987. Like those facilities that followed, it is a low-rise structure sited on a wooded parcel to minimize its visual impact on The Woodlands' natural setting.
Courtesy of The Woodlands Operating Company, LP/Ted Washington

George Mitchell and former President Jimmy Carter at a conference held in The Woodlands on business relations between Mexico and the United States sponsored by HARC. At a separate meeting, Carter presented Mitchell with the developer's most prized recognition, the Lorax Award for environmental achievement, which was inscribed with a quote from Dr. Seuss: "I speak for the trees because the trees have no tongues."
Courtesy of The Woodlands Operating Company, LP

To Roger Galatas with respect and with high regard – G. Bush

This 1994 photograph taken during the ceremony for the first graduating class of the John Cooper School, the first private school to open in The Woodlands, is signed by former President George H.W. Bush, who gave the commencement address. On the podium from left to right are Roger Galatas, George Mitchell, President Bush, and Warren Butler, chairman of the school board.
Courtesy of The Woodlands Operating Company, LP/Ted Washington

Roger Galatas received this note of thanks from George H.W. Bush following the former president's 1995 induction into the Texas Golf Hall of Fame, which is located in The Woodlands.
Courtesy of The Woodlands Operating Company, LP

GEORGE BUSH   11-15-95

Dear Roger,
  Thanks for a great evening at the Hall of Fame event; and thanks, too, for "Woodlands", a beauty.
  I sure enjoyed Monday night out there.
  I want you to have the attached. I'll keep the other one - happily.
      Sincerely,
      G. Bush

At a news conference held June 13, 1997, Gerald Haddock, chief executive officer of Crescent Real Estate Equities, and George Mitchell announced the purchase of The Woodlands Corporation and all of its assets by Crescent and Morgan Stanley.
Courtesy of The Woodlands Operating Company, LP/Ted Washington

Houston Chronicle

Vol. 96   No. 243   Friday, June 13, 1997   50 Cents   ★★★

Mitchell selling The Woodlands

Partnership to buy community for $543 million in cash

By RALPH BIVINS
Houston Chronicle

The Woodlands, the largest master-planned community in the Houston area, is being sold for $543 million to a partnership of Fort Worth-based Crescent Real Estate Equities and Morgan Stanley Real Estate Fund II.

The Woodlands, which had more than 1,000 new home sales last year, is being sold by Mitchell Energy & Development Corp. as part of a plan

Mitchell Energy's George P. Mitchell envisioned The Woodlands concept years ago.

to focus on its oil and gas business.

Stock analysts have long said Mitchell Energy's shares would be worth more if it exited the real estate business.

Crescent is not expected to tamper with the formula that made The Woodlands a success — leaving a lot of forest in place as new homes and stores have been carefully nestled amongst the trees.

"The overall plan for The Woodlands is now well-established and most of the critical elements are now in place," said Mitchell Energy

chairman George P. Mitchell, who envisioned the concept for The Woodlands years ago.

"I am confident that Crescent and Morgan Stanley . . . will carry forward with the same quality-of-life criteria we've established over the last two decades," said Mitchell, who is 78.

With The Woodlands acquisition, Crescent, a publicly traded real estate investment firm, becomes an even bigger force in Texas real es-

See **WOODLANDS** on Page 24A.

George Mitchell's $543 million sale of The Woodlands Corporation is reported in the *Houston Chronicle*.

George Mitchell, his shoulders slumped, walks away from the news conference in which he announced the sale of The Woodlands Corporation. The only remorse Mitchell ever expressed about The Woodlands was the decision to sell it.
Courtesy of the Houston Chronicle

Woodlands' Art in Public Places program currently includes 25 outdoor sculptures exhibited throughout the community's villages and commercial centers. The pieces are acquired and maintained through fees collected from the sale of commercial land and the construction of certain commercial buildings in The Woodlands. Among the pieces on display are *Jungle Gym* (top), artist Jane A. DeDecker's bronze casting of children playing that was installed in the Sterling Ridge Village Center in 2002; *Boy With Hawk* (bottom, left), a bronze metal casting by Charles Park that is located in Grogan's Mill Village Center; and *Rise of the Midgard Serpent* (bottom, right), a welded metal construction by Marc Rosenthall that was purchased and donated by Cynthia Woods Mitchell and installed in 1985 in Lake Woodlands off The Woodlands Parkway.

The Woodlands Waterway is the centerpiece of the Town Center and marks its latest phase of development. The corridor will connect commercial, residential, and entertainment facilities via three modes of nonvehicular transportation: pedestrian walkways, trolleys, and water cruisers.
Courtesy of The Woodlands Operating Company, LP

The first of six water cruisers was put in service on the Waterway in July 2004. Operated under an agreement with Brazos Transit Autho the cruisers provide transportation among office, shopping, restaurant, and entertainment venues in Town Center, and can be rented for catered events.
Courtesy of The Woodlands Operating Company, LP/Ted Washington

Waterway's turning basin for water cruisers is adjacent to The Woodlands Mall and a street-level landscaped retail plaza offering upscale s and a variety of restaurants.

Waterway Lofts, a condominium property, is the first residential complex to be developed in Town Center. Other residential projects, ding townhomes, are under construction in Town Center. Future plans call for approximately 2,000 residential units to be built extending along the Waterway to Lake Woodlands.

Looking east toward Interstate 45, this aerial view of The Woodlands Waterway shows its initial length of 1.5 miles. In the foreground is Teflon-coated white tent structure of the Cynthia Woods Mitchell Pavilion. East of the pavilion on the north side of the Waterway lie the Marriott Hotel and Convention Center, Town Center office buildings, the Anadarko Petroleum Company building, The Woodlands Mall, an 17-screen movie theater. A mix of office and urban residential properties line the south side of the Waterway.
Courtesy of The Woodlands Operating Company, LP/Ted Washington

AARP here, and all the seniors' organizations that you've seen now develop. We started the YMCA. We started the scouting programs for kids. We started Overeaters Anonymous, Alcoholics Anonymous. We put together a health committee that started the hospital." Gebert also started something called the Green Teen Machine, which was a program for youngsters in the Settler's Corner neighborhood. "Some company from Houston was mowing the lawns and I went to Mr. Mitchell and said, 'Hey, why are you paying somebody outside to do that? Our teenagers need a project that they can work on and begin to earn some money of their own. How about turning that contract over to us, and [the kids will] have something constructive to do instead of writing graffiti on the bike paths.' He agreed." The program lasted for five years.

Gebert brought this kind of innovative thinking beyond the confines of The Woodlands. "It doesn't a take genius to understand that The Woodlands is not an island. The truth of the matter is, it's deeply involved with the county and county politics are deeply involved with The Woodlands. You've got to build connections. So we started with family services that would take care of the needs of families, not only inside The Woodlands, but also outside. That was Interfaith's first jump into the services that connected the people in [nearby] Tamina, the [existing] black community, for example, with people here in The Woodlands. Then we saw that we had huge problems with our teenage population—not only here, but also all over the county. Again, it didn't take a genius to know that we needed a countywide organization to deal with that. We formed what became Montgomery County Youth Services."

Montgomery County Youth Services is not a part of the county government. "We would not allow that. We were determined that the government was not going to take over what we could do ourselves. If the government begged us to take some money with no strings attached, we'd be happy to take it. When I was at Interfaith, we had no government grants and neither did any of the organizations that I started."

Today, Interfaith has a $16 million annual budget. The largest part of its budget now comes from government. Worksource, its job-retraining program, is the largest of its kind in Texas. It's a federally funded program with 12 centers across the state.

"That came out of a thing that started way back in the early days called the Employee Assistance Center, which Mr. Mitchell asked us to set up so that he would have a place outside his company to send employees with alcohol and drug problems and those kinds of things. We set that up for him on an enrollment basis with each company putting in $4 a month for each employee, and not only did Mitchell join it, but a whole bunch of other companies around here joined it. And we were able to provide expert services for free."

When started, Interfaith had one employee. It now has hundreds—plus thousands of volunteers. It's still a nonprofit corporation established to help churches develop in The Woodlands. But it is much more. Interfaith volunteers visit new residents to provide information about the community. Its services for senior citizens range from transportation for shopping and medical visits to pairing seniors with student writers so the older person can record his or her life story. Interfaith provides those in need of financial assistance with rent, food, and clothing. Its annual programs include adopt-a-school, a school supplies and backpack drive, and an adopt-a-family drive at Christmas. Its information and referral services provide assistance to area residents, both via telephone and the Internet.

"I'm very proud of what the organization has become," states Gebert. "Our motto from the beginning was for a more loving and caring community. And when the Houston Golf Association came along many years ago and [bought] vans for Interfaith to use to transport people who needed health care and to transport children for the child development center, I put a slogan on the [vehicles] with just three words, 'Because we care.' Because everybody was asking me, 'Why are you knocking yourself out doing all this?' And the answer was 'Because we care.' " Gebert is especially proud of Faith Together, another independent organization established under his leadership. It has Hindus, Muslims, Buddhists, Jews, and Christians all working together. "When 9/11 came," noted Gebert, "we were able to have the rabbi praying for the Palestinians and the Muslim leader praying for the Jews. This community is special. And it's special because of stuff like that. It's amazing."

There is some dissension in the community about Interfaith. When it was just the Christian and Jews, everybody got along. When the Far Eastern religions started growing and wanted to be part of it, there was a little rift. Some of the more conservative Christians could not live with that and still can't. Some of those who were part of the group in the early days are no longer part of Interfaith. "I wish I were still there because I think I could have worked through that with them," Gebert said. "Because our agreement always was cooperate on what you can cooperate on. Don't cooperate on what you can't cooperate on, but don't be mad at the other guy for being different. But that broke down."

And remember that four-page book with a list of residents? Today it's a 1,700-page telephone directory. It started just for the residents to get to know each other. It is still that, but is also a tool for businesses to advertise to the people. The first year the residents' book sold advertisements was 1981. Owen Marsh, a local businessman and Interfaith supporter, told Gebert he needed a decent cover for the directory, and offered to pay $500 for one if he could put an advertisement on it for his business. The next year, other companies wanted to advertise. The latest book has 898 pages of advertising that brought in $1.7 million to Interfaith. Gebert, who retired from the organization in 1989 and still lives in The Woodlands, volunteers with Interfaith and is in charge of distributing the directory to the residents, working with six teams to deliver it door to door.

What made Interfaith a success? Part can be attributed to the first people who moved to The Woodlands, the pioneers. "George is the real hero," Gebert said. "I was maybe his front man on the people stuff, but it was his vision that I bought into. It was that vision that was proclaimed to me over the telephone while I was sitting there in my office in Philadelphia, that I said if that vision is real, I would be there. And it was George's vision and it was real."

Chapter 9

GOVERNANCE

———— • ◆ • ————

The Woodlands probably has more residents per capita setting government policy than any place outside a New England town meeting. Basic governmental services for The Woodlands residents come from a smorgasbord of government and quasi-governmental agencies. Almost 200 residents of The Woodlands serve on policy-making boards. Despite the fact that, or maybe because, power is so dispersed in The Woodlands, there has been a remarkable lack of political strife.

The rather peculiar governmental structure for The Woodlands goes back to an early decision by George Mitchell—to tie the new town to the city of Houston. The state of Texas gives cities strong powers of annexation. Cities can establish extraterritorial jurisdiction (ETJ) in areas outside their boundaries and prevent people in those areas from forming their own cities. At the central city's sole discretion, and after following required notice and hearing procedures, it can annex any area within its extraterritorial jurisdiction over the objections of those annexed. The new citizens don't have a vote on the matter.

Before The Woodlands was started, Mitchell asked the Houston City Council to extend its extraterritorial jurisdiction over the new town. There just happened to be a problem with that decision. The city of Conroe also had extraterritorial jurisdiction over part of what was to become The Woodlands. "Mickey" Deison, then the mayor of Conroe, recalled a meeting with Mitchell about the conflicting jurisdiction. "Mitchell always talked to me like I worked for him," Deison said. "And he said, 'Now you go up there and tell your council that I want y'all to release all your ETJ down here because I'm going to bring it all under the umbrella of Houston.' And I said, 'Well, Mr. Mitchell. . .if I do that, I'll probably never be able to run for public office again in Montgomery County.' "

The decision by Mitchell resulted in a lawsuit between the parties, but it was settled and, as a part of the process, residents living north of The Woodlands were allowed to incorporate a small portion of Mitchell's property into the city of Shenandoah. The Conroe council thought that this new city would serve as a buffer to the expansion between The Woodlands and the city of Houston. In the end, Mitchell got almost everything he wanted. About 95 percent of The Woodlands wound up within Houston's extraterritorial jurisdiction. Basically, that means that under existing state law, while The Woodlands is not a part of Houston, it cannot incorporate as a city on its own or be annexed by the nearby cities of Conroe or Shenandoah without the permission of the city of Houston.

Mitchell had two reasons for seeking the city of Houston's embrace. One was altruistic, the other very practical. The primary reason Mitchell started The Woodlands was his fear that central cities were being drained of their tax bases by the movement of affluent residents to suburbia and outside city limits. He wanted The Woodlands to be part of Houston's solution, not part of its problem. Thus, Mitchell envisioned that Houston would eventually annex The Woodlands. The practical reason was the experience of other large developers who saw the early residents of their projects incorporate, then stymie further expansion efforts by the developer. It's called the drawbridge mentality. I like it the way it is. Let's pull up the drawbridge and not allow others to move in.

But as a result of Mitchell's strategy, some method had to be found to deliver basic city services, without a city. The first challenges involved how to provide water to drink and get rid of sewage. Mike Page, a young lawyer then with the large Houston firm of Vinson & Elkins, worked on these issues. Now with his own firm, he's still working on them.

"One of the first choices was who is going to be in charge of providing a public water supply system and a wastewater treatment system. . .that would serve all The Woodlands—would be there, reliable, not be reluctant to act, not subject to political whims, and would be a steady provider whenever demand was made," Page said in a 2003 interview with the authors.

Page's firm came up with a twofold solution. Retail water and sewer services would come from Municipal Utility Districts (MUDs), which are special districts with limited governmental powers formed under authority of state law. They would build the water and sewer lines, distribute the water within the villages of The Woodlands, read the meters, and collect the fees. The wholesaler of water and sewage treatment services would be the San Jacinto River Authority. It had the advantage of being an existing state agency with its board appointed by the state, so it was largely sheltered from local politics.

"We made our recommendations to management and they promptly fired us," Page recalled. "After thrashing about for a couple of years with other alternatives, we were rehired and we ended up implementing those suggestions. That's how the San Jacinto River Authority came to be our central service provider for a variety of reasons, mostly because they were governmental, tax exempt, and rather apolitical. And they had a responsibility for both water supply and water quality in the river basin, of which The Woodlands was a part."

Another reason for teaming up with the River Authority was that it was a long-standing governmental entity eligible to receive federal and state grants for water and sewage treatment projects.

The Woodlands' MUDs were not unique. They had long been a favorite of suburban developers for a number of different reasons. MUDs, being governmental units, could sell tax-exempt bonds to finance the water, sewer, and drainage infrastructure. That allowed the property developer to borrow money at a lower cost. In states with their own income taxes, that's an even more desirable situation. However, it makes no difference in Texas, which overwhelmingly regards state income tax right up there with the works of the devil. With tax-exempt bonds, the developer charges less for his lots since his infrastructure cost is lower. Residents who buy those lots pay taxes to the MUDs, which in turn pay off the bonds, and they can deduct those taxes on their federal income taxes.

According to Page, The Woodlands MUDs—there are now 14 of them—were somewhat unusual, because they were very large as those districts go. Typically, developers of individual subdivisions of 300 to 500 acres would set up a MUD. Those in The Woodlands were five times that size or more. Each one of those MUDs has an elected board of five who set policies for the district.

Turning sewage treatment over to the San Jacinto River Authority also resulted in large plants that are inherently more efficient. It also meant that The Woodlands had only three such plants, instead of the 15 or 20 that might have been built in a typical development pattern. That also helps sell lots for housing. No one wants to live next to a wastewater treatment plant, even one that is well operated.

Page credits Michael Richmond for a decision that resulted in a financial penalty for The Woodlands Corporation in the early days but resulted in large savings to residents in succeeding years. Richmond decided not to have a MUD sell tax-exempt bonds at the beginning of the community's development. Instead, The Woodlands Corporation fronted the money to build water, sewer, and drainage facilities. Bonds were sold only after there were enough residents that potential investors could see that there was a sufficient population and tax base to retire them. Reassured bond buyers were willing to accept lower interest rates, which in turn meant lower taxes. The Woodlands Corporation was reimbursed for those upfront costs after the bonds were sold.

"As it turns out, that practice that The Woodlands adopted of a developer advancing funds and then being reimbursed for its costs when the tax base was more firmly established, came to be a part of the rules of the state some 15 years later," Page noted. "When we had the [economic] downturn in the 1980s and some of the municipal utility districts in the area outside of The Woodlands weren't doing very well, the state concluded that risks need to be shifted more to the developer at the front end. So by rule they prohibited districts from issuing bonds until a certain level of development of a tax base had been reached, which meant, of course, that the developer had to advance its money to be reimbursed later. That was the first piece of the model that I think The Woodlands was probably responsible for. And it's still in the rule book today and we've not had a financial failure [of a MUD] in the Houston area since the rule was adopted in 1987."

Due to the decision of The Woodlands Corporation to pay the upfront costs for infrastructure and wait to be reimbursed when bonds were sold, taxes in the 14 MUDs in The Woodlands generally have been lower than in competing housing developments.

Under state law, The Woodlands' MUDs could impose a tax up to $1.50 per $100 of property value. "The Woodlands has never thought that [rate] was tolerable," Page said. "So the target [here] has always been a $1 per $100 or less and they've always been able to maintain that. I think for maybe one or two years we had one district that was $1.05 or something like that, but they have always been able to start out at the $1 level or lower. The rates today range from about 25 cents to 70 cents."

Consistent tax rates among districts have always been a target for The Woodlands Corporation. That's been done, Page explained, "so that buyers and Realtors weren't confused. There wasn't neighborhood or village jealousy or envy over tax rates, so the tax rates really weren't driving the market. The company decided early on that wherever a problem existed with the tax rate of one district being noticeably higher than that of its neighbors, the developer would help make additional land, sometimes noncontiguous land, available for annexation by the district so that they could in effect create some more value and lower the tax rate. It's worked very well."

The Woodlands has used other types of special purpose governmental districts to help build or maintain both infrastructure and special needs. Two of the most prominent include a road district and an improvement district for Town Center, The Woodlands' main commercial area, which includes a regional shopping mall.

In 1991, The Woodlands Corporation knew that because of rapid growth it needed to do something to upgrade streets, roads, bridges, and traffic signals. They had in the 1980s set up a general road-building special district, supported by taxes levied on all residents. With state and federal funding, the special district had spent $48 million on road improvements. The bonds for that special district were then paid off and the district abolished. But more money was needed.

"Rather than impose additional taxes upon the resident population, The Woodlands could foresee a significant growth about to occur in the commercial and retail areas, particularly with the opening of the mall. So the decision was made to create a road district centered on the commercial areas only. [These] areas would serve as the tax base for that district, which would have tentacles reaching out on all major thoroughfares," Page said, adding that the new special road district was "kind of an octopus-looking thing, with the center being the main commercial district and the arms being all the major thoroughfares that extended out to the village commercial centers. And the idea was to get citizens not only to the mall and commercial areas, but [also] to get them off the freeway and into the neighborhoods and in and about The Woodlands."

The special road district set a tax of 50 cents per $100 of property values. "It obviously benefits the business community by bringing their customers over to their places of business, but it has been a tremendous benefit to the residents as well. That's been going on now about ten years and at last count that district accomplished, along with leveraged state and county funds, about $100 million worth of local improvements."

The Woodlands Corporation persuaded the Texas Legislature to enact special legislation to make the road district possible. Then they had to hold a local election to approve the bonds. The district's board members are elected every two years. So how many people were actually living within the bounds of the road district when the first election was held? Two. The bonds passed by a landslide. At the time of the writing of this book, The Woodlands Corporation is busy building condominiums, apartments, and townhomes within Town Center, which is part of the special road district. How will those people vote in the future for that extra 50-cent tax? The reality is they won't. The road district board has de-annexed areas that have turned residential to avoid taxing residents for road improvements, replacing that land with property from the expanding commercial district of The Woodlands.

The second special district, the Town Center Improvement District, was another case of special needs and growing pains, Page said. The Woodlands Corporation had seen security problems at other major shopping centers in Houston. For example, the Greenspoint area, which is closer to downtown Houston, saw sales plummet because of security concerns of their customers. Greenspoint is working to solve its problem. The Woodlands Mall did not want to see a similar problem develop in Town Center. It also did not want to add to the tax burden of local residents.

The answer was a special district financed by a sales tax. All of the economic projections indicated that a majority of sales in the mall would be to nonresidents. The idea that nonresidents can pay part of home folks' taxes is always attractive.

The improvement district levied a 1 percent sales tax on every dollar spent at the mall and surrounding commercial district. About half the money levied went for enhanced security— a private security force, including some horse-mounted patrols. The rest went for economic development, marketing programs, and enhancement of the area.

One reason for the continuing success of the MUDs and other special districts within The Woodlands, according to Page, is that they have stuck to their mission. Since The Woodlands has no city government, due to Mitchell's original decision, who takes care of the problems that normally would be resolved by a city council?

The majority of The Woodlands is in Montgomery County, with one village in Harris County. But counties in Texas have very limited power to pass ordinances. Since there is no state-sanctioned government in The Woodlands, aside from the county and the municipal utility districts, its developers and people have turned to an array of nonprofit associations. All residents of The Woodlands 18 or older are automatically members of these associations and eligible to vote in elections. At the bottom of the food chain, so to speak, are the village associations. Each of the seven villages has an elected board of ten members. They have limited powers, primarily over residential neighborhoods and village issues within their borders. They don't set or collect taxes. Any money they receive comes from associations higher on the food chain.

The real city government entities in The Woodlands are the community associations. They are a story within themselves. In the beginning, there was just one, The Woodlands Community Association. Then in 1992, two more were added: The Woodlands Association and The Woodlands Commercial Owners Association.

Joel Deretchin, who was The Woodlands Corporation's liaison to the community associations for years, said in a 2003 interview, "The community associations provide the services and perform functions that you would normally associate with a city government. Because we are in the extraterritorial jurisdiction of Houston, The Woodlands cannot incorporate without the city's permission.

"I was involved in taking the concept of the community association and creating an administrative structure and the service delivery mechanisms for providing what the associations now do in The Woodlands." That includes fire protection, augmenting police protection (principally by Montgomery County), municipal services such as garbage collection, streetlighting, streetscape maintenance, development, operation of parks and pathways, and covenant administration, which is a Woodlands euphemism for what a building and code enforcement department would normally do. The community associations' boards of directors act like a city council.

When Deretchin was first hired in the mid-1970s, the developer handled all the community association tasks. "I actually created an independent organization under the corporate structure of The Woodlands Community Association to do that. And today there are about 175 people in that organization, plus the fire department that is about another 120 to 130 people, so it's not insignificant. There's a combined budget of about $30 million today."

The Woodlands' Community Association gets its operating money from property assessments, very much like a city tax. The taxable value of the property in The Woodlands is established by the Montgomery County Appraisal District and the community association determines the assessment rate.

As the land was developed, more and more residents were elected to the original association's board of directors, replacing those appointed by the developer. The master plan for The Woodlands anticipated a 20-year buildout. At the end of those two decades, in August 1992, the residents would control The Woodlands Community Association. The developer would no longer have a voice in running the community.

"Well, a couple of things happened along the way," Deretchin said. "One is that The Woodlands grew from [just over 17,000 acres] to 27,000 acres, so there was no way it could be substantially developed in 20 years. Second, the development projections that were used upfront were unrealistically high. If The Woodlands had ever hit that pace of development, it would exceed anything ever done in the United States, before or since. In the early 1990s, we would have been selling about 4,000 units. There's no community in the country that's ever done that.

"So 20 years came and went and The Woodlands wasn't fully developed and we were faced then with a decision," Deretchin said. The decision—and it was vital to the future of The Woodlands—had to do with the covenants in all the deeds, which controlled what kinds of buildings would be allowed, the number of houses to be built in each area, and whether or not the things that make The Woodlands distinctive, such as saving the trees, would continue.

Interpreting the deed restrictions was the business of the Development Standards Committee, essentially an architectural control committee. It was part of The Woodlands Community Association but was still under control of the developer. The executives of The Woodlands Corporation feared that if they lost control of the Development Standards Committee, the value of undeveloped property could fall. The resident-controlled Woodlands Community Association would also appoint members to the separate Development Standards Committee (DSC) and could stymie future construction in The Woodlands.

That could put The Woodlands Corporation under severe financial strain. Remember, developing a property like The Woodlands means huge upfront costs. Typically, developers don't recover their costs and start making profits until the final stages of the project.

To avoid a diminished role, The Woodlands Corporation decided to create two additional associations. One, The Woodlands Association, was the governing body over the then-undeveloped residential land. It would allow the developer to maintain control of the Development Standards Committee in the land yet to be developed. The developer would appoint a majority of the members of The Woodlands Association board until property within its jurisdiction is 75 percent developed. The original Woodlands Community Association retained control over the developed land. Its 13-member board has one person appointed by the developer.

Formed in 1992, the second community association governs certain commercial areas in community. "The commercial marketing people and the development company said that the people they talked to when they sell commercial property really wanted covenants that are styled more for commercial property owners than the residential covenants that we had been imposing in the commercial areas," Deretchin recalled. "We created a Commercial Owners Association with its own covenants." In order to keep a single identity for all of The Woodlands and to achieve administrative efficiencies, the associations, the developer, and the fire department entered into an agreement, called the Mutual Benefits Agreement, which is the glue that holds all the associations together.

Instead of each association having its own staff, all city-like functions were moved into a nonprofit corporation called The Woodlands Community Services Corporation. Each association contracts with the services corporation for staff support. None of the associations has its own staff, which means that all sections of The Woodlands receive the same level of services. The Woodlands Community Services Corporation has its own board, which is composed of appointees of the three community boards. They set policy and hire what is, in reality, a city manager to oversee daily operations.

Needless to say, many residents opposed this new plan. It took two years of negotiations between the developer and the residents before it was implemented.

That was not the end of the conflict between the developer and the community associations, or among the associations themselves. Conflict is part of the political process. Deretchin said there have been members who sought to achieve dominance of one association over the other, mainly The Woodlands Community Association over the other two associations. Some of those same people have sought to use the Mutual Benefits Agreement as leverage over the developer and that caused a lot of controversy. When Mitchell Energy & Development Corporation sold its interests in The Woodlands to Crescent Real Estate and Morgan Stanley, the sale triggered an opportunity to renegotiate provisions of the Mutual Benefits Agreement. That was a long and hotly contested negotiation, Deretchin said. The Woodlands Community Association representatives sought more authority and control than they originally had. Some on The Woodlands Community Association board also tried to use the sale to leverage their position in other negotiations over financing of capital acquisitions for the service corporation and the fire department and how that would be shared and financed.

The outcome of the negotiations, according to Deretchin, was that the developer gave up on some points but kept what they regarded as the crown jewel—control of the Development Standards Committee until the entire development is completed.

Deretchin deserves a lot of credit for the operation of The Woodlands Community Association. It was his patience, perseverance, and professional approach that kept relations working between the developer and the residents. In my judgment, being a resident and not now actively involved in the process, it works very well from a service delivery standpoint. I don't know who's on the board. Most people in The Woodlands don't know who serves on the board. But we do know that the garbage gets picked up, the landscaping looks good, and the parks operate well.

Because people are generally satisfied with services in The Woodlands, voter turnout for elections to the boards is low. While political scientists decry such low turnouts, the reality is that people who like the way things are going generally don't bother to vote. When there is a very large turnout, you can bet that the incumbents are in trouble. Because turnout is low, a few neighbors can and do get together to elect someone who shares his or her views. Those are the kinds of people who often have their own agendas. That creates a potential for strife on the community boards, but generally members work well together. Political noise in The Woodlands is pretty much the way it is elsewhere. It picks up around election time for the community associations, but dies down until the next visit to the polls.

In the years since the governance structure changed in The Woodlands, people have learned how to become political. And as Deretchin said, "If The Woodlands ever becomes a municipality, they will have honed some of their skills and set the stage for more conventional politics."

So what is the political future of The Woodlands? If the majority of its residents have their say, it won't be part of Houston. Mitchell's original plan to have the city eventually annex the town is more than unpopular. Over the years, The Woodlands Corporation has done polling of its residents to help them deliver the kinds of services residents want. They have also, on occasion, asked the annexation question. Generally, about 95 percent of residents have consistently opposed annexation by Houston.

Still, under current state law, if Houston wants to annex, it can. Over the years, there have been efforts in the Texas Legislature to change the annexation laws. State representatives from primarily suburban areas in danger of being annexed have sponsored those changes. But so far, the cities have managed to beat back those efforts.

The city of Houston, however, seems to be in no hurry to annex The Woodlands. In the past, the city has annexed two large master-planned communities in suburban areas, Clear Lake to the south and Kingwood to the north. The ears of city council members are still ringing from the griping of those new residents.

Right now, the city of Houston has entered into a moratorium agreement with The Woodlands' utility districts, effectively promising not to annex the community until the year 2014. Page, a lawyer for The Woodlands, recalled how that came about.

"Lee Brown had been mayor [of Houston for] about six months when we went to see him and his first question was, 'What's in it for Houston?' And we said, 'Well, $10 and other good and valuable consideration.' He didn't appreciate the humor. But our real pitch to him was, 'You took a real black eye over the Kingwood annexation, there's going to be lots of healthy discussion about the annexation laws in the next session of the [state] legislature, and it would probably do the city of Houston some good to [remind] the legislature that you're not just grabbing territory right and left. You do things on some kind of rational basis and that you were able to come to a reasonable understanding with The Woodlands as a demonstration of your good faith and good judgment.' "

At first, Page said, Brown was not that interested in the proposal. But as the Texas Legislature went into session, his interest picked up. "It turned out to be a really bloody session," Page said. "There was lots of rancor and pressure to just dismantle the unilateral annex-ation ability of the city. So the city's representatives came back to us while the session was on, and said let's examine that idea some more and we did and came up with a piece of legisla-tion that in effect says that we will pay to the city the sum of $200,000. They will share with us planning information that they develop on long-term water supply and regional waste-water treatment and drainage issues in consideration for that $200,000. And the city agreed not to annex The Woodlands before 2014."

A committee of stakeholders in The Woodlands is currently engaged in a two- to three-year effort to try and come up with positions that the majority of residents would support and would also gain acceptance by the city of Houston. State law does allow for some kind of power sharing among cities and surrounding unincorporated areas. One possible compromise could be that The Woodlands agrees to pay the city of Houston for various services such as regional water and wastewater, support of the regional port and airport, and the like. The Woodlands would retain control of fire and police protection, garbage pickup, and other close-to-home services. Another possibility is that the state legislature might indeed one day curb the powers of cities to annex. The least likely outcome is for residents of The Woodlands to agree happily to become part of the city of Houston.

Or we might just see a continuation of the status quo. The city of Houston now has a majority of minorities residing within its boundaries. But while racial politics is always pres-ent, it has not approached the acrimony seen in other cities. For example, Houston elected an African American mayor, Lee Brown, who garnered a substantial portion of the white vote as well as the support of the predominantly white business community. In 2003, it elected a white mayor, Bill White, who also had a substantial slice of both the black and Hispanic votes. The annexations of Clear Lake and Kingwood showed that it is legally possible to annex pre-dominantly white areas without running afoul of the U.S. Voting Rights Act that forbids the dilution of minority votes. Still, there is some evidence that future annexations could be chal-lenged on such grounds.

The Woodlands might well remain far into the future with a government that is not a gov-ernment at all, but a collection of nonprofit corporations and special purpose districts. It does seem to work.

Chapter 10

HEALTH CARE

———— •◆• ————

From its inception, the developers of The Woodlands knew that attracting first-class medical care for their new town would be an important quality-of-life asset. But as we were to learn, getting good medical care for the people of The Woodlands was no different from building any other part of its social infrastructure. It would be a hard slog with a rewarding outcome.

Building a health care system in The Woodlands was an important element for the growing community. But the process under which it was done was important for another reason. The experience we gained really became the formula by which other community institutions were developed. So a brief overview of the process may be worthwhile. Working out a system for health care delivery gave us confidence to try a similar approach in development of the John Cooper School, the Cynthia Woods Mitchell Pavilion, the Houston Advanced Research Center, and other major institutions.

So how did we approach health care? By 1978, enough people had moved to The Woodlands to establish a nucleus of community leaders interested in future growth and services such as health care. Don Gebert, the original director of Interfaith, served as a facilitator for community discussions and it was on the patio of his home that the early informal conversations about health care took place. This led to productive discussions with the development company, which was also looking at the health care issue. The creation of a study committee consisting of community volunteers and company representatives soon followed. The Woodlands Corporation provided initial funding and human resources to support the study committee and resident members provided the community connection. As discussions progressed, The Woodlands Medical Center, Inc., a nonprofit corporation, was established to carry forward the community's vision for health care. Its board of directors consisted of 12 volunteer members, including those experienced in community organizations, qualified community leaders, members of the health care profession, and representatives of The Woodlands Corporation.

The nonprofit first identified the need for a clinic that would attract doctors to serve in the community. There were none at the time. There were several doctors who resided in The Woodlands but had offices elsewhere. There was no substantial health care delivery system in the community, even though 5,000 or 6,000 people were living here by the late 1970s. The first approach was to design and build a clinic that would serve to attract doctors and provide outpatient services. Because both Medicare and some insurance programs provided payments for certain procedures only if the patient stayed in the hospital overnight, the clinic was designed with two beds.

In those days, the state of Texas required developers of health care facilities to get a certificate of need issued by the state. This was part of a federal effort to prevent the overbuilding of hospital beds, which would drive up costs. We hired a health care consultant to help guide us in designing the clinic, identifying doctors, and preparing an application to secure the certificate. We hired an architect, designed a clinic, and started construction.

The Woodlands Corporation then recruited Dr. Jack Lesch as the first medical director of the clinic. Lesch was just finishing his family medicine residency in Houston. He had already decided he was going to sign on with a multispecialty medical group in the Bryan–College Station area when he got the offer from The Woodlands in December 1978. The head of his family medicine program at St. Luke's Episcopal Hospital in Houston told him that The Woodlands Corporation was trying to organize a health care program in the new town.

"I had no real particular interest in the position," Lesch said. But he looked at the vision for this new town and decided he wanted to be a part of it. So he turned down that nice, safe, secure setup he had waiting for him in Bryan. The Woodlands "was a big, wide world of unknowns. But I couldn't imagine being over there [in Bryan] always wondering, what would have happened or what could have happened in The Woodlands because it was just in the beginnings of developing health care."

Fortunately, as it turned out for Lesch, the planned clinic never opened. It became entangled in the state's medical bureaucracy, which had turned down the application by The Woodlands for a certificate of need on the grounds it duplicated other facilities outside The Woodlands. The 10,000-square-foot family practice clinic, already built, couldn't open. Young Dr. Lesch was about to arrive at the clinic he was to head but that could not be used.

Lesch was told that The Woodlands Corporation would help him find space to set up his own office. "And that was what I was wanting to avoid," Lesch said.

But it turned out to be the greatest thing that ever happened. The Woodlands Corporation solved the problem of office space for Lesch. There was a small, unused corner in the Information Center, the place where prospective homebuyers stopped to find out what was available for sale. "It had three-story ceilings and on the second floor we built three rooms to see patients. It was very inefficient, but comfortable," Lesch said. The Woodlands Corporation charged him $500 a month for the space, much less rent than he would have paid elsewhere. It took only a couple of months after moving into the center to build a viable practice, Lesch said. "There were a lot of folks who were looking to see somebody or have their care locally and not have to travel around." He kept expanding, taking in more cubbyholes in the building, until 1985 when he constructed a building of his own where he continues to practice today.

These days, Lesch is seeing the babies of the babies he delivered in the early days of his practice. "It sort of makes you feel old," he said, wryly.

In the early years, as the number of physicians practicing in The Woodlands increased they still lacked a vital part of the practice picture: a hospital. There were hospitals in Conroe, and certainly many of them in Houston, but they were inconvenient for patients and physicians alike. Residents, doctors, and The Woodlands Corporation all wanted a hospital for their new town. As with houses of worship in the beginning stages of The Woodlands' development, there was a critical mass problem. Hospitals require huge investments. They need patients filling beds to pay for the facility and its operation. The Woodlands simply did not have enough residents in the early days to provide that critical mass.

I joined The Woodlands at the beginning of 1979 and had the good fortune to be involved in its health care program from that time until today. Prior to joining the company, I had served on the board of directors of the Montgomery County Hospital and was asked to use that experience to coordinate efforts underway to establish Woodlands Medical Center, Inc.

The quest for a hospital was started in late 1979 not only for the good of the community, but also because the Humana Corporation wanted to build a for-profit hospital on Interstate 45 adjacent to The Woodlands. Rather than challenge the rejected certificate of need for the two-bed clinic, we moved to secure a certificate of need for a hospital. We felt that if the Humana hospital was built, a Woodlands facility would be delayed for many years. We wanted a not-for-profit hospital that would be affiliated with the Texas Medical Center. Officials from Baylor College of Medicine and St. Luke's Episcopal Hospital, both in the Texas Medical Center, helped us plan a new hospital for The Woodlands. But it was the Methodist Hospital, a major Texas Medical Center facility, that played an unbelievably important role. Methodist's CEO Ted Bowen, Executive Vice President Bill Moreland, and his successor Mike Williamson committed personal time and corporate resources in successful support of The Woodlands hospital, which is owned by The Woodlands Medical Center Inc. They led the way for the nonprofit's certificate of need application, architectural design, initial staffing, and opening of the hospital in 1985. Methodist managed the facility for several years.

Mitchell approved $500,000 of corporate funds for the preliminary design and legal work necessary to obtain the certificate of need from the state to build a hospital.

In order to secure the $20 million needed to build the hospital from a consortium of ten banks, Mitchell agreed to pay up to $12.5 million of any operating losses. Methodist Hospital signed on to manage the new hospital. With Methodist leading the way, we on our hands and knees begged these ten banks to lend $20 million to us, and they did. And not one of those ten banks is in business today and the hospital has flourished. Some of the banks disappeared as a result of the economic downturn of the mid-1980s. Some merged with other institutions, but they did not fail because of the hospital loan.

Obtaining a certificate of need for the new hospital in The Woodlands was by no means a slam dunk. Montgomery County had recently created a hospital district and built the new Conroe Regional Hospital. They were concerned about competition for their new facility. But they were more concerned about the proposed for-profit facility than they were about a nonprofit hospital that would be built by The Woodlands.

We gained the political support of the board of directors of the Montgomery County Hospital District, primarily because they feared competition from a for-profit hospital. They could see a better relationship with a nonprofit hospital in The Woodlands. But that was politically tough for them. They had their own hospital that just opened. They needed to protect their cash flow. They didn't want us to pirate away doctors and patients. But they supported our certificate of need. Board members Rigby Owen, Jr.; John Holmes; and Walter Jolly were especially helpful. Two conditions of their support were to cap the number of beds at The Woodlands Hospital at 100 and to locate the new facility on Interstate 45, not actually within The Woodlands, so it wouldn't look as if they were doing us a favor but were instead helping to bring health care to the southern part of Montgomery County.

Originally, the new facility was to be named The Woodlands Hospital and located deep within the town. When it was moved to Interstate 45, the only place we could find a workable site without disturbing our commercial development was within the corporate limits of the city of Shenandoah. And Shenandoah really didn't want us to hang a sign with "The Woodlands Hospital" on a building at the front door to their community. So the applicant name that we went forward with was Southwood Community Hospital. The application was granted and the hospital was built. Prior to its opening on January 19, 1985, it was renamed The Woodlands Hospital to avoid confusion with a nearby professional building named Southwood Tower. Shenandoah was not thrilled with the change, but the benefits of convenient health care soon outweighed the name problem.

The new hospital quickly ran into problems. Some were expected. Some were not. The first problem was there simply were not enough people using it. When it opened, there were 25 doctors with admitting privileges at the new hospital. But only five or six physicians were actually using the 100-bed facility regularly, and the average daily census, patients actually occupying beds, was 21.

In those days, the hospital was so empty that the parking lot was deserted. Carpooling had become popular and vanpools were used to transport people from The Woodlands to work locations in Houston. We volunteered to let the vanpools use our parking lot at the hospital and that gave the general appearance of activity. You'd be amazed how effective marketing can be when you have a crowded parking lot.

That helped, but what really improved the situation were the recruitment of some good doctors and the population growth of the community. The other problem was one we could not have anticipated. Methodist was named in a lawsuit filed against another hospital in east Texas. A baby born prematurely went into distress and was blinded by the oxygen that was administered to save its life. While Methodist provided only limited advisory services to the hospital, the case resulted in a significant financial settlement by the hospital and Methodist in the early 1990s. Because of this, the Methodist Board elected to stop managing community hospitals.

That decision left The Woodlands' hospital with a board of 12 volunteer laypeople, including me. None of us knew how to run a hospital. For about two years, however, we ran the hospital as a nonprofit. Luckily, Pat Peyton, the administrator, John Black, the financial officer, and Margery McIntyre, the head of nursing, all of whom were originally hired by Methodist, elected to stay on. And a couple of years later, Memorial Hospital System bought our hospital for $21 million; we paid off the $20 million of debt, and used the extra million dollars for charitable purposes.

The hospital in The Woodlands has continued to grow. The $20 million hospital is now a $145 million one. It's been expanded twice by Memorial. The original building is used for administrative purposes. A new tower with 165 hospital beds is complete. The recently expanded hospital now averages more than 80 percent occupancy. A new professional building for physicians is now adjacent to the hospital and additional land has been purchased for future expansion.

Along the way several interesting stories developed. After the structural steel framework for the hospital had been erected, George Mitchell became concerned about whether the building's architectural character fit The Woodlands' image. Methodist had selected a notable hospital architect and plans had been reviewed extensively prior to start of construction, but Mitchell wanted a second opinion. And I had the unpleasant job of telling the hospital's architect that we had engaged another designer to take a look at his work. Fortunately, Mitchell's architect agreed that the hospital was too far along in construction to make any major changes and that the design fit the character of The Woodlands. I am really not sure what we would have done with a different finding.

But as we progressed toward the grand opening, Reverend Robert Gipson, a board member, asked a perfectly good question when reviewing a set of blueprints. Where was the chapel? There wasn't one. During the week prior to the hospital's official opening, Bruce Monicle, who was managing interior finishes for portions of the building, converted a janitor's broom closet to a tastefully designed and furnished chapel. It still functions as such today.

It has been a wonderful experience. There are now 500 doctors on staff and 1,000 total employees at The Woodlands Hospital.

And success breeds success. St. Luke's recently constructed and opened the second hospital in The Woodlands. And primary care physicians and specialists have developed independent practices to serve residents in the community and surrounding region.

Chapter 11

EDUCATION

———— • ◆ • ————

Developers of successful master-planned communities know it's vitally important to provide quality educational opportunities for residents. Families with school-age children want to live in communities that have great neighborhood schools. Companies want their employees to have access to continuing education and job training programs. A successful community provides the school system with an expanding tax base. Neighborhood schools reduce transportation costs for the district. Of course, the real winners are the students who benefit from a safe, challenging learning environment.

George Mitchell's concept for The Woodlands embraced the full range of educational objectives. Much effort went into fostering a system that would include high-quality public schools, private schools, and institutions of higher education. There were disappointments along the way. But in the end, he succeeded.

When Mitchell bought land for The Woodlands, it was without regard to city, county, or school district boundaries. It was just land available for sale that had some proximity to Interstate 45. For the most part, it was in Montgomery County. However, the land was within the extraterritorial jurisdiction of the cities of Houston, Conroe, Oak Ridge North, and Shenandoah, and it was in two counties and the portion in Montgomery County was in two school districts. The two school districts were the Conroe Independent School District (CISD) and the Magnolia Independent School District (MISD). Note carefully the word "independent" in those titles. Unlike those in many other states, school districts in Texas—with few exceptions—are political agencies in their own right established under the laws of the state. While they receive oversight from the Texas Education Agency along with some state funding, locally elected boards govern day-to-day affairs. Local school districts may or may not have the same boundaries as the city in which they are headquartered, meaning that the Conroe and Magnolia districts were responsible for education in areas beyond the towns from which they took their names. Conroe had jurisdiction over the east half of The Woodlands and Magnolia over the west half.

While it would have been more convenient to have just one school district within The Woodlands, we were satisfied with the academic quality of both districts. But there was one big hitch. The value of assessed property within the CISD was much higher than that in the Magnolia district. Generally, local school districts in Texas received money from the state for part of their operations, but they must use their own property taxes to cover the balance as well as pay the bill for new school construction. The first school there, before The Woodlands was established, was Lamar Elementary, which was built by CISD to serve children in neighboring areas. In anticipation of the new town's growth, Wilkerson Intermediate School was also built before any substantial development took place in The Woodlands.

The CISD committed to building a high school for The Woodlands before the new town opened. Mitchell made an arrangement with the superintendent at the time, J.L. "Mac" McCullough, to provide a 50-acre site for the project. The site was deep in the woods. The first trip the members of the Conroe school board made to inspect the lot was in a marsh buggy—there was no road.

The board members agreed to build the school and Mitchell agreed to provide vehicular access before it opened, including a bridge across Panther Creek, which required a substantial capital outlay. CISD started construction, despite the absence of a road and utilities. This was in 1974, when cash flow was a problem for The Woodlands Corporation. As the story goes, McCullough threatened bodily harm if Mitchell didn't get the bridge built across Panther Creek in time for the school to open. While that's probably an overstatement, McCullough was more than a little upset. Here was a brand new high school designed to accommodate 2,400 students and no road. The road and bridge were completed just before school opened. That was the first real friction between The Woodlands and the public education system. It would not be the last. The new high school was named for McCullough.

For the first ten to 12 years of development, the corporation was building neighborhoods that fell within the Conroe Independent School District. As we began to develop land in the western portion of The Woodlands property, we had to build a relationship with the Magnolia Independent School District. And while that was a good school district, it didn't have the financial resources to expand its physical plant in a timely way. MISD was not focused on building neighborhood schools as CISD had been in The Woodlands. It was obvious that our marketing of The Woodlands' newest residences was going to be hampered because we were moving into a new school district whose physical school plant was located no fewer than 45 minutes away from homes to be built. It would take a number of years before the Magnolia district gained enough financial capacity to build an extensive physical plant in The Woodlands, so we sought a better alternative.

The Conroe school district was wealthy compared with the Magnolia district. A lot of the tax base in the Conroe district since the 1930s came from the Conroe oilfield. As The Woodlands grew, production in the oilfield started to decline. Fortunately, the growing commercial and residential tax base in The Woodlands made up for the drop in oil production. The Woodlands' tax base became a source of funding and financing for the school district, replacing the declining values in the Conroe oilfield.

One of the important concepts of The Woodlands plan was to place an elementary school in each of the residential villages. As it turned out, most villages now contain several. It would have been difficult for MISD to build the first school in a timely way because there were no students in the Magnolia School District who resided in The Woodlands. There would not be an appreciable school population for a number of years after our development started in that district. We looked at a number of alternatives. State law at that time did not allow landowners to petition for the change of a school boundary. It gave that power only to parents of students who resided in the district. So there was a problem that could be solved only by anxious parents petitioning the school districts to change the boundary, but without building a school, the odds were homes would not be sold and there would be no parents.

To solve the problem, we needed to change the state law. It became quite a political challenge. We worked closely with both the Magnolia and Conroe school districts to get them to agree that a boundary exchange could be done in a way that would not harm either district. The existing school boundary ran along survey lines through undeveloped, wooded land, following no roadway or any other system of natural division.

We approached our state senator, Carl Parker of Beaumont, and asked if he would help us resolve the school boundary problem by supporting legislation in the Texas Senate that would allow landowners to petition for the change in school district boundaries. And the senator, while his political views were not always closely aligned with those of The Woodlands community, thought that this was a reasonable thing to do. He said he would help get it done, and he did. I credit much of the success of that bill's passage to Senator Parker and his ability to maneuver it through the Texas Legislature.

State law was amended and school districts can now change their boundary upon petition by landowners. The Woodlands then had to convince both Magnolia and Conroe to alter their boundaries. The new law required both districts to agree that the petition for boundary changes was acceptable to them before it could go forward. The school boards would then have to vote on it. We spent many nights in public meetings at Magnolia High School explaining why we thought this was something that needed to be done and how Magnolia could be compensated if it gave up some of the land in its district.

The new legislation stated that when land is detached from a district's jurisdiction, the annexing school district would assume a share of the losing district's bonded debt. But Conroe wasn't going to take on that liability. It would take the land and serve it, but CISD wasn't going to take the pro-rata share of the debt. That's where The Woodlands Corporation stepped in as a third party, underwriting the debt over time.

The compensation came in the form of a $12 million payment by The Woodlands Corporation to the MISD at the rate of $500,000 a year. We also agreed to donate a number of school sites to Magnolia on land we owned outside The Woodlands. Then we had to convince Conroe that annexing the land from the Magnolia District was a good financial deal. Following public debate, an economic impact study, and further negotiations with CISD and MISD, the boards of both districts voted in favor of the boundary change.

There was little organized opposition in the Conroe district to the change. There were individuals who asked good questions. We tried to provide good answers, but I think the economics were fairly transparent. If the population grew, the commercial base would grow, and the tax dollars would be there. We also agreed to donate some additional school sites to them at no cost, to make a $250,000 contribution to the CISD, plus we agreed to support some ongoing educational programs with financial contributions.

There was more opposition in the Magnolia School District. One opposing group was the Magnolia Volunteer Fire Department, which was something I didn't expect. The firefighters' concern was that they would not be allowed to provide fire protection for that part of The Woodlands to be excluded from the Magnolia School District. We were able to successfully explain that there was not a direct relationship between their concern and the de-annexation proposal before the school district. Other opposition came from residents in the Magnolia District who saw the proposal as a "land grab" conspiracy by The Woodlands and the Conroe School District. Conspiracy theories fueled by emotion are always hard to defeat, but we argued the point and made progress. Others had a legitimate concern that the transfer of land from Magnolia to Conroe would harm the long-term tax base for Magnolia. Economic studies performed by independent consultants disproved this concern.

On balance, there was enough opposition to cause the Magnolia School Board initially to vote against the de-annexation proposal. The new state law allowed a landowner to petition the State Board of Education for relief in cases where one school district votes to approve annexation and the other school district votes against the proposal. Petitions were prepared and the legal battle was joined, but a sweetened financial offer from The Woodlands Corporation resulted in a final approval by Magnolia, thus avoiding a court fight, which would have been very harmful to future relations. As it turned out, everyone was a winner.

I do recall one incident that was comical in hindsight, but not so funny when it happened. We were in a public meeting in the Magnolia high school auditorium. We worked hard to maintain a professional but low-key approach. We did not want to appear as The Big Woodlands coming forward to dictate how the MISD should make its decisions or run its business. We provided all the information necessary, and we answered all the questions.

In one well-attended meeting, late at night, someone came into the meeting and announced in a loud voice, "There's a car in the parking lot, a Jaguar, with headlights on, so would the owner of that Jaguar go turn your lights off." It turned out to be our attorney's car, and that was not the image we had intended to portray—that we had a high-priced attorney, obviously able to afford a Jaguar, representing us in that meeting. But after the laughter died down, it turned out not to be a big deal in the final discussions. The attorney who owned the Jaguar was Karen West. She's now the general counsel for The Woodlands Operating Company and she's doing quite well in that job, and she was very effective then, too. She had received the Jaguar as a special gift from her husband for graduating from law school after first raising their family. And she still drives a Jaguar.

In hindsight, all the projections that were made about growth of the commercial base in The Woodlands have come true. The Conroe Independent School District has built schools in neighborhoods in that part of The Woodlands that formerly was part of Magnolia. They function well. The Conroe district has been able to successfully pass future bond elections to build high schools and regional facilities. Magnolia has really come to the forefront. It's one of the fastest-growing school districts in the state of Texas now. It has constructed and opened a number of high-quality schools, and would have done a good job in The Woodlands, save and except for the timing of having to do it. Their financial base has grown considerably on development within their district after that de-annexation occurred.

Mike Page, an attorney for The Woodlands who helped shepherd the legislation through the Texas Legislature, said the MISD hesitated to let go of the potential they saw in the tax base growth in The Woodlands. "It's one of these things that if I could have afforded it, I would have been rich. But I couldn't afford it because I would have been poor before I had a chance to be rich."

The Woodlands now faces another challenge with school boundaries. Much of its residential development in the future will be in Harris County's Tomball School District, which is a very good progressive school district, but its facilities are located a 45-minute bus ride away from the lands being developed by The Woodlands. Tomball has agreed to build an elementary school in the new Village of Creekside Park, south of Spring Creek in Harris County, but the middle school and the high school are still quite a distance away. I think that the school district boundary issue is going to be a challenge to the future development of The Woodlands in Harris County. I don't think anyone in The Woodlands Corporation has the stomach to address another school boundary relocation. It was that traumatic and the memory remains vivid in the minds of many people who are still there. But had that boundary adjustment not been made, The Woodlands would be a different community today. Residential growth would have slowed considerably. We actually converted some commercial land we held to residential use because we were running out of lots in the Conroe school district. We made the conversion so that we would not run out of our residential product during that year or so when we were discussing the boundary issue with both the state legislature and the local school boards.

The school boundary shift was one of the major defining events in The Woodlands. It would rank up there with the acquisition of lands upon which The Woodlands was built. While the Corporation sought the best public schools possible for its residents, George Mitchell also realized he needed to do more. While the CISD had excellent programs, Mitchell felt a private school was needed in the community. Recruiting companies to move to The Woodlands, particularly biotechnology companies and venture capitalists, would be easier if we also had a private college preparatory school. It should complement the public school system and not compete with it.

John Cooper was the headmaster of Kincaid School, one of the top private schools in Houston. Some of Mitchell's children went to Kincaid. When Cooper retired, Mitchell convinced him and his wife to move to The Woodlands and be sort of an ex-officio adviser about education matters.

When it came time to help set up a private school, I got the assignment since I had served two terms on the elected CISD board. I knew something about the public education system and Ed Lee asked if I would help John Cooper. We formed a nonprofit corporation and recruited a board of directors. Some leaders in the community volunteered to serve and we did the preliminary planning. Before the school was actually built, its site moved three times as development consumed the proposed parcels. Finally, we agreed on a location for the school and Mitchell agreed to donate the land and provide $2 million to build the first classroom building.

Prior to the public announcement of the private school, Cooper and I visited the superintendent of CISD to make sure he knew we were not dissatisfied with his schools. We thought that our private schools would complement the stock of public schools and really raise the standard of education in the area. Conroe school officials were somewhat less than enthusiastic, but as it played out over time, the public and private systems established a good working relationship; there never has been any antagonism between them.

After construction started on the first building, it was time to recruit a headmaster. Mitchell said, "I have somebody in mind for that." It was Mitchell's niece. Now George Mitchell is not a person who believes in nepotism, but I was still a little apprehensive. His niece was Marina Ballentyne, the daughter of his sister, Maria Ballentyne. Marina was getting her PhD at Stanford. As it turned out, that apprehension was totally misplaced. The young educator came in, did a superb job as the first headmaster, and worked well with both the parents and the volunteer board of directors. She recruited an outstanding faculty and staff and got the school up and running with Cooper's help. We started out with kindergarten through fourth grade and added a grade each year. Funds were raised through foundations, corporations, and parent groups, largely because we changed the name of the school. Its original name was to be The Woodlands School, but we found that nobody wanted to donate to something called The Woodlands School because they felt that George Mitchell should pay the bills. So we prevailed upon Cooper to let us use his name, which he did with great reluctance and humility. We changed the name to the John Cooper School and opened under that name in 1988. The first graduating class from the upper school earned their diplomas in 1994. The ceremony was a story in itself.

Some of George H.W. Bush's children had gone to Kincaid along with some of Mitchell's children. Cooper took it upon himself to call President Bush, who was still in office, and asked him to give the address at the first graduation. Bush agreed. But before that could come to pass, Bush had been defeated for reelection and Cooper had died.

Marina Ballentyne, knowing the story and having a passing acquaintance with the former president, reminded him of his promise. Bush not only gave the address, but he also personally visited with each of the graduating students and posed for pictures with them.

The John Cooper School was followed by another private school, The Woodlands Christian Academy. It was formed by a group of parents with children at the nonsectarian Cooper school who wanted an institution with good academics but which also taught religious values. The Woodlands Corporation helped them acquire land at a bargain price and provided some utilities such as water and sewer connections and other services, but they raised their own funds for design, construction, and operation of the school. Greg Brenneman, then president of Continental Airlines, who lives in The Woodlands, was the leader in that effort. He contributed a portion of his own money to it and encouraged others to do the same. The school is now in its second decade and goes through the 12th grade.

Mitchell was not as successful in his initial effort to locate a college campus in the community. In January 1971, before construction started on The Woodlands, Mitchell met with Philip G. Hoffman, then the president of the University of Houston (UH), about locating a branch of that school in the new town. Mitchell took Hoffman and Coulson Tough, a vice president of the university who later came to work for The Woodlands, on a tour of the property.

The next day, Mitchell formally offered the university 300 acres of free land at The Woodlands, with an option to purchase 100 acres more at below-market rates. Three months later, Hoffman notified Mitchell the university would accept the property in principle if details could be worked out. Mitchell then upped his offer, saying he would give away the entire 400 acres, free. Nearly a year later, the school's regents formally accepted Mitchell's offer.

Coulson Tough, who retired from The Woodlands Corporation in 2003, in an interview that same year, remembers how the offer from Mitchell came about. The Coordinating Board for Higher Education of Texas said the University of Houston had to establish two new campuses to meet the anticipated growth of the student population—one to the south and one to the north of Houston, Tough said. "I began negotiating with Friendswood Development Corporation [the developer of Clear Lake City near the Johnson Space Center]. And finally we did get 400 acres from Friendswood to establish that campus." The south campus was supposed to be an upper-level school, offering the last two years of undergraduate education as well as graduate programs. The north campus was to be a four-year institution with a limited master's degree program.

"Then I had to try to find land to the north of Houston. The Coordinating Board said it had to be at no cost to the university and roads and utilities had to be accessible. That's not really very easy, so someone said we ought to talk to George Mitchell, and I said, 'Who's he?' I was told he was going to develop a community north of Houston someplace." Mitchell was invited to make the offer of land to the University of Houston. "I had quite a few meetings with [officials from The Woodlands Corporation] and we negotiated for land. The funny thing about it was that they were going to give me all the land along the west side of what was going to be Lake Woodlands." Tough said he told the officials they were giving up a lot of valuable real estate along the lake. They agreed and offered the 400 acres further north.

It didn't happen. In the summer of 1974, UH bought a building in downtown Houston that had formerly been the campus of South Texas Junior College. Unhappy with the university's move downtown, the coordinating board argued that the purchase fulfilled the university's requirement to open a branch north of the city.

But the real problem was opposition from Sam Houston State University in Huntsville, 40 miles north, and Texas A&M University in College Station, approximately 80 miles to the northwest. "When it came right down to getting the approval, Jimmy Edwards, who was our state representative, was a graduate of Sam Houston State. Sam Houston was very worried that if the University of Houston got a campus up here, that would hurt them. [Edwards] came out against it. . .and that was the end of getting the University of Houston campus."

There were other moves to again seek state permission to allow UH to establish a campus at The Woodlands. The Texas Legislature at one time approved a $200,000 planning study to look into the matter. But it was vetoed by then-Governor Mark White, although not on its own merits. This time the study was killed by a dispute involving Texas Southern University, a historically black state college in Houston, which said expanding the UH system while Texas Southern was underfunded was unfair.

Talks between UH, the state, and The Woodlands Corporation continued off and on for years. The final blow came after Mitchell made yet another offer—this time it was 200 acres of free land and a donation of money for the first building. A UH official replied, "Well, we really have to do a study to determine whether it's feasible for us to accept a donation of land and the feasibility study would cost $35,000, and Mr. Mitchell, we would love for you to pay for that study." That's when Mitchell said, "You know, if you can't really agree that you want us to give you 200 acres of land. . .then I'm not going to pay for the study."

We next focused our attention on securing a community college campus for The Woodlands. The North Harris Community College was exploring the possibility of expanding its jurisdiction northward to cover the Conroe school district, including The Woodlands. To achieve this objective, an election of voters residing in the Conroe district was required to allow the community college the authority to impose a property tax and build facilities within the district. An election was called, but the vote failed in part because no specific plans were presented to define where the future campus would be located, and there was suspicion among voters that either Conroe or The Woodlands would have the upper hand in determining campus locations.

Another election was called. This time a specific campus was identified. It was a 100-acre site located at the far northern edge of land owned by The Woodlands Corporation but well beyond development underway at the time. It had the acceptable appearance of being midway between The Woodlands and Conroe and it was centrally located in the school district. But as had been the case with the first high school site in The Woodlands, the parcel proposed for the community college was served by neither an existing major thoroughfare nor any utilities. Commitments were made by the corporation to build or facilitate the building of the necessary infrastructure. With the campus location identified and with considerable effort by community leaders in Conroe and The Woodlands, voters approved the proposal. Bonds were sold to finance the construction of an architecturally attractive 4,000-student community college campus that opened in 1995 with Governor George W. Bush in attendance. The Woodlands Corporation fulfilled its obligations with respect to roadway and utility construction just in time for the opening.

Its location works well for the entire county. It is near Interstate 45, the major north-south corridor, and fronts on State Highway 242, a new east-west thoroughfare connecting major populations to the campus location.

With encouragement from Mitchell and leadership from John Pickelman, chancellor of North Harris Montgomery Community College, and Bill Law, president of the Montgomery County campus, an innovative additional step was taken for higher education. The community college, working with six universities, created the University Center to provide the final two years of undergraduate study resulting in a bachelor's degree program (the first two years provided by the community college). The Woodlands Corporation donated ten acres of land and $2 million toward the construction of a 70,000-square-foot learning center to house the program. Rather than a ground breaking at the start of construction, the six participating universities staged a "ground spreading" event. Buckets of dirt from the campus of each university were brought and spread upon the University Center site to ensure that no degree would be granted unless the student had first walked upon that university's soil. The University Center opened in September 1998. The building is named the George P. Mitchell Building in recognition of his significant contribution to this educational institution. The six university participants are Texas A&M, Prairie View A&M, Sam Houston State University, Texas Southern University, the University of Houston, and University of Houston Downtown. Not only did Mitchell get his wish of a UH presence at The Woodlands, but he gained financially by not being able to make his original donation of acres to UH when the community college campus land was purchased by the community college district in 1993.

The community college has been a wonderful asset to the area, providing job training programs for companies, lifelong learning opportunities for seniors, and a local option for high school graduates. The University Center is one of only a handful of such programs in the United States and is a model for others to follow.

Chapter 12

THE NAME GAME

———— •◆• ————

There was one unforeseen problem with The Woodlands' status as an extraterritorial jurisdiction of Houston, which George Mitchell had pushed so hard for back in the 1970s. It complicated the naming of our streets, because all names had to be approved by Houston's planning department and none could duplicate those already in use in the city. Originally, members of The Woodlands' planning department named the streets, recalled Susan Vreeland, a marketing executive with The Woodlands Corporation. "They came up with some really outlandish names like Wolly Bucket and Crinkleroot, so [we] thought maybe the marketing people ought to take that on that job. And we've been doing it ever since the opening of the Village of Panther Creek up to the present day, so that's about 20 years."

There's never been a written policy about street naming in the town, Vreeland said. "But in keeping with the way The Woodlands has been developed as a community in harmony with nature, of course we always have kept to the nature theme." Despite the fact that most tree names had already been allocated in Houston, Vreeland found a way to keep using them. If you add enough words together, you can come up with something like Oak Pond, Oak Court Place, and Woodhaven Wood. In other words, Vreeland said, "We cheat."

"But frankly, in the present day we're kind of running out of ideas," she admitted. "You know we've done every species of bird, butterfly, tree, and wildflower. For example, in our new gated community, Carlton Woods, I resorted to silver patterns because we needed something that was very elegant and unique. We came up with names such as Cartouche and Electra, and believe it or not, they came out of the silver department in Dillard's [department store]. Musical terms are another [approach] that we've come up with, like Etude, Largo, and Aria. We look for names that have a very fluid, lyrical sound—something that looks good on engraved stationary and makes you want to buy a home on that street. It's all part of the marketing process."

The Woodlands Corporation has tried to fit names of streets and neighborhoods with the names of The Woodlands' seven residential villages. It is useful to review those village names and their status at the time of this book's publication. The first to be established was the Village of Grogan's Mill. It's essentially built out. Some of the original residents still live there. The village, in existence since 1974, is currently seeing a period of extensive remodeling by homeowners, including a few teardowns to make way for the construction of bigger houses. It's an attractive village. It has three golf courses—more than any of the other villages—and is the closest to Interstate 45. The original land purchased for The Woodlands was from the Grogan Cochran Lumber Company. Grogan's Mill is named for one of the families that owned that company.

Since Grogan's Mill was the only village for the first several years, it got the full attention of everyone on the team, including planners, marketing people, management, residents, and George Mitchell himself. The decision was made to adopt a system of names for streets, parks, and neighborhoods that reflected not only the land's connection to the timber industry, but also the names of birds, flowers, trees, shrubs, and animals. To remain consistent with the environmental theme, neighborhood entry markers were sandblasted wooden signs finished in earth tones. Street names were inscribed vertically on posts without cross arms. To read the names people had to cock their head to the side. There was a joke among some within the county that you could recognize residents from The Woodlands by the way they held their head.

To the west of Grogan's Mill is the second village to be developed, the Village of Panther Creek, which was named for the creek that runs through it. It's also complete. It has a full range of housing, neighborhood shopping facilities, and schools. Ann and I live in Panther Creek. It's centrally located and occupies a stretch of land along the western shore of Lake Woodlands. It is the smallest residential village in the community.

The third to be developed was the Village of Cochran's Crossing, also named for one of the families who owned the lumber company. It opened in July 1983 on a very hot day. We had the grand opening in a park and George Mitchell was present. He had been down on Galveston Island for a weekend visit, his typical routine, and he came in his fishing hat, light blue trousers, and a slightly wrinkled shirt. He didn't know it was going to be a formal event. Members of the Cochran family were also there. Cochran's Crossing is also essentially complete, including the 27-hole Arnold Palmer Golf Course and Galatas Elementary School.

Following closely on the heels of Cochran's Crossing, the Village of Indian Springs opened in 1984. There was modest archeological evidence suggesting that an Indian tribe hunted and perhaps camped within the floodplain along Spring Creek, which formed the southern boundary of this village. Thus, street and neighborhood names such as Flintridge, Rushwing, and Shawnee Ridge were used to recognize the site's history. The Spring Creek floodplain remains protected.

Next to be developed was the Village of Alden Bridge. Its grand opening was in 1995. It provides the full range of housing, neighborhood shopping, and schools as the other villages do, and it's reaching its capacity in terms of development. The Village of Alden Bridge was actually named for a sawmill near where I grew up in Benton, Louisiana. The original town of Alden Bridge had a millpond that I fished in when I was a little kid. The mill is gone, the town is gone, and the forest has reclaimed the entire place. Alden Bridge was where a railroad bridge was built across the stream and Philo Alden built a sawmill, a general store, and houses. Later, Alden was elected the sheriff of the county—Bossier Parish—and shortly after his election he met an early death. He was kicked in the head by a mule and died.

The sixth village is Sterling Ridge, which includes the neighborhood of Carlton Woods, a gated golf course community. Sterling Ridge was named in celebration of The Woodlands'

25th anniversary. The year was 1999. It's still under active development today. It has a higher percentage of upscale housing than the other villages because of its two signature golf courses, one designed by Jack Nicklaus and the other by Gary Player.

The next village in the sequence of development is the Village of College Park, a mixed-use village that has a significant amount of housing but also a major commercial component. The housing is primarily on the east side of Interstate 45, which separates it geographically from the heart of The Woodlands. It benefits, however, from being part of the community and its amenities are consistent with the quality and the style of those typical of The Woodlands proper.

The portion of College Park west of Interstate 45 includes a 100-acre community college campus and the University Center from which it derives its name, St. Luke's Community Hospital, and a substantial retail component. Housing on this side of the highway is found primarily in the age-restricted neighborhoods of Windsor Hills and Windsor Lakes. Dwellings for residents over the age of 55 were intentionally located near the college to provide easy access to lifelong learning opportunities.

The seventh and last residential village, currently under development, is the Village of Creekside Park, which is the only village in The Woodlands not located in Montgomery County. It lies entirely in adjacent Harris County. Public education will be provided to village residents by the Tomball Independent School District as opposed to the Conroe district that serves all other villages. A centerpiece of the village will be a Tom Fazio–designed golf course constructed as an extension of the country club experience provided by The Club at Carlton Woods, which has two golf courses—one in the Village of Sterling Ridge, the other in the Village of Creekside Park.

This seventh village was originally named the Village of Harmony Bend to relate to the name Harmony Bridge, which crosses Spring Creek at Kuykendahl Road as it connects Harris and Montgomery counties. The bridge's name was selected to express the good relations between the two counties. The opening ceremony for Harmony Bridge in 1986 included a festive event at the center point of the bridge. The band from McCullough High School in The Woodlands marched south across the bridge and was met by the band from Klein High School marching in the opposite direction from Harris County. Elected officials from both counties met in the middle of the bridge, shook hands, and cut a green ribbon as an expression of harmony and good will. I recall sitting on the speakers' stage with a sense of apprehension as the rhythmic cadence of the marching bands created a noticeable vibration within the structure. This was my first major public event after being named president of The Woodlands Corporation. I had to think about what I would do if the bridge collapsed. But it held up without a problem. The new owners of The Woodlands elected to change the village name in 2003, but that is what owners get to do.

Public schools in The Woodlands are named to honor heroes of Texas history (Mirabeau B. Lamar), famous American leaders (Sally K. Ride, Colin Powell, Barbara Bush), and former school board members and school administrators (Ned Knox, Sam Hailey, Don Buckalew, Coulson Tough, W.D. Wilkerson, Mac McCullough, and Roger Galatas). And appropriately, one school is named in honor of George Mitchell.

One is also named for David Vetter, the courageous youngster who lived his entire life in a plastic bubble to protect his weakened immune system from disease and infection. David, who spent his 12 years living in the adjacent town of Shenandoah, received special education assistance from the public school system. His father, David Vetter, Sr., currently serves as mayor of Shenandoah and as a board member of the Town Center Improvement District. The plastic bubble that was home to David for many years is in the collection of the Smithsonian in Washington, D.C.

The school system invited each honoree to attend its school dedication and most did. Colin Powell came to the special opening event at Colin Powell Elementary School. He began his presentation by first apologizing to the assembled elected officials, school administrators, community leaders, and parents to say that on this day with their indulgence he would tailor his comments to the students. And he did. He walked into the crowd of smiling youngsters seated on the floor of the assembly room and talked about responsibility and leadership in terms they could understand.

Barbara Bush came to the opening of Barbara Bush Elementary School. The event was held in the late afternoon and as I recall she arrived in a rather plain, unmarked automobile, driven by what appeared to be a Secret Service agent. As her car entered The Woodlands, an alert local security officer on routine traffic duty pulled her car over for entering a restricted parking area near the school. He approached her car, looked into the back seat, and quickly recognized his dilemma. But he recovered by saying, "Welcome to The Woodlands, Mrs. Bush. May I escort you to your school?" And he did. They arrived on time.

Having a school bear my name is something I still don't know how to deal with. It is a great honor and I appreciate it more than I can express. I visit the school from time to time each year and remain impressed with the quality of its learning environment. The faculty, staff, and students are all so bright and enthusiastic. It is a school with great participation by parents, which is such a key element in education. On one visit to the school, a student raised his hand and volunteered, "I know what your middle initial L stands for. It stands for elementary." At a different time, my wife Ann was cashing a check at the grocery store and the clerk, recognizing her name, asked if she was named after the school. It's a great thrill to see youngsters wearing T-shirts with Galatas Greyhounds inscribed across its front.

Three schools in The Woodlands are named in honor of three individuals who played a visible role in the development company: George Mitchell, Coulson Tough, and me. I think we all believe that this primarily recognizes an element of trust between the community and the company rather than a personal accomplishment.

Part IV

---◆---

PRODUCTIVE RELATIONSHIPS

George Mitchell recognized from the beginning of The Woodlands that building productive relationships with others would be vital to the development's success. No single person or team has the expertise—or the necessary funds—to build a new town. Relationships are necessary, whether they are with homebuilders who can turn lots into places for new residents to live, or with nonprofit agencies that can be called upon to help build the necessary social infrastructure so crucial to any community. He also knew that facilitating relationships between residents was critical to the long-term vitality of The Woodlands.

Chapter 13

HOMES IN THE
NEW COMMUNITY

———— • ◆ • ————

Most developers of large-scale communities will agree that construction quality, diversity of architectural styles, and a wide range of house prices are important factors in attracting homebuyers in large numbers. And the majority of homebuyers will tell you that their decision to purchase a particular house is influenced by the character of the surrounding environment.

Community developers will also likely agree that the most profitable part of their business, particularly in the early phases of a project, is the development and sale of building sites to homebuilders. And it is the sale of homes to families or individuals that creates the demand for other profitable development opportunities, including retail centers, restaurants, office buildings, membership clubs, health care facilities, lodging, and other commercial uses. As the homes and commercial facilities increase in number and value, so too does the tax base required to fund community services.

A visitor driving along major thoroughfares in The Woodlands may be surprised to find that there is not a house in sight, though more than 75,000 people live there. Even on a trip through neighborhood streets, a driver would not be exposed to rows of houses and garage doors. Why? Because we preserve the natural vegetation along major thoroughfares, and ensure through community deed restrictions that trees and understory in a portion of the frontyards of homes are preserved. There are fewer manicured lawns and more songbirds.

That didn't happen by chance. The residential program in The Woodlands was carefully managed, from market research to determine the preferences of potential homebuyers to the planning, design, construction, and promotion of the town and its housing stock. Our company deliberately created the living environment where homes are located. We developed lots and building sites that were sold to homebuilders who could produce high-quality homes within a specified design and price range. Homes are arranged in small neighborhoods connected to each other and to the village shopping and schools by greenbelt pathways and residential streets.

Housing in The Woodlands covers the full market range from very affordable to very expensive and includes rental apartments, condominiums, townhomes, duplexes, patio homes, and single-family homes—from bungalows to expansive estates with lakefront or golf locations.

Today, with its demonstrated success, attracting qualified homebuilders to The Woodlands is easy. But that was not the case during the startup years. Also, the fairly restrictive rules under which The Woodlands Corporation sold lots and imposed construction standards frightened away some of the more independent-minded homebuilders. It was, however, the imposition of rules, standards, and inspections that later distinguished The Woodlands as a place of high quality. Unincorporated areas of counties in Texas have very limited authority to impose quality standards; therefore, it is left to the developer to set standards through covenants and contractual agreements with homebuilders. Developers of smaller residential communities with relatively short marketing lives generally do not establish design guidelines for fear of driving away the very homebuilders they are trying to attract. It was the long-term, phased development of The Woodlands that motivated us to enhance the future value of land yet to be developed.

During the first several years of development, The Woodlands Corporation dutifully imposed construction standards and architectural review of house plans. But for reasons not now clear, it had no building inspection system for residential construction. Frankly, during those early years construction quality was less than perfect. One apartment project built by a contractor was so sub par it had to undergo extensive rehabilitation before it could be acquired by default from the original investor-owner and successfully managed by us. It was that incident that convinced us to build, own, and manage future apartment properties.

It was not until 1979 that Gil Fehn, a building contractor who retired to The Woodlands, was persuaded to form and manage a residential building inspection program. Fehn had gained most of his construction experience in the Northeast, where strict building codes are rigidly enforced and structures are designed to withstand the weight of accumulated snow. Quality improved greatly under Fehn's program. Some homebuilders complained. But standards were uniformly applied to all, so no one was at a competitive disadvantage and we all benefited from the greater market acceptance of quality.

One of the first production homebuilders to move to The Woodlands was Ryland Homes, whose origin was in the master-planned community of Columbia, Maryland. It was there that Jim Ryan founded Ryland and saw the advantages of building in master-planned communities, where the supply of lots and a relationship with the developer could last for decades. As Ryland sought to expand its program to the Houston market, it was natural to explore opportunities in The Woodlands, where so many members of Columbia's development team had been hired. Ryland struck a deal with The Woodlands that has lasted to this day, but the company had to modify its business approach to succeed in Houston. When he first came to our city, Ryan had a very conservative financial plan for his operation. Ryland would only build homes under contract to a purchaser. This apparently worked well in Maryland but had limited potential in Houston, where a large number of homebuyers came from corporate relocation. Families moving to town on short notice did not want to wait for a new home to be built, so they opted to buy speculative homes—houses built before a buyer is identified. Eventually, Bob Salcetti, who ran Ryland's Houston operation, got approval from his corporate headquarters to build a very limited number of spec homes in the new town, a move that increased home sales for Ryland and lot sales for The Woodlands at a time when both needed the revenue.

Ryland also brought innovation to home construction. The company built an assembly plant in north Houston to manufacture wall panels and roof trusses that could be delivered to the building site on a flatbed truck. This shortened construction time and reduced the cost of housing so long as sales volume remained high enough to support production at the plant. Unloading and stacking the house panels and trusses, while respecting our environmental mandate to save trees on the wooded building sites, caused some grief, but that was eventually managed in a reasonable way. The lower cost of panel construction was consistent with affordable housing goals of The Woodlands. But that advantage disappeared during Houston's economic downturn in the 1980s, when housing starts plummeted. Ryland closed its factory permanently.

Life Forms Homes, founded by George Mitchell's son, architect Scott Mitchell, was an early leader in developing residential neighborhoods with all the housing constructed by a single builder and following a common architectural theme and customized neighborhood amenities. Life Forms' early neighborhoods include Slash Pine, Moss Rock, The Arbor, and Trace Creek, dispersed throughout the villages. Prior to the creation of Life Forms' business model, it was common practice for several different builders to construct homes in the same neighborhood using compatible, but nonuniform architectural design. While multiple builders are still used in many neighborhoods, the Life Forms approach blended architecture, land planning, and building construction to create more unique neighborhoods of slightly higher density. Other builders now follow the Life Forms approach in selected neighborhoods throughout The Woodlands.

To support the custom home effort, The Woodlands Corporation operated a central sales office that marketed new homes for all custom builders. We also managed the advertising program and featured custom home exhibits in our Information Center. This left builders free to concentrate on home design, construction quality, and warranty work.

As the community developed, the custom program expanded along with it. Early builders increased their efforts and additional builders were added to the program. Thirty years later, the custom home program is a significant component of the residential business. I have great respect for those early builders. They took a financial risk along with the development company. One mistake could have put any one of them out of business, but they followed the developer's rules, worked hard, and produced a high-quality product. Most succeeded financially and some are still at work in The Woodlands.

From time to time, The Woodlands Corporation looked into the possibility of forming its own homebuilding division to finance and construct innovative housing types that other builders were not prepared to tackle, including condominiums, townhomes, and zero-lot-line patio homes. We always found one reason or another to leave the building to others, but a tragic event finally led us into the homebuilding business. On a Sunday afternoon in the 1980s, Harris Lieberman, owner of Harris Development Company, a builder in The Woodlands, and his wife perished in a helicopter crash in the countryside west of Houston.

As the shock of that event diminished over the next several months, The Woodlands Corporation purchased the assets of Harris Development Company, assumed its obligations in The Woodlands, and hired its professional staff, including Larry White, who became the general manager of our newly acquired homebuilding entity.

We renamed it Hometown Builders and launched our homebuilding effort in The Woodlands. We constructed the affordable condominiums at Creekside in the Village of Panther Creek, the initial phase of both Parkside Apartments and Forrest Lake Townhomes, the Huntington Woods patio home neighborhood in Cochran's Crossing, and about 200 single-family homes in Panther Creek. Outside The Woodlands, Hometown Builders also coordinated the construction of the 14-story San Luis Resort Condominiums on Galveston Island.

The homebuilding effort went well, but our timing could not have been worse. By 1986, Houston's economy was in a tailspin and housing starts were off dramatically. With home sales down 50 percent in The Woodlands, we had to decide whether or not we should become the dominant homebuilder in the community or terminate our program in favor of other builders. We elected to discontinue Hometown Builders and concentrate only on community development.

We had another interesting building adventure. Prior to forming Hometown Builders, we used a general contractor to build apartments for our account in The Woodlands. A contractor headquartered in Brownwood, Texas, built Holly Creek and Wood Glen Apartments. Its president was Ben Barnes, former lieutenant governor of Texas and business partner of former Governor John Connelly. They did a great job for us, but that is not the interesting part. Barnes is absolutely the most captivating, charismatic person I have ever met. He would come to my office to review construction reports and within five minutes he would be sitting in my chair with his feet on my desk talking on my phone to a business associate or political ally in gosh knows where while I sat in the visitor's chair just enjoying the conversation. In just a few minutes, he would be up and gone without talking about apartment construction. But I was somehow convinced that things were in good hands. I'm still amazed that his run for governor was not successful.

Construction of upscale housing has always been part of The Woodlands. Wilding was the first golf estate neighborhood in the new town. Mitchell believed that wealthy individuals were far more likely to spend the money required to retain talented architects, so we did the necessary federal filings to allow us to sell lots to individuals to encourage better architecture. That was in 1975, and residential lots on golf courses were then priced below $30,000, so the measure of wealth was relative. But some very attractive, substantial homes were constructed in Wilding and that added value to the rest of The Woodlands. The next upscale neighborhood was Doe Run, which was followed by Grogan's Point.

The neighborhood of Grogan's Point includes 800 acres of property not directly contiguous with other landholdings of The Woodlands. To reach this land, one had to exit The Woodlands and travel a short distance along an existing county road. Various alternatives were considered for development of this property, including an enclave of affordable housing under a separate name. But the beauty of the land, the size of the parcel, and our ability to extend the third nine of an existing golf course into the property, suggested an upscale golf community of estate homes would offset any minor location problem. Grogan's Point has become one of the more popular neighborhoods for executive homes in town.

As in other estate neighborhoods, we sold lots to both homebuilders and individuals to achieve a more diverse mix of good architecture in Grogan's Point. The neighborhood is also where we held our first lottery for lot sales. In 1982, we held a drawing to determine who got to buy 25 lots offered for sale. All 25 were sold on the day of the lottery. In hindsight that does not sound like such a big deal, but it was impressive at the time. Today, there are 465 homes in Grogan's Point.

The latest and most exclusive upscale golf neighborhood is Carlton Woods, which opened in 2000 after The Woodlands was purchased by Crescent and Morgan Stanley. I make that distinction because the concept for Carlton Woods seeks to capitalize on Crescent's experience at Desert Mountain, a successful golf resort community they bought from Mobil Land Company near Phoenix, Arizona.

Carlton Woods is the first and thus far the only gated neighborhood in The Woodlands. It is among the larger neighborhoods, with approximately 500 building sites surrounding an 18-hole Jack Nicklaus Signature Golf Course and a 50,000-square-foot country club facility of attractive Mediterranean design. Carlton Woods was named in honor of the late Carlton Gipson, the golf course designer who was associated with The Woodlands from 1972 to 1984. The Club at Carlton Woods has a membership capacity of 450. It is among the more expensive clubs in the Houston region. Pricing for lots and homes around it lead the market.

Development plans for The Woodlands had always included a more exclusive country club in the western portion of the community where The Club at Carlton Woods is located. But if George Mitchell had continued his ownership, I'm not sure it would have been a gated community. While this approach accommodates a certain market sector, the original plan was to have an open environment where everyone shared community amenities and benefits. Safety and security were provided to the entire community, making gated enclaves unnecessary. For example, George and Cynthia Mitchell live in an attractive, well-appointed wood frame home in a neighborhood on a public street. Others, however, may prefer to live in a more private setting.

Pat Moritz, a real estate agent who specializes in properties in The Woodlands, says that gated communities appeal to certain kinds of buyers. Most buyers, she says, aren't worried about crime. "It's the prestige that's important, especially to young professional in their 30s and 40s."

Another niche in the housing market is the age-restricted neighborhood for active adults, which we began to focus on early in the 1990s. We've located them within walking distance of the shopping center and parks. Their residents are part of the community, but also protected from it in the sense that there are no tricycles in driveways. The largest developer of age-restricted housing is the Del Webb Co., with its massive Sun City projects in which the population is homogeneous and isolated from other communities. The Woodlands chose a different route. Our research indicated that there is a large segment of retirees over 55 who did not want to live in a Del Webb–style community. These are people who want to live in age-restricted neighborhoods near more diverse communities where their children and grand-children can live.

Our research found that a smaller neighborhood, ranging in size from 70 homes to slightly over 400 homes, was the most acceptable to the greatest segment of the homebuyers we interviewed in the 55-plus category. We teamed up with Lennar Homes, which had extensive national experience in retirement living communities. Our first neighborhood was Ashley Greens, which included 68 homes, and it was nestled among non–age restricted developments. Our next experience was with a larger community—Windsor Hills, with 450 homes, located adjacent to the community college in The Woodlands. Lennar constructed amenities exclusively for this community: a clubhouse, meeting rooms, and swimming pools. But in all cases, people who live in Windsor Hills and Ashley Greens can also use the broader array of amenities within The Woodlands.

The plan to offer homes across a broad range of price points in customized neighborhoods has paid off in more sales. Currently, about 1,300 to 1,500 new homes are started each year. Addressing many market segments within a broad range of prices has been important in establishing an economically viable residential program in The Woodlands. But the environment within which homes are placed, providing convenient access to community amenities and services, has been a key factor in attracting a large volume of buyers. New homes in The Woodlands sell for a premium of 15 to 25 percent over similar homes in other areas of Houston. This premium is partially related to upgrades in interior finishes, compliance with design requirements, and a higher lot cost. But it is achievable because of the value of the living environment.

Chapter 14

AFFORDABLE HOUSING AND AFFIRMATIVE ACTION

———— • ◆ • ————

I n an era when residential segregation was just starting to fade away, both in Houston and
also across the nation, The Woodlands welcomed people regardless of their race or ethnic
background. One reason for that policy was financing. The Woodlands obtained a $50
million loan guarantee from the U.S. Department of Housing and Urban Development
(HUD)—money used to buy the initial 17,460 acres of the development. "Clearly, the HUD
program had social objectives," recalled Joel Deretchin, who was hired in 1977 as The
Woodlands director of government relations and is now vice president for residential operations.

"HUD and Congress were interested in making sure that the new towns developed under
the program would meet the needs of people of modest income and the community would
be open to people of all races," he explained. Under the terms of the HUD agreement, The
Woodlands Corporation was obligated to conduct an affirmative action program. The agreement set levels for employment of minorities and the hiring of minority contractors. It also
required The Woodlands Corporation to enforce equal opportunity housing by requiring
homebuilders to sell their properties to anyone regardless of race or ethnicity.

The agency's intention was for the corporation to produce a population profile roughly
equal to that of the five-county Houston Standard Metropolitan Statistical Area. The agreement also required The Woodlands to ensure that annual targets for the construction of low-
and moderate-income housing units were met.

Another impetus for making The Woodlands a home for more than the upper tier of the
market came from George Mitchell himself. He was determined from the beginning to make
The Woodlands into more than just a successful real estate development. One of the reasons
Mitchell started the project came from what he saw as the decline of America's cities in the
1970s. Mitchell wasn't naïve. He could not solve the problems of racial and economic stratification with one new development on the outskirts of Houston. Instead, his goal was for The
Woodlands to be a demonstration project. He wanted to show other developers that an eco-

nomically and racially integrated community wasn't just the right thing to do. It also brought real financial benefits to the developer.

So what about Mitchell's dream? Was it realized? The short answer is not completely. Mitchell gives himself good marks for providing homes for a diverse economic range of the population, but he also concedes that his campaign to fully integrate The Woodlands racially was not as successful. Given the realities of both the times and the funding available, the outcome was probably as good as could be expected.

From the first, The Woodlands set out to build homes for a wide range of income levels. Throughout its years of development, there have been as many as 59 separate price points for homes, ranging from modest houses to mansions. Mitchell's aim, he said later, was that a teacher in a public school in The Woodlands could be able to afford to buy a home in the community where he or she worked. Mitchell worked diligently with builders to ensure that a selection of inexpensive homes was always on the market. The Woodlands, by its very design and size, could better accommodate a wide variety of housing stock than more conventionally built developments. Generally, those who buy homes want others in their neighborhoods to have similar characteristics. The owner of a large home would not look kindly on a much smaller house built next door. The Woodlands now comprises seven different villages. Each is built with numerous residential neighborhoods, each generally containing 50 to 100 homes. Between each neighborhood within a village are bands of trees and natural foliage. Thus, each neighborhood has a distinct look, while each village can contain a wide variety of housing.

But even the best planned and executed blueprint using only privately built and financed housing won't satisfy all housing needs. "There's a predicate based on the realities of development that, without subsidies, it's virtually impossible to provide housing at rent levels or sales prices that low-income people can afford," said Deretchin. "Fortunately for The Woodlands in its early days, the federal government was actively involved in rent subsidy programs for apartments and it also dabbled for a couple of years in mortgage subsidy programs, trying to make homeownership available to people of limited means."

Those subsidies were used for both multifamily and single-family homes for sale, although most were in the former category such as apartments and condominiums. "And that's a fact that is little known because The Woodlands has been perceived because of its marketing as an affluent community," Deretchin noted. The Woodlands Corporation decided early on that it would be the sole owner-manager of subsidized apartments for low-income residents in the new town. We took notice of the way subsidized units across the country had fallen into disrepair, because they were neither well managed, nor well maintained. Most of the problems came from absentee ownership. The Woodlands Corporation had a vested interest in the larger community. It would be in our best interest to manage and maintain the apartments and make sure prospective tenants were objectively screened following guidelines established by HUD. The corporation was not as concerned about projects for the elderly. Seniors, of course, are not as hard on the physical plant. Most subsidized housing for the elderly in The Woodlands was built by nonprofit and religious organizations. Again, these developer groups were carefully selected to find organizations interested in high-quality construction and maintenance.

"The family projects around the country would fall into disrepair because kids are hard on them and people don't take care of them as well. There's not a whole lot of money built into the economics of those projects to care for them," Deretchin said. "So we did the family units ourselves as a company and made sure, using our own internal management operations, that they were well maintained. On the one hand, we really and truly believed in providing housing for people with low incomes. But we also didn't want that to detract from the marketability of the rest of The Woodlands. We wanted these projects as integrated into the community as possible so that the kids would go to school with other kids. You know, part of enabling youngsters to achieve in life is giving them contact with others who may not have the less fortunate background that they have. If they would go to school with the other kids and go to the same schools, same classes and so forth, they would acquire not only the same education, but also the kind of outlook that makes them believe that they can break out of the less fortunate circumstances that they were born into. And there are plenty of examples of that. My wife grew up in the low-income projects in New York [City] and has gone on to earn a PhD and is well recognized in the Houston area for her work. Well, that's what we wanted these kids to have the chance to do as well.

"We wanted to integrate lower-income residents into a broader social and economic fabric that would help them get jobs and become self-sufficient," Deretchin continued. "And the Interfaith organization in The Woodlands has always lent a helping hand to all of the folks in subsidized apartments. Interfaith offers a food pantry, rent and clothing assistance, and school supplies, and it has also set up a computer training program in the Copperwood Apartments so people can develop marketable job skills. So there has been, through Interfaith, through the churches and others, a support infrastructure, social and economic support to help these folks who, even though they're in subsidized apartments, still need help with the rest of their lives. We, The Woodlands Corporation, provided financial and other support to organizations like Interfaith, who in turn would provide support for these people in need."

It's an interesting point, too, that this affordable housing really helped build a stronger community. When I first came to The Woodlands, I was apprehensive about it. When I got here, the program was already in place. I came from a development company that didn't embrace affordable housing. And I was concerned personally that the affordable housing would deter affluent people from buying the more expensive properties in The Woodlands. Not true. The affordable housing really makes it a stronger community. For example, many grandparents who want to live near their families do so in affordable or subsidized apartments. That makes families stronger. Many people who provide important services in the community—sell groceries, teach school, patrol our streets, staff the libraries, and work for county government—qualify for affordable housing, and live in nice neighborhoods.

Of course, there are some who object to rental apartments in the community and the thought of subsidized apartments is just more than they can bear. I have had to deal with this issue for many years, but it is an easy argument after the emotion fades into rational discussion. Many who have first objected to rent-assisted housing may later find it to be very suitable for their retired parents living on a fixed income and it is hard to stay upset with the place where your mother lives.

Unfortunately, the kinds of rent subsidy programs that helped build most of the affordable housing in The Woodlands fell victim to budget cuts. These programs are still around.
There just aren't as many now. According to Deretchin, The Woodlands, working with nonprofit groups, continues to apply for subsidized housing and is sometimes successful. In 2003,
for example, rent subsidies were authorized for 60 new units in The Woodlands.

The Woodlands also built some housing using the Tax Credit Program. According to
Deretchin, this (federal) program didn't replace the cut in rent subsidy programs, but it did
provide some help. Under this program, the builder of rental apartments received a tax credit from the government that he could then sell to someone else. In return, the housing developer agreed to keep rents below market rate. Those rents weren't as low as those paid for other
kinds of subsidized units, Deretchin said, but it did make them affordable for lower-middle-
class working people.

Today, the federal government continues to reduce its housing subsidy business, and that
includes the termination of subsidies for existing apartments. Deretchin explained, "I think
the subsidies were guaranteed for 20 years in every project. As the subsidy agreements
expire, HUD is choosing not to renew them and the properties are being converted to
market rate. There are two age-restricted rental projects here in The Woodlands: Tamarac
Pines and Copperwood, which are both being turned into tax credit projects, meaning
they'll have a modicum of subsidy but not enough for most of the people who live there.
And that's a disgrace. The federal government is literally turning people out on the street all
over the country."

Meanwhile, The Woodlands continues to do what it can to keep a portion of its housing
affordable. We develop lots and price them for builders to produce single-family homes at
the lowest market rates in affordable neighborhoods. We do the same with duplexes. I'm not
sure there are very many people in Houston building duplexes, if any, but we do that because
you can lower the price. Let's say a single-family home, at the low end, comes in around
$130,000. We can bring in a duplex probably for about $100,000. We do the same with
townhouses and condominiums. People can buy a home starting at $80,000 or $90,000 in
The Woodlands.

Given The Woodlands Corporation's efforts to create a healthy mixed-income community,
did we meet affirmative action goals mandated by the federal government as a condition for
the HUD loan guarantees? "The project agreement had requirements for actively going out
and seeking minorities to live and work in The Woodlands," Deretchin noted. "The overall
objective was that The Woodlands new community should mirror the complexion of the metropolitan area in terms of racial diversity. We were required to have programs and show
progress in attracting minorities to live here, and we also had to use minority firms in the
development of The Woodlands. And we did very well in that regard. We advertised in minority newspapers and sought out minority builders and contractors.

"And we made sure that the general contractors would hire minority subcontractors and
so forth. We were very active. We attended a lot of the meetings of the minority contractor
organizations to let them know that there was business to be had in The Woodlands and how
to deal with our bidding and procurement procedures and policies. And we promoted our

community at housing fairs down in Houston that we knew would attract minorities. We linked up, for example, with minority organizations like the Association for the Advancement of Mexican Americans."

Another way The Woodlands Corporation encouraged minorities to move to the new town was to help establish institutions that appealed to them. "We encouraged the formation of an African American church," noted Deretchin, who also nurtured a relationship with a Hispanic social club within the Catholic Church.

Over the years, the percentage of African American and Hispanic residents of The Woodlands has averaged about 10 percent. That compares to Harris County (which contains most of the city of Houston) with an 18.5 percent black and 32.9 percent Hispanic population. The Woodlands is, however, primarily in Montgomery County to the north of Houston, where African Americans make up 3.5 percent of the population and Hispanics 13.6 percent.

During the second half of the 1980s, Houston saw a very large number of low-to-moderate-income minorities move to the suburbs. This was brought about primarily by the collapse in real estate prices for housing, mirroring the same kind of collapse in prices for petroleum—Houston's long-dominant industry. At that time, many developers had over-built suburban housing. There were thousands of vacant homes, many of them never occupied. This, coupled with an unprecedented number of mortgage foreclosures, drove down suburban housing values, making them more affordable.

The radical change in the fortunes of the housing market had a milder effect on The Woodlands and other master-planned communities. We also saw a drop in housing prices, but they fell much less than in other areas. The bargains were elsewhere.

Under the HUD loan agreement, The Woodlands Corporation submitted an annual report on how we achieved compliance with affirmative and low-income housing mandates. "We never got dinged for not doing a very conscientious job," said Deretchin. "And we were probably one of the few and maybe the only developer in Houston that really worked at attracting minorities into our community. I thought by now it would have more rigid stratification, but it doesn't. You can move into just about any aspect of Woodlands life regardless of whether you have money or you don't, regardless of whether you're a minority or not, and assume positions of leadership just because you want to do some good for the community. Nobody's excluded, at least not that I'm aware of."

Deretchin admitted that when it comes to The Woodlands he is biased. "I moved here 28 years ago. Raised my kids here, they went off to college, and now one's come back, raising her kids here. Three generations of family are commonplace now."

Generational differences are also accommodated at The Woodlands. In addition to subsidized apartments for the elderly, The Woodlands also developed a number of market-rate housing alternatives for this group. We worked with one developer to build a nursing home and with another to build a facility that combines assisted and independent living quarters for couples or single individuals over 55. This facility has a health care clinic and cafeteria.

The broad range of housing options not only has helped to develop a strong residential community, but also has bolstered efforts to attract businesses and jobs. The requirements of the HUD agreement turned out not only to be the right thing to do, but they also supported the business plan of The Woodlands to be more than just a residential community.

According to Deretchin, "There has always been a symbiotic relationship between our residential development and our commercial development. In the first half of The Woodlands' life, it was the residential side that really supported the company and generated interest with people settling here and moving their businesses here. In the second half of the community's evolution, the commercial component has hit its stride, which brings in employees who in turn support the continued growth of our homebuilding program."

Chapter 15

RESEARCH FOREST

⎯ ◆ ⎯

George Mitchell has always been an effective combination of dreamer and man of action. He dared to dream big and had the ability and the money to make his dreams come true.

One of Mitchell's dreams for The Woodlands was the Research Forest. Another was the yet-to-be-fulfilled Houston Advanced Research Center (HARC), an institutional program envisioned by Mitchell.

Mitchell and his team recognized that the Research Forest could capture a share of the value that came from the commercialization of discoveries made at Houston's famed Texas Medical Center, and from other major research institutions. He thought the kinds of high-value jobs found among companies dedicated to capitalizing on the commercialization of such research would benefit The Woodlands. But Mitchell's interests went beyond his pocketbook. He had a deep intellectual interest in research and a desire to benefit mankind. He backed up that interest and deep conviction with his own money. Over the years, Mitchell has donated millions of dollars to support research efforts, primarily at Texas Medical Center. The Research Forest he envisioned would benefit society by making available the fruits of university and medical research.

In its first ten years, the Research Forest was just a collection of acreage. Using outside consulting firms, we did some early studies to learn from what others had done. Our models were Silicon Valley in California and its relationship with Stanford University; Route 128 in the Boston area, where abandoned textile mills were converted into office space for technology companies that capitalized on research from nearby universities; and Research Triangle in North Carolina. I made a trip to the Research Triangle and surveyed what was being done there.

We found that three critical elements were needed to make a research park work. Clearly, proximity to major universities conducting extensive research was required. That was a challenge for us because Rice University and the University of Houston were 40 miles to the south, Texas A&M University was 90 miles to the north, and the University of Texas at Austin was 150 miles to the northwest. What we didn't have was a research university in The Woodlands.

The second element we needed was an institute to coordinate university, corporate, and government research efforts. To create such an institution, Mitchell used both personal and corporate funds—and tapped his contacts—to establish and implement what was first called the Houston Area Research Center and later became the Houston Advanced Research Center. He gained the support of 12 universities, including the University of Texas, Texas A&M, Louisiana State University, and the University of Oklahoma. He recruited an executive director, Dr. Skip Porter, from Texas A&M, who became president of HARC and set about putting together a good team of people. They planned to do contract research for clients such as the Department of Defense, private groups, universities, and corporations.

We set aside a 100-acre campus for HARC. The Woodlands Corporation agreed to donate the land to the research institution on an as-needed basis as HARC expanded. HARC's objective was and continues to be to attract the best scientific minds from its 12 university supporters to conduct research. HARC did well for a number of years, but as the Department of Defense reduced funding for its contract research programs, HARC's activity also declined. The fortunes of HARC were also hurt by the collapse of the Superconducting Super Collider Project, a high-profile science program designed to explore high-energy physics. HARC was hired to develop the giant magnets needed for the project, but when the federally funded program was abruptly shut down by Congress in 1993, it was a massive financial and morale blow to HARC.

HARC's existence did spark a clear interest in the Research Forest. About 30 companies started up as a result of research in the Texas Medical Center and similar endeavors set up shop in the Research Forest. Some did well. Some didn't make it.

The third element for making the Research Forest a success was venture capital, which was especially important for startup companies in what was then the new and promising field of biotechnology. The payoff from biotech developments in terms of both profits and results could be huge. But biotechnology, then as now, is on what one wag called "the bleeding edge of science." Bringing these kinds of products to market could take years, even decades, of research. They would also have to leap high regulatory hurdles. To make matters worse, statistics showed that a majority of biotech companies were destined to fail, making their efforts to raise capital all the more challenging.

George Mitchell stepped up to help with funding. He and Mike Richmond, who also helped finance and deal with university projects in the Research Forest, formed a source of venture capital funded by $18 million from Mitchell Energy, The Woodlands Corporation, and some from Mitchell personally. It provided seed money for startup companies. Other venture capitalists provided some funding as well.

The startup companies also need homes. We learned that they typically don't have a long planning horizon. They need buildings when they need them and seldom think ahead of time about the process required to secure new space. Most executives of startup technology companies have little or no real estate experience, so we designed spaces tailored to their needs. We made space available at affordable prices to entice companies here. The buildings were very attractive and have become a model for others to use.

Buildings were constructed in a cost-effective way. We had the land so we could set them in generous environmental surroundings, save the trees around them, and excavate ponds and lakes to give the area surrounding the buildings an attractive setting. Excavated dirt from the ponds was used to elevate the building pad itself. We favored tilt-up construction, wherein concrete walls were poured in place on the ground and then raised into vertical position. Clad in finishes of granite, glass, or marble, the buildings had offices in front and laboratory space in back. Typically, they comprised about 70,000 square feet and could be divided into modules so that individual companies could use 2,000 or 10,000 square feet or the entire building, depending on need. Each user would pay its own utilities. There were no common spaces in the building. They were single-story structures, so they needed no elevators and accommodated the disabled in a cost-effective way. In other types of markets these might be known as flex buildings, with offices in the front and warehouses in the back.

We built many of the buildings in the mid- to late 1980s. It was during that period that Houston lost 200,000 jobs, the economy tanked, and downtown Class A office buildings were renting for only $14 to $15 a square foot. We couldn't build a high-rise office building and economically compete with downtown giveaway space, so we had to develop buildings that could rent for $12 to $14 per square foot and be competitive. Those were the two elements that drove us into single-story, but less expensive office buildings that could compete with downtown space but also be affordable for startup companies. To this day, it has been the model—and a very successful one—for designing buildings throughout the Research Forest.

Baylor College of Medicine was an early tenant in Research Forest. It set up a magnetic resonance imaging center. Others followed suit, including the biotech company Life Cell and Surgimedics, a manufacturer of disposable operating room instruments used in open-heart surgery; and Zonagen, which sought to develop a drug competitive with Viagra, but which, unfortunately, did not make it through certification by the Federal Drug Administration but continues with other drug research.

There was an unexpected factor that has hampered the growth of Research Forest. Successful companies often don't stick around. Blame that primarily on the finances of these small companies and the way the pharmaceutical industry works. If a biotech company develops a promising product, it still usually faces more years of development and millions more in expenses before it can get that product to market. At the same time, giant pharmaceutical companies stand willing to buy small biotech firms and assume the financial burden. That can be very attractive to the owners of small companies, and especially to the venture capitalists that put up the seed money to start them. It provides an attractive exit strategy for them. Quite often, biotech companies that started in The Woodlands have disappeared, having been swept into the maw of an industry giant seeking expertise and potential valuable discoveries.

Still, the Research Forest continues to grow, but not as fast as in the early days. Most of its buildings were realized during the economic boom of the late 1980s and early 1990s. Without George Mitchell at The Woodlands' helm, the Research Forest is no longer a top priority for the corporation; the current owners have not continued his emotional and monetary investment in the research community. Plus, his significant contacts within research institutions and personal contributions are no longer available.

While the Research Forest is, at least, a qualified success, HARC's viability remains in doubt. In the last decade, its size, scope, and financing have decreased. The institution still exists, but the 100-acre campus that we made available to HARC was acquired by the North Harris Community College system, which uses the facilities to house its operational needs. It's a very attractive campus. HARC is now a tenant of the college and occupies a single building.

An outsider's view of HARC could lead to misinterpretation. To some, it was viewed as a tool to bring prestige to The Woodlands more than to do research. But that was not really true. It helped to create jobs and fueled real estate sales. But I think George Mitchell felt that it was something much bigger than that. He really wanted to create a research presence that made a difference in the world. In fact, he still funds activities at HARC. In an interview early in 2004, he admitted that HARC has been a disappointment to him, saying that it should have made itself an invaluable coordinator of research projects among its university supporters. Mitchell's son, Todd, is now chairman of the HARC board. "He has enough gumption to make it work," Mitchell says. "And I think there's a good chance he will."

Chapter 16

TOWN CENTER

———•◆•———

There's an old story about a bright young graduate of the Harvard Business School invited to interview at a crusty, New England insurance company. The president of the company was looking to leaven his organization with some new, well-educated blood. The two men had lunch and things went well until dessert was served. Then the president told the young man he was sorry, but he just wouldn't fit in. Why? The young grad had eaten his pie starting at the front instead of with the crust. This indicated to the president that the young man was too interested in immediate gratification.

When George Mitchell and his team planned The Woodlands they resisted biting from the front, specifically a 1,200-acre tract of land that flanked Interstate 45. It had the easiest access to the highway. Conventional suburban planning would have earmarked a good portion of the land for housing, because it would have provided the least expensive way to initiate development. But the Mitchell team reserved that prime parcel for future development of a commercial district. The land would remain vacant until both The Woodlands and the areas north and south of it along the highway had a sufficient resident base to support commercial uses. When the time was right, the land, dubbed the Town Center, would become the central business and urban-style residential area for southern Montgomery and northern Harris counties.

Robert Heineman, one of the original planners of The Woodlands, said that there was no doubt that reserving this choice freeway location for future commercial development would add more long-term value to the community.

Town Center was planned to be a regional destination—the downtown for all of north Houston, serving the 1 million people who today live within 20 miles of The Woodlands. Our original planners sought to avoid the problems associated with nonresidents driving through residential areas to get to major shopping areas or job locations. Town Center's location on the Interstate 45 edge of The Woodlands made it accessible to both the region's population and the residential villages of the new community. We recognized that this location for Town Center would mean there would be competitive retail development along Interstate 45 on property we did not own. That would likely have occurred anyway, and the overall benefits outweighed that drawback.

By the late 1980s, the construction of Town Center was underway; it will continue for another 15 years. Eventually, there will be some 18 million square feet of occupiable space there, roughly equal to the downtown of Kansas City or Miami. That includes the property set aside for office, retail, entertainment, hospitality, health care, and urban residential development.

One of the most striking features of Town Center today is The Woodlands Waterway. Over the years, the Waterway went through a series of planning changes, according to Heineman. "That sketch I did back in 1972 wasn't the Waterway. It was the drainage corridor through the middle of Town Center." Later plans included a linear park with a series of water features rather than a continuous Waterway. "That evolved into a transportation corridor over time because of the availability of grant funds for transportation programs." And public transportation will further enhance the quality of visitor experience in Town Center.

"Over the years," Heineman said, "Town Center had grown into a major destination that people want to visit. It has a mall, the Cynthia Woods Mitchell Pavilion, lots of offices, employers, and jobs, restaurants, and the like. What we hadn't done was tie all of these uses together other than by automobile." Heineman and other planners did not want to emulate the Galleria–Post Oak area of Houston. "There you've got offices, residential, shopping, entertainment, and parks with a fountain and a lake. You have all of the uses, but the connections are only by automobile. Now, you wouldn't walk from one side of Post Oak to the other for fear of your life. Plus, you must make your way across big parking lots. So the idea of the Waterway was to preserve a corridor with the buildings in the proper place around it for future transit or pedestrian activities. It was dream on a map for years."

While The Woodlands Corporation figured out just what to do with the Waterway, the corridor served mainly as a drainage ditch. "The idea," Heineman explained, "was to take a drainage ditch and turn it into a linear park, which would also serve as a transportation route. We had to look at transportation as more than just getting from point A to point B, because for that you can't beat the car. You have to make it festive, an entertainment."

The first building constructed along the proposed Waterway was for the Municipal Utility District's office. The original plan was to build it facing a street, its back turned to the Waterway, which would have given the building's Dumpster a waterfront site. "We were able to convince the district to change its plan." Heineman and his colleagues were also able to convince others to place their Dumpsters and parking lots out of view of the Waterway.

Throughout the years since 1972, Heineman has been a champion of the evolving Waterway, as was Dick Browne, who headed The Woodlands' planning department for a number of years. Browne was the more vocal supporter and challenged others to understand its value to the community. I would say he was passionate about it. Heineman was also very effective in his more subdued, professional approach. It was Heineman who understood and spoke the language of transportation planners working for the local and federal agencies that reviewed and approved transportation grants. Securing federal grants was the key to constructing the Waterway. Thus far, about $20 million in grants have been used to build and equip the Waterway.

The Woodlands Corporation is not eligible to receive federal grants, so it had to work with the Brazos Transportation Authority. Brazos was chartered to provide transportation services in a number of less-populated counties in east Texas, including Montgomery County, the home of The Woodlands. Our first dealings with Brazos occurred in 1987 and involved the successful operation of a park-and-ride commuter bus service from lots in the community to downtown Houston. It naturally followed that the authority would make a good partner for the Waterway project. In the mid-1990s, The Woodlands granted Brazos a 300-foot-wide transportation easement in the Waterway, together with certain exclusive rights to run transportation services in Town Center. This made Brazos eligible to apply for and receive grants to construct the Waterway and to purchase vehicles to serve the community. The establishment of this transportation corridor in the early stages of planning will likely eliminate the need for costly revamping in the future.

In looking around the country for successful examples of waterway development, Browne and Heineman found that the San Antonio Riverwalk stood out. It is the biggest tourist attraction in the state and most people who visit San Antonio say the Riverwalk was the main reason that they traveled to the city—more so than the Alamo, as irreverent to Texans as that might sound.

Boone Powell of Ford, Powell & Carson Architects had been a principal planner and adviser to the San Antonio Riverwalk for many years, so it was obvious their talent could help the Waterway in The Woodlands. We did not want to copy what had been done in San Antonio, but we did want to understand what made it successful. We looked at things such as the width and depth of the water; width and location of sidewalks; height and design of bridges; function and shape of public areas; and landscaping, lighting, and the correct interface between businesses and the water's edge. Over several years, Powell conducted planning sessions for our development team and hosted site trips to explore the Riverwalk by day and night. We also had useful discussions with the San Antonio city departments that operated the Riverwalk to understand what to expect and prepare for in Town Center.

In the late 1990s, construction finally started on the initial 1.5-mile segment of the Waterway, extending from the Cynthia Woods Mitchell Pavilion to the west to the mall on the east. Water cruisers now operate on the Waterway, although they function more as a form of entertainment than as a transportation system. The real transportation will be a fleet of motorized trolley cars on an adjacent trolley way to move people from one end of Town Center to the other. The Waterway itself already provides a pleasing visual element for the Town Center.

From the very beginning, the anchor for Town Center was to be a regional shopping mall. But getting a mall proved to be a formidable task. In 1982, The Woodlands installed a large sign on Interstate 45 proudly announcing that a new regional mall would be built there. The mall did not open until 1994. The sign was repainted every year. We felt that a crisp, clean sign was better than an old, faded one. It was a joke throughout the county that the biggest item in our budget was paint for the sign. We changed the message from time to time, but it always said something about "Coming soon."

That sign was, in part, a defensive measure. There was a competing site for a mall about ten miles to the north. Had that one been built, the mall for The Woodlands would have been history. The DeBartolo organization, based in Cleveland, Ohio, was behind the competing mall. They had talked to The Woodlands Corporation about the Interstate 45 site, but those discussions were terminated because we felt that DeBartolo really preferred the Conroe location. Instead, we focused negotiations on Homart, which at the time was a wholly owned subsidiary of Sears.

The real barrier to the mall's realization was the usual one—the lack of enough population to support it. There were three other malls to the north of Houston. The Woodlands also had a real disadvantage because it didn't have any intersecting east-west highways to bring traffic in from those areas of Montgomery County. Another holdup in building the mall was getting the approval and funding to build an overpass that would lead the traffic going north on Interstate 45 directly into the mall site. The Woodlands did get the overpass built, but it sat there for several years without a mall on one end.

Our plans for the proposed mall always involved a partnership with an experienced operator. We would supply the land and, in this case, the fill dirt necessary to build the parking lot and building pad. That dirt ultimately came from Lake Robbins, a new 20-acre lake adjacent to the mall. And that's part of the efficiency of a master-planned community. You excavate lakes and drainage ways and then you can use that material to build golf courses, parking lots at malls, overpass embankments, or elevated sites for buildings. So there's really an efficiency to be gained when you are part of a comprehensive effort with a large piece of property.

The key to developing the mall was securing anchor tenants. They are the primary draw to bring shoppers to the mall. In the case of a neighborhood shopping center, that anchor would be a supermarket. For The Woodlands Mall, we needed at least four anchors—and that was Homart's responsibility. The firm first secured an agreement with Dillard's department store. Sears agreed to open a store in the mall. And Foley's came along, too. We couldn't get the fourth anchor because many of the major retailers were locked into long-term leases in Greenspoint Mall, which is about ten miles south of The Woodlands. The tenants there, particularly JCPenney, were also reluctant to relocate. Facing the prospect of having to give up three committed anchors, Homart agreed to count Mervyn's as the fourth anchor, even though Mervyn's is not considered an anchor store by mall development standards. With those four anchors in hand, Homart was willing to go forward, assuming it could fill enough leasable space with small shops in the mall to make the mall viable.

The turning point to get Sears to agree to count Mervyn's as a fourth anchor was a trip we took to Chicago. George Mitchell, Mike Richmond, and Ben Love, who was then chairman of Texas Commerce Bank and also a member of the board of directors of Mitchell Energy, and I flew to Chicago, met with the chairman of Sears and his executive staff in their private lunchroom in the top of the Sears Tower, and made the plea for moving ahead on the mall. We got the commitment.

Construction of the mall was completed in 1994. The Woodlands Corporation was a passive investor, but we did participate in planning, design, landscaping, lighting, signage, and other elements that had an impact on the community. The design of The Woodlands Mall was unique for Houston. A portion of the parking lot was elevated so you could enter the two-level mall from the second level or from ground level. It's not spread out like a typical suburban mall that requires you to walk all day to get from one end to the other. A shopper can stand in the food court in the center of The Woodlands Mall and see all of the department stores from that one location. Having it on two levels cuts down on the walking distance and just makes it a friendlier, easier place to shop.

The mall opened to great fanfare and a huge crowd. All the senior officers from Homart and The Woodlands were there. There was a ribbon cutting inside the mall in the center court about 10 a.m. As we approached the ring road around the mall, we could see people waiting for the doors to open so that they could experience the first day of shopping and take a look at the commercial development in their hometown. By some estimates, 50,000 people turned out for the event. George Mitchell and I were in the car along with Mike Richmond and some of the Homart people, and as we drove in, people were saluting us as though we were the star attractions in a Mardi Gras parade.

When we got inside, people began to tug at George Mitchell's coat sleeve to get his attention and say thanks for bringing the mall to The Woodlands. It was almost a love fest. The expression of appreciation to George Mitchell for bringing something of value to the community was just unbelievable.

Within a week, we went from the heights of opening the mall to the depths of a major flood throughout the Houston region. It was a 500-year flood—one that's calculated to occur only once every 500 years. Rainfall exceeded 35 inches in a 36-hour period and was the first major test of our drainage system. The storm system worked wonderfully well, except for a neighborhood or two that fronted on Spring Creek, whose extensive watershed expanded beyond designed controls in The Woodlands. Approximately 200 homes got wet. Ninety-nine percent of the system worked well. That 1 percent didn't fail; it just wasn't designed to accommodate that quantity of water. The flooding led to lawsuits and acrimony, but all were eventually resolved.

The mall has expanded since its opening. The first time involved the addition of JCPenney as an anchor store, which left Greenspoint Mall when its lease expired in 1998. Recently, the mall has undergone another expansion that includes a number of upscale restaurants and shops along the Waterway corridor.

We also developed a retail power center immediately to the north of The Woodlands Mall called Pinecroft Center that includes Target, Toys R Us, Best Buy, and other examples of what retailers call big-box stores. It was tastefully done. It doesn't have a massive parking lot and a sea of cars. Landscaped areas were retained in parking lots. Trees were planted. The fronts of buildings were screened from the streets. The mall also generated an opportunity to expand the menu of restaurants around the ring road. For many years we had a dearth of restaurants. Now there's quite a collection of them. They're all full and every time a new one opens, the line is so long you can't get in. I don't know where people ate before, but there was certainly a pent-up demand for restaurants throughout The Woodlands.

The mall also helped with the development of the 17-screen movie theater that has done quite well. It shares parking with office buildings that have been built adjacent to the mall and the theater. A fourth major shopping area called Market Street, which is immediately west of the mall, is also under construction.

In addition to retail and entertainment, Town Center is a major regional employment center. Of the 30,000 jobs located in The Woodlands, most are in Town Center or its neighbor, the Research Forest. Major employers include Anadarko, Chevron Phillips, Memorial Hermann Hospital, Hughes Christensen, Hewitt Associates, CBI, and the Marriott Waterway Hotel and Convention Center.

This commercial growth was sparked by the Town Center Improvement District. The district itself isn't unique. Such business improvement districts, or BIDs, as they are known, have long been used in towns and cities around the country. What's unique about this one is the way it's financed.

Municipalities can establish these special improvement districts. In The Woodlands, with no city government, that wasn't possible. However, if 51 percent of the property owners in an area petition the Texas Legislature, a BID can be established. And that is what businesses in The Woodlands' Town Center did. The district then set up a mandatory taxing program for all property owners, spending its revenues on public safety, economic development, and capital projects.

The BID for commercial areas of The Woodlands also promotes job creation and business development. However, it has stayed away from areas that districts often get involved in, such as water, sewer, and drainage—all of which are managed by existing municipal utility districts in The Woodlands.

"We are a local government, we are a political subdivision of the state of Texas," said Frank Robinson, the president of the Town Center Improvement District. "We're a body politic with all of the corporate rights, privileges, and powers found under the Texas Government Code with few exceptions: We don't write ordinances, we have no police powers, and we have no powers of condemnation. We have expanded the role of this district over the last ten years and have gone back to the legislature at least twice, tweaking and enhancing our legislation to give us additional powers" to create economic development zones.

Essentially, said Robinson, the improvement district brings a focused management of government services to an area. It serves as a catalyst to help local governments work on specific problems.

"This district, like many districts, doesn't really replace anybody else's responsibilities when it comes to funding for capital improvements or operational expenses," Robinson said. "We're here to enhance what others already do. A great example is our public safety effort. We employ, through the sheriff's department, additional deputies to patrol this area. They work for the county. We simply supplement the county's treasury and they have added deputies to the number they would already have on patrol in the area. We also have agreements with Shenandoah and Oak Ridge, incorporated cities adjacent to The Woodlands, through which we provide some funding for their police departments and in return, they patrol parts of Town Center from time to time."

Robinson, a former assistant city manager of the enclave city of West University Place in Houston, said that his former job included oversight of the police and fire departments. The first thing Robinson did when he arrived was come up with a public safety master plan using the assets of the entire region. Using taxes from the improvement district, he financed a police radio net that allows all of the agencies patrolling the Town Center to talk to each other. The improvement district bought mobile data terminals for all of the sheriff's cars that were assigned to The Woodlands, as well as those belonging to the cities of Shenandoah and Oak Ridge so the whole region was electronically connected. (Eventually, that system was superseded by a countywide radio system.) The improvement district also hired a private security firm to provide horse-mounted security guards in Town Center. That, according to Robinson, was both a security and public relations move. The unarmed guards are extra eyes and ears for law enforcement officers. "It was so well received by the local police community, primarily the sheriff who controlled the radio frequencies, that he put the mounted patrol on his radio channels."

Most improvement districts derive their revenues from property taxes. The Town Center Improvement District decided to go another route: a 1 percent sales tax. "We were the first improvement district in the state to collect a sales tax," Robinson said.

Over the years, the improvement district has upped its sales tax rate in Economic Development Zones. In these zones, an additional sales tax in increments of one-eighth of a cent can be levied. The Cynthia Woods Mitchell Pavilion is an example of one. "The pavilion was ten years old; it needed to expand or it was going to become a second-rate entertainment venue," Robinson said. "It could no longer compete with other big outdoor theaters in the region, so we created a zone around it." An additional 1 percent is collected on sales within the pavilion and is used to pay off bonds sold to expand the pavilion by 4,000 seats and add new dressing rooms, concession areas, and other upgrades.

Following the tax-funded upgrades to the pavilion, two more economic development zones were established—one for the Market Street Project and another for the expansion of The Woodlands Mall. Both of these zones reflect a new trend in retail: open-air lifestyle shopping.

In both cases, the stores in the two zones, like those in the pavilion, will charge an additional 1 percent sales tax on goods. That means shoppers will be paying a cent more on the dollar in sales tax than they would in stores just a few hundred yards away. In the pavilion, that might not be a problem, where shoppers are in effect a captive market. But will shoppers in the two new zones pay 1 percent more for a retail item or restaurant meal than they would for the same thing nearby?

According to Robinson, studies on shoppers and sales tax show that most people don't pay much attention to the numbers. And it seems to be true. "At the Cheesecake Factory, which is in one of the higher tax zones, you can't get a seat at lunchtime."

Another reason why the sales tax is not likely to cause much resentment among residents of Town Center is they probably won't pay all that much of it. More than 60 percent of the customers who come into Town Center do not live in The Woodlands or in the immediate area, according to mall tracking services.

The Town Center Improvement District also has been active in economic development. "That's why we built the convention center, both for economic development as well as job creation," said Robinson. "The convention center, when it's fully operational by 2005, will have somewhere in the neighborhood of 550 to 700 employees. And the economic development zones that we have in place add another 1,000 jobs within the improvement district over the next two years."

Through its economic initiatives and other activities, from Independence Day parties to the annual installation of the largest temporary outdoor ice rink in the Southwest, the Town Center Improvement District's policy "all along has been to keep this a pristine, safe, and secure place. We want to be a regional destination. We want to create exciting experiences for people when they come," Robinson said.

Chapter 17

TRANSPORTATION AND MOBILITY

———— •◆•• ————

N o one would want to move to The Woodlands if doing so meant a stressful daily battle with traffic, so transportation and mobility needs were a large part of the planning and development of the new community. A network of major thorough-fares was included within the community's general plan. Schedules for initial construction, and later expansion, of roads were tied to growth projections. Design approval and funding support required a close working relationship with local, state, and federal institutions and agencies, including Montgomery County, the city of Houston, the Texas Department of Transportation, the Houston-Galveston Area Council (the metropolitan planning agency), the Brazos Transit Authority, local road districts, and others. Success in working with outside agencies required both knowledge of their programs and rules and the building of mutual trust and respect.

The Woodlands' location on Interstate 45 provided excellent access to the city of Houston. But from the beginning, we lacked adequate east-west connections. Within The Woodlands, two major thoroughfares were in the original plan. Woodlands Parkway bisects the commu-nity from east to west, starting at Interstate 45 and terminating at a farm-to-market road on the far west side. Late in 2004, the parkway will be connected to FM 2978, a farm-to-market road on the western edge of The Woodlands, which will provide access to the town of Tomball and western parts of Harris County. A second east-west route is Research Forest Drive.

In addition to the recent construction of a third east-west artery, State Highway 242, the original two roads are being widened and improved as population and traffic increase. Woodlands Parkway, for example, is being widened from four divided lanes to six, a project that's going to cause some consternation in The Woodlands. While the improvements will ease mobility, they'll also add a traffic burden from outside the community. That's why it's been important to keep tree screens and buffers of greenbelts along the major thoroughfares, so that the heavier traffic will be screened acoustically and visually from the adjacent neighborhoods.

When The Woodlands opened in 1974, we were not worried so much about people being able to get here in their cars but whether or not they could afford the gasoline to commute to Houston, 27 miles to the south. The first oil crisis, when OPEC boosted the price of fuel, was in full swing at the time.

In response to the crisis, we initiated a vanpooling program. The corporation helped fund and secure grants to purchase 12-passenger vans. People parked their cars in lots at office buildings and other designated sites, where the van would pick them up. The person driving the van was in charge of servicing it and in return, drove free. The other 11 commuters paid a fee, which was much less than the cost of commuting alone in a car. In short order and working with the Brazos Transit Authority, we built park-and-ride lots that are serviced by larger, 50-passenger buses. There are now 30 buses in the fleet, each painted with the name Woodlands Express, which is a good mobile billboard. Those buses take 2,000 cars off the road every day. Local shuttles, trolleys, and water cruisers were added to facilitate convenient transportation within Town Center. We didn't have the luxury of a public transit system when we started to develop The Woodlands. But with the help of federal grants and effective partnerships with the county and the transit authority, we have created a system that fits our needs and can grow along with the population.

Master-planned communities are good places for mass transit solutions; the systems can be put in place through public/private initiatives, serve a large number of people, and reduce the number of automobile trips, contributing to the conservation of natural resources.

Chapter 18

GOLF

———◆———

In its early years, The Woodlands had another problem: How to become known to potential customers without spending a fortune on advertising. As we have in many other instances, we turned to a nonprofit institution for help. This time it was the Houston Golf Association (HGA).

From the beginning, the developers of The Woodlands perceived golf as a prime component in the new town. There were many good reasons to connect the future of The Woodlands to the sport. First, there's the obvious attraction of the game to potential homebuyers.

Second, the golf courses themselves—ultimately there would be seven in the 27,000 acres of The Woodlands—fit well into the plan for the new town. The original master plan for The Woodlands called for 25 percent of the new community to be open space. Golf courses add to the open space objectives. And the third reason to emphasize the sport is that homes built around or near golf courses generally command higher prices.

Indeed, a golf course was among the first things built at The Woodlands. Before it was even completed, the course was used to gain publicity for the new town. Bringing the Houston Open, a stop on the national men's national Professional Golfers Association (PGA) tour, to The Woodlands was a major objective.

The HGA, then and now, sponsors the Houston Open. The association's aim is not only to bring the PGA tour to Houston, but also to raise money for charity. Its goal was to give local charities as much money each year as the golfers won in prizes. In 1974, the tour event was played at the Quail Valley County Club in Houston. In years past, it had been staged at the municipal golf course in Memorial Park within the city of Houston. The tour event at Quail Valley was struggling. The purse for the event, the amount of money the pro golfers could earn in total, was $150,000. Its main problem was it had no title sponsor—a corporation interested in paying a substantial sum in return for putting its name on the event. The HGA was looking for a new site. Its first choice was to go back to Memorial Park, but local resistance to using the city golf course for the PGA tour soon made that impossible. Enter George Mitchell.

He invited members of the HGA to play a round at the new golf course at The Woodlands in 1974. It was so new that its country club building had just been topped off. HGA members playing that day remembered looking at the steel frame of the country club building and seeing the evergreen tree that ironworkers, as per tradition, had placed atop the building after completing the frame. The HGA members agreed that, for a brand new golf course, the one at The Woodlands was in good shape. One reason for the condition of the course was the late Carlton Gipson. For many years, Gipson was in charge of all Woodlands courses.

Terry Russ, a longtime member of the HGA, said of Gipson, "I've never come across a man who knew more about golf course work, design, and maintenance than he did. He was one of the finest gentlemen I've ever known."

Satisfied with the course, the HGA made a deal with Mitchell. He wrote the HGA a check for $50,000. That money was used to pay HGA bills and for its charity commitments. The Houston Open relocated to The Woodlands course in 1975. It stayed there for 28 years.

The move proved to be a good one for both the HGA and The Woodlands. To understand why, we need to digress briefly to discuss the finances of a stop on the PGA tour. At the top of the revenue heap is the contract to televise the tournament. How much that contract pays depends on a number of factors. Foremost is a tournament's ability to attract players home viewers want to watch. The Houston Open, which usually takes place in April, has always had a problem attracting the very top players simply because of its place on the schedule of events. It usually came two weeks after the Masters Tournament, which is considered one of the top four events on the tour, along with the U.S. Open, the British Open, and the PGA Tournament of Champions. Many of the biggest names on the tour take a couple of weeks off after playing in the Masters. Sponsors of tour events have little say in when their tournaments are scheduled. That's up to the PGA, which plans its tournaments in consultation with the television or cable network carrying the event.

Attracting the players often depends on the purse. There has been a huge escalation in the size of purses over the years. Remember, the purse at Quail Valley in 1974 was $150,000. In 2003, according to the HGA, the average purse was close to $5 million.

Next comes the contract with a named sponsor. The sponsor pays a rights fee to the tournament's sponsoring organization. Depending on negotiations, the rights fee can pay up to 80 percent of the prize money the sponsor awards to the golfers. The amount the title sponsor pays often depends on timing. For example, in the fall, when the major broadcast networks are carrying professional and college football games, a tournament might be televised on a cable network and the title sponsor would pay less for the privilege of sponsoring the tournament. The title sponsor must also agree to buy 36 units of 30-second commercials from the television or cable network to be aired during the tournament.

According to Terry Russ, the HGA had held its annual golf tournament without a title sponsor for 33 years, and that was still the case during its first two years at The Woodlands. "Over a period of time, the handwriting was on the wall: We were not going to be financially successful." The HGA obtained its first title sponsor in 1980. Michelob beer, an Anheuser-Busch brand, signed a three-year deal. Coca-Cola was next, a two-year sponsorship. Then for two years, the Houston Open once again had no title sponsor. In the argot of the tour, the HGA went "naked." Being naked means you are losing your shirt. During those two years without a title sponsor, the HGA ran into severe financial difficulties. "The news media stated publicly that the Houston Golf Association lost in excess of $100,000 with their tournament that year. It was true, but it wasn't accurate," Paul Wahlberg, another HGA member, said. "We actually lost $350,000." The charities that depended on HGA donations were concerned about the precarious position of their patron. But they need not have worried. "We went to the bank and borrowed $100,000, which we distributed to our core charities. You know, in hindsight, a lot of people say that that was HGA's darkest hour, but I think it was our brightest hour—doing something that we believed in, which was helping the community."

Fortunately, the HGA soon acquired a title sponsor, the Independent Insurance Agents of America. When that contract expired, Shell Oil Co., which has its U.S. operations headquarters in Houston, became the sponsor.

For years, tournament sponsors made their real money on the Pro-Amateur events held in advance of the tournament itself. Amateurs pay to play a round of golf, either with professional golfers or with celebrity golfers. Just how much they pay usually depends on those who agree to play with them. That, incidentally, is slowly changing. Increasingly, corporate entertaining is overtaking the money brought in by the pro-ams. Corporations pay substantial fees for tickets and special handling at the golf tournaments, including elaborate tents, stands, food, and drink. Members of the sponsoring organization, in this case the HGA, spend a great deal of time going out and soliciting either foursomes to play in the pro-am or people to rent those entertainment venues.

Paul Wahlberg remembers that in 1959, the year he joined the HGA, the most expensive sponsorship package sold by the organization cost $100. For that you got 20 tickets to the golf tournament and access to the clubhouse. In those days, says Wahlberg, "Our clubhouse was a big open-air tent.

"Every morning we put 1,000 pounds of ice at each end of the tent and ran a big fan, which blew across the ice. People felt privileged to come into that clubhouse. It had sawdust floors and at the end of the day it was a muddy mess." These days, the HGA uses a two-story tent. The upper floor overlooks the course. Food and drink are served on the lower floor, which is air conditioned.

By moving to The Woodlands, the HGA found a not-so-secret weapon in hiking the turnout and fees paid for its pro-am event: Doug Sanders, the golf director in charge of The Woodlands operation. Not only was Sanders a big name on the PGA tour, but he also had solid ties to the entertainment industry. He used those ties to attract some of the top stars in movies, television, and politics to play in the Houston Open Pro-Am. People who attended the tournament got to see Bob Hope, Andy Williams, and ex-President Gerald Ford teeing up. Of course, those people did not come free. True, they did not charge appearance fees. But their airfare, lodging at The Woodlands Conference Center Hotel, meals, and drinks were provided gratis. They also received a per diem. Some spent more than they were allotted.

One year, Evel Knievel, the motorcycle daredevil, played in the tournament. The first thing he did after checking in was to buy an expensive set of golf irons at the pro shop, charging them to his room. An assistant in the shop called tournament officials, who then retrieved the clubs from Knievel's room. Wahlberg remembers, "The only way we could get him to check out of the room was to shut off maid and room services. He was going to stay there until next year. He liked it so much."

Still the pro-am was very successful. At one point, there were so many people participating, it had to be held simultaneously on five of The Woodlands' courses. However, in at least one incident, those who played the pro-am had troubles of a different sort. To play one year, a prominent Harris County official took time off from work, missing an important public vote. When his picture appeared in the *Houston Chronicle* the day after the event, he found himself having to come up with a quick explanation.

Even after Sanders left his position as golf director, he continued to be associated with the pro-am event for a few more years. After Sanders bowed out, country singers became the dominant celebrity presence at the pro-am. Darrell Royal, the former head football coach at the University of Texas, and Willie Nelson, the Texas country legend, rounded up guitar players both to play in the pro-am and to perform at an informal concert on the indoor tennis courts at the Conference Center. Several thousand people would crowd around the courts to listen to the music that went on for four or five hours. Any show that features Willie Nelson is likely to be long. Nelson is known for getting on the stage and singing every song he knows at least once, if not twice. After the show, the musicians would retire to their rooms and hold an all-night picking party, then get up the next day and play golf.

Putting on the tournament took a tremendous volunteer effort. During the tournament, some 3,200 people would volunteer to do everything from crowd control to cleanup patrol on the course and surrounding grounds after play. While all were committed to work at least four hours every day, many would work double shifts. It was not at all unusual to have the same people take a week's vacation to volunteer every year.

In 2001, the agreement between The Woodlands Corporation and the HGA ended. There were a number of factors that brought about the divorce. According to HGA officials, the number-one reason for the termination was parking. Over the course of a tournament as many as 230,000 people attended the Houston Open each year. In the early days of the new town, there was ample space for visitor parking—attendees just put their cars on the shoulder of one of the major thoroughfares. However, as more houses were built and sold, parking became a problem.

The HGA was forced to run shuttle buses from less convenient parking areas. There was also a disagreement about rental fees for the course. By this time, The Woodlands Corporation had been sold to the Crescent–Morgan Stanley partnership. The new owners proposed a new multiyear contract that more than doubled the fee over the years of the proposed agreement.

But there were other reasons why the partnership fell apart. The truth of the matter was that neither side really needed the other as much as they had 28 years earlier. The HGA came to The Woodlands when the new town was struggling. The golf tournament brought immediate recognition to the fledging community. Conversely, the HGA needed a fresh start for its troubled premiere event.

Perhaps the fact that George Mitchell no longer owned The Woodlands also had something to do with the split. Mitchell quietly expressed his disappointment at the departure of the golf association from an arrangement that had served both so well, but wished them much success in their new location. Still, while it lasted, holding the Houston Open at The

Woodlands was a boon to both sides. Or as Russ pointed out, "It helped. . .[The Woodlands] because we were on national television. It helped Houston and The Woodlands because [the broadcasters] would leave you with these fancy panoramic views of Houston and The Woodlands. . . .I think it was good for the golf association, good for Houston, and damn good for The Woodlands."

Indeed, golf has become a major amenity and business activity in The Woodlands. We have six signature courses and a seventh under construction. The use of notable golf course architects helped gain market recognition and creditability for the community. It also produced an outstanding collection of golf facilities, including courses designed by Joe Lee, Von Hagge–Devlin, Arnold Palmer, Jack Nicklaus, Gary Player, and Tom Fazio. The Von Hagge-Devlin course was later modified to become a TPC (Tournament Players Course) designated facility, the third one so designated in the United States. While famous names are attached to each, it was our golf superintendent, Carlton Gipson, who quietly oversaw the construction and maintenance quality of the first four courses built in The Woodlands.

Arnold Palmer added a personal touch to golf in The Woodlands when he arrived to celebrate the opening of the third nine on the course that bears his name. Palmer and Ed Seay, the chief operating officer of the Palmer Course Design Company, arrived by private jet in the early morning at Hooks Airport, a small airfield a few miles south of The Woodlands. Jim Ball, executive director of The Woodlands Conference Center and Resort, and members of his staff met Palmer and Seay in a shiny limousine at the airport to personally escort them to the course. In all the excitement, Ball gave incorrect instructions to the driver, so instead of going toward The Woodlands they were driving in the opposite direction. Fifteen minutes later, Ball caught his mistake and told the limo driver to reverse course. Soon they passed the airport they had just left, at which time Palmer politely remarked that Houston seemed to have a lot of small airports. Ball responded, "Mr. Palmer, we just wanted to give you a sense of the neighborhood." They arrived at the golf course an hour late.

But the late arrival did not diminish the quality of the day, which was a sunny but freezing cold day in March. Without any complaint, Palmer changed into his golfing attire and played a nine-hole exhibition with Jeff Maggert, a Woodlands native who represented us on the PGA tour. We had named the third nine "The Deacon" in honor of Palmer's father, and he seemed touched. Following the exhibition round, Palmer signed autographs for almost two hours. At lunch, he gave an entertaining discussion of his philosophy about golf course design, promoting the idea that it "should be both challenging to the pro and enjoyable for the everyday player." He also made a tongue-in-cheek public pitch for his firm to design all the remaining courses in The Woodlands—he received a big round of applause.

During this visit, Palmer heard that a national collegiate golf event was being held that day on the TPC course in The Woodlands. Following his generous donation of time to the opening event of The Deacon nine, Palmer and Seay made their way to the TPC course where he shared his thoughts about respecting the values of the game. Tiger Woods was among the college players on the course that day.

Chapter 19

YMCA

———— • ◆ • ————

Building a YMCA in The Woodlands is an example of how community volunteers and employees of The Woodlands Corporation worked with an established organization to add a substantial amenity to the town. The corporation provided some initial help and donated land but was able to reduce its involvement as residents stepped up their support of the organization. The Woodlands YMCA started without any facilities, recalls Steve McPhetridge, who was in charge of sales of residential and commercial land for the company. It was the focal point for youth sports activities such as T-ball, soccer, and basketball—the kinds of activities that didn't require a building.

"Under the auspices of the YMCA, you would gather together 15 little kids and they'd all go off and play soccer with another 15 little kids. We had an organization and some cash flow from program fees. But the Houston Metropolitan Y was leery about doing something so far away," says McPhetridge. "It took a while to convince them that The Woodlands was a good place to establish a Y."

The home base for The Woodlands Y was an abandoned retail store that at one time sold mattresses. "It was out on Interstate 45 and if it rained, you couldn't meet because the roof leaked like a sieve and there were rats running around. Then we moved to a singlewide trailer on Sawdust Road, because a landowner there allowed us to make some athletic fields on the property. The community and local businesses—homebuilders mostly—helped with funding and in-kind services."

The breakthrough in securing a permanent home for the YMCA came with the donation of a 12-acre tract of land from The Woodlands Corporation. The site was not perfect. Of the 12 acres, only four were not in the floodplain. "But we filled it for free [using material] from all the road construction and ditches," McPhetridge recalls. With funds from the Houston Metropolitan Y and the community, the project got underway. A group of local residents, landscapers, and golf course people did all the site work, from irrigating the fields to grading and drainage.

For opening day, recalls McPhetridge, "We expected 150 people, but we had cars backed up for two miles trying to get to the Y. You couldn't get near the place. We must have had 3,000 people. It was really a testament to how The Woodlands feels about youth sports activities, the role of the Y, the religious overtones—all those kind of things mixed together.

"From the corporation's standpoint, the last thing it wanted to do was get in the kind of business where someone else could do a better job. We found the Y to be a great partner to provide that important infrastructure with community support and encouragement from the company. It became a tremendous asset and since then a second Y has been built and opened."

Chapter 20

THE PAVILION

———— • ◆ • ————

W hen there were no outside institutions to help, such as the publicly funded Brazos Transit Authority, the private Houston Golf Association (HGA), or the YMCA, The Woodlands created its own. That was the case in the construction of the Cynthia Woods Mitchell Pavilion, named for George Mitchell's wife.

Some sort of performing arts pavilion was always part of the plan for The Woodlands. It was on the menu of projects that Dick Browne, one of the original consultants and later the head of planning at The Woodlands, thought was important. It was part of George's vision of the town. It was a labor of love for Cynthia. But it took a long time to come to fruition. Following years of financial setbacks, the proper conditions for the pavilion's realization finally appeared. The actual genesis of the pavilion relates to the golf course where the Houston Open was played. The HGA and the Professional Golfers Association (PGA) wanted to build stadium seating on The Woodlands course designed by Robert Von Hagge and Bruce Devlin. We spent a lot of time on this project. We visited Ponte Vedra, Florida, to look at the Sawgrass Course, which was the first course with such seating built under PGA sponsorship. Sawgrass built mounds around the greens and tee boxes and along fairways to make golf more of a spectator sport.

We constructed the same kind of seating mounds around the greens on our course. Several weeks before the first tournament was going to be played on the revamped course, Dick Browne and I went to lunch at the Tournament Players Clubhouse. We each bought a hot dog. It was a beautiful sunny day, so we decided to eat our hot dogs on the mound at the 18th green, a perch from which we could envision how the tournament might look when it played there in a few weeks. I don't remember who started the conversation, Dick or myself, but we realized that we could model a small community pavilion on the mounded seating around the golf green. We could replace the green with a concrete surface, build a larger mound, mount a tent over the green, and create a small community pavilion. Perhaps that would be the start of the music pavilion that the Mitchells had proposed for The Woodlands. We approached George with our concept. He suggested we talk to Cynthia about it. We did, and she liked the idea. An architect Browne talked to about the pavilion had suggested a Teflon-coated tent. We met with Pace Entertainment, which was at the time the leader in booking outdoor entertainment events in the United States on "the shed circuit." The first thing Pace pointed out to us was that construction of a facility for 1,500 people, which is what we had planned to build, was not commercially viable. To attract commercial artists, whose performances might help pay for the symphony, opera, and other (money-losing) cultural events, we needed seating for at least 10,000 people. Well, that was considerably more than we thought we would build. The smaller venue might have cost $1 million. Cynthia immediately championed the bigger pavilion. So we built it.

We used a 501(c)(3) corporation for the pavilion. We recruited knowledgeable people from both inside The Woodlands and the greater Houston region to serve on the nonprofit organization's board. Joe Kutchin, the retired public relations director for Mitchell Energy, was the first chairman of the board. Danci Ware, who handled many of the personal public relations chores for Mitchell, helped with some of the early planning and promotional activities. Once again, we used fill excavated from the Town Center waterway system to build the mound seating. We did it during the second-wettest season in the history of The Woodlands. The wettest season was when Plato Pappas supervised construction of Woodlands Parkway. The second time was when he was trying to transform 300,000 cubic yards of fill into a seating mound for the pavilion. He succeeded. Construction was completed and the facility opened in April 1990. Instead of $1 million, the pavilion cost $10 million, all paid by The Woodlands Corporation as a gift to the community. Those were $10 million hot dogs that Dick Browne and I ate at the 18th green.

In addition, George and Cynthia Mitchell personally donated $5 million to the Houston Symphony to make the pavilion its summer home. He and Cynthia also gave money to the Houston Ballet and the Houston Grand Opera to help stage productions in The Woodlands in the summer.

The Houston Symphony presented the first performance in the new pavilion on a Friday evening. A squall line arrived just about the time the symphony started playing. There were flashes of lightning and thunder and trees were blowing. The lights in the trees made them vivid. It was just a wonderful experience for that opening night, if you were sitting under the tent. For those on the lawn it was a drenching experience. The second night saw a Frank Sinatra performance and the third night the group Alabama played. Since then, about 50 touring acts each year perform at the pavilion and the profits from their appearances support cultural events like the symphony and ballet.

Since its inception, the pavilion has been expanded twice. It now seats 18,000. It was built because George Mitchell thought it was the right thing to do. Over a long period, it would add to the profitability of The Woodlands Corporation and enhance the value of its properties. It's a long-term investment that some developers might not have made. But it made The Woodlands a better place, an achievement that holds great value for Mitchell.

Chapter 21

ART IN
PUBLIC PLACES

———◆•———

In 1973, The Woodlands adopted a formal program to provide art in public places throughout the community. That came from a recommendation by Coulson Tough to George Mitchell. Prior to joining Mitchell's organization, Tough was in charge of developing facilities at the University of Houston, where he initiated a similar public art program funded by setting aside 1 percent of the construction costs of new buildings on campus. He recommended a similar approach for all commercial buildings in The Woodlands.

Mitchell bought into the proposal and supported it faithfully. But given the early marketing challenges in attracting commercial users to the new community, he felt that spending 1 percent of construction costs could drive prospects away. Instead, he agreed to impose an art fund fee of 0.25 percent of the cost of all commercial building construction in The Woodlands, including that undertaken by the corporation for its own account. In addition, he agreed to add a half-percent of all commercial land sales earned by The Woodlands to the fund. To date, slightly more than $3 million has been collected to purchase pieces of art for public places. Of that amount, The Woodlands Corporation has contributed approximately $2 million, while third parties contributed the remainder.

An informal committee composed of Mitchell and Tough, with Mitchell's assistant, Joyce Gay, serving as an art adviser, initially made the selection of specific pieces of art and their location. After Gay left the committee, it became somewhat more structured and included Tough as chairman, with Cynthia Woods Mitchell and myself as members. Sally Sprout, former curator of the Transco Energy Company art collection, served as adviser to the committee, but George Mitchell always participated in final decisions. Artists were selected based on their national or regional reputation and exhibition of work in well-regarded museums.

Steve McPhetridge, who was responsible for negotiating commercial transactions for the company, indicated that with a few exceptions, imposition of the art fee was not a problematic issue for commercial users. Most saw the contribution as an investment in the community that would accrue to their benefit. However, he also observed that collection of the art fee was more successful when paid in conjunction with the land purchase rather than trying to collect it after the building was complete. Therefore, an estimated building cost was used to calculate the required payment. Some entities are exempt from the art fee. For example, public facilities constructed by the county or school district do not pay the fee. Nonprofit institutions such as hospitals do not pay the fee either, but they have generally agreed to include pieces of art on their campus. Several of the very large commercial property owners in The Woodlands have negotiated a lower art fee in exchange for their agreement to include works of art as part of their landscaping program that's visible to the public.

For the most part, the selection and placement of art have been well received by the community, but there have been some vocal exceptions. One that I recall is the piece installed in the median of Research Forest Drive near the HARC campus. It is a modern painted steel sculpture that Tough had originally planned for placement within a nearby retail center. But Mitchell had suggested to Tough that the roadway leading to HARC deserved attention from the art program. Since this piece was ready for installation, Tough moved it to the public street location and that is when we started hearing from the neighbors.

The piece happened to be painted bright orange. Motorists complained that it looked like a confusing traffic barricade. Local graduates of Texas A&M were most vocal because to them it looked like a salute to the University of Texas—its school color is burnt orange. Residents called my office, Tough's office, and, I would guess, Mitchell heard the complaints, too. The solution we finally agreed on was to paint the sculpture a dark green. It now blends into the colors of the natural vegetation and is hardly visible to anyone.

A very popular piece of art is the *Dragon*, which was personally acquired by Cynthia Mitchell and donated to the community. The challenge with this very large serpentine piece was finding a place to put it. It was green and red and resembled the Loch Ness Monster, which suggested that a watery site would be a suitable home for it. We considered several lakes on the golf courses but decided it would be too much of a distraction to serious golfers.

Finally, Matt Swanson, an urban planner in our planning department, suggested locating it near Tea Cup Island in Lake Woodlands, which is visible from Woodlands Parkway. And that is where the *Dragon* found a home. It has become a recognizable symbol of The Woodlands for those who travel the parkway. It also has become a sporting target for graduating high school students who come out under the cover of darkness to paint it a different color in celebration of their special day. This prompts a repaint to restore it to its original hue. Thanks to its many layers of paint, the *Dragon* will likely never rust. I just hope no accident occurs from student activity.

Tea Cup Island, by the way, is a small, circular artificial landmass near the spillway and dam for Lake Woodlands that came about through the imagination of a caffeine-addicted land planner. One day as Lake Woodlands was being designed, a planner set his cup of tea on a paper contour map of the lake. Upon removal, the cup left a circular stain on the map and the planner embellished the drawing with a bulkhead, a bridge, landscaping, and an observation tower. It was so attractive that we added it to the construction plans for the lake.

One piece of art that seems especially appropriate for The Woodlands is titled *Giant*. Inscribed on its base is a quote from Isaac Newton that reads: "If I have seen farther, it is because I have stood on the shoulders of giants."

Chapter 22

THE WOODLANDS AND ITS NEIGHBORS

———— •◆• ————

One of the first things Joel L. Deretchin did when he came to work for The Woodlands Corporation in March 1977 as director of governmental affairs was to go out and buy himself some cowboy boots and a western hat. Deretchin wasn't returning to his roots. He was from the East Coast, or as Texans call it, the "right coast."

Before coming to The Woodlands Corporation in 1977, Deretchin had acquired an extensive background in development and government work, including stints in Minneapolis's housing and urban renewal department; a nonprofit engaged in the redevelopment of downtown Detroit; a privately sponsored new town in Dayton, Ohio; and, finally, HUD.

"I was representing HUD in some negotiations with The Woodlands Corporation. Rob Lap was on the other side of the table. He was the vice president for governmental relations. And some time after those negotiations were concluded, Rob let me know he had an opening in his department and asked me if I'd want to work for him at The Woodlands Corporation, which I did. After a few years, Rob left the company, and I assumed responsibility for the department."

As to the hat, and, in Texas-speak, "manly footwear," well, Deretchin just wanted to fit in. "I was dealing with officials in Conroe on a regular basis. And in those days, Montgomery County was more rural than it is today, so everybody up there wore western-style clothes. I felt out of place going up there with a suit and a tie. When Ed Lee became president of The Woodlands Corporation, he instituted a dress code. We had to wear a tie and jacket, but I received permission to wear jeans and an open shirt—and I took advantage of that."

At first, Deretchin found Montgomery County to be a strange place. One of the problems was the language. "The first meeting I attended here was between county officials and The Woodlands team regarding the development of a fire station and police station on Grogan's Mill Road. The Woodlands had sought a HUD grant, so the agency's people were there, too. They had done a study and it was called Study to Explore the Feasibility of a Fire and Rescue Station in The Woodlands—FAR. So I'm sitting in this meeting. I didn't know any of the players. I knew that on this side of the table were the county folks and that HUD and the developer folks were on the other side. You could tell them apart because the county people were wearing boots and the developer and HUD people were wearing black shoes and black socks.

"The county folks were talking about the fire station—except to the ears of the HUD people it sounded like "FAR"—and HUD and the development people were also talking about the FAR station. The developer and HUD people were talking about the FAR—Fire and Rescue Station—the FAR station, and the county people were talking about the fire station—f-i-r-e—the fire station. They were communicating, but they sure as heck were talking about two different things."

Montgomery County was a far different kind of place when George Mitchell started assembling the land for what was to become The Woodlands in the 1960s. Though adjacent to Harris County, home of Houston, the state's most populous city, the residents of Montgomery County had very different attitudes than their urban neighbors. Many people were concerned that Houston would encroach on the countryside. More than a few had moved to Montgomery County to escape the city. Their attitudes about The Woodlands were mixed. While there was hope that The Woodlands would increase the tax base and provide needed amenities to all residents of Montgomery County, there were also suspicions that it would change their way of life.

R.A. "Mickey" Deison, who was mayor of the adjacent town of Conroe when The Woodlands started, believes that most residents of the county were more curious than resentful about Mitchell's plans, although the county government quickly became a fan of the developer's efforts.

The Woodlands, Deison said, transformed the process of land development in Montgomery County. The county, located directly in the path of Houston's northward growth, would have developed in any case. But Deison believes that, without The Woodlands, it would have looked very different. "It would have been a piecemeal process without oversight or true planning." As a result of the example of The Woodlands, Deison said, the county government has imposed controls over how new property developments are planned and built.

The Woodlands, like most successful master-planned communities, has produced positive benefits beyond its physical boundaries. To understand the magnitude of its influence, we need to look at the economic, political, and demographic nature of the region where The Woodlands is located, and understand the time period over which it has been developed. Located 27 miles north of downtown Houston, adjacent to Interstate 45 and near Houston's George Bush Intercontinental Airport, The Woodlands has enjoyed the benefits of a growing regional economy. The migration of people from Houston to places that offered a better environment in which to raise and educate their children started in the 1960s and continues today. Corporate relocations to Houston, which also continue today, added to the number of families who sought homes in its suburbs.

When Ann and I moved to Montgomery County in 1968, before I came to work at The Woodlands, the county population was less than 50,000. The center of political power and social activity was in Conroe; the county seat was located approximately ten miles north of land George Mitchell was quietly buying for his new community. All elected officeholders were registered Democrats; only Dr. Wally Wilkerson publicly confessed to being a

Republican. He was that party's county chairman, and still is. The Conroe Independent School District that served the Conroe area was well rated and improving. It had a single high school campus located in Conroe. Interstate 45 had recently opened, connecting Montgomery County to Houston and Dallas, which is 200 miles to the north. Lake Conroe, a major freshwater reservoir for the city of Houston and recreational amenity for the county, had not yet been constructed, although plans for its development were underway. Timber, oil, and gas production had been major economic engines in Montgomery County for many decades. Suburban growth would have occurred whether George Mitchell had undertaken The Woodlands or not. The question is: Did The Woodlands have a positive impact on the larger community in which it is located?

The formal opening of The Woodlands occurred on October 19, 1974. (This was two months after the resignation of President Nixon, the man who signed legislation establishing the program through which The Woodlands received significant funding.) There were no residents in the new town other than several employees of Mitchell's. The tax base was minimal, there were no permanent jobs, and its political influence was minor.

According to a study conducted in 1986 by Dr. Barton A. Smith, professor of economics at the University of Houston, the region had changed dramatically during the first 12 years of The Woodlands' development. "The transformation of Montgomery County from rural to suburban continues. The Woodlands has been an integral part of the process. Today, The Woodlands encompasses 29 percent of all county employment; 61 percent of county retail sales; 31 percent of county property values; and 21 percent of county population."

Smith credits The Woodlands for the county's substantial economic gains since 1975, including 32 percent of the county's population growth, 42 percent of all new county jobs, and thousands of additional jobs in the county but outside The Woodlands can be attributable to spillover effects. In addition, the economist showed that The Woodlands' property tax base in the 1980–1986 period accounted for 114 percent of the gains in the county tax base. "Excluding The Woodlands," noted Smith, "the Montgomery County tax base would have actually fallen. Within the 1980–1986 period, 78 percent of all new retail sales in the county occurred within the boundaries of The Woodlands."

Smith also forecasted a strong future: "Montgomery County and The Woodlands' share of regional population and employment will continue to rise throughout the next two decades. While both the county and The Woodlands are dependent upon the regional economy, their economies are becoming less sensitive to the region's overall economic growth rate. These areas are approaching the point where growth and development could continue even in the absence of rapid economic expansion in Houston per se."

He was right. Benefits generated by The Woodlands continued to grow after 1986. By 2003, the taxable value of all real property in The Woodlands increased sixfold to $6.5 billion, or 37 percent of all taxable property in the county. The number of residents in The Woodlands had increased to 75,000, or 25 percent of the county's population. Since the county's annual budget is largely funded by property taxes and services provided by the county are based in part on a per-capita cost, one could conclude that 37 percent of property taxes paid by property owners in The Woodlands produce a surplus compared to the cost of services for 25 percent of the county's population living in The Woodlands. During the early years of development, The Woodlands was a net user of county resources, but that shifted in the 1980s and the community became a producer of surplus resources. That trend continues as commercial development—and its related tax value—expands.

For a number of years, the accounting staff at The Woodlands Corporation would analyze the annual county budget in an attempt to identify direct or allocated expenditures that would benefit The Woodlands and its residents. Armed with this analysis and the calculated amount of surplus property taxes paid by The Woodlands' property owners, Joel Deretchin, representing The Woodlands Community Association, and I would schedule a meeting with county judge Alan "Barb" Sadler to appeal for a "fair share" of the tax pie.

The judge was always cordial, but I'm sure he did not look forward to our annual visit. He believed that budget allocations should be based on need and not ability to pay, and there is merit in that argument. But we did establish the premise that The Woodlands was paying its way and then some. We were never able to gain any adjustments in the county budget, although our discussions may have affected future resource allocations.

Property taxes paid by our homeowners have an even greater impact on the Conroe Independent School District, which serves The Woodlands and other parts of Montgomery County. The Woodlands' $6.5 billion in taxable value constitutes almost 60 percent of taxable values within the district today. Currently, 43 percent of the school district's students reside in The Woodlands. The school funding formula in Texas is a convoluted mathematical equation, which makes it difficult to describe the direct relationship between tax collection and school finances. However, it is safe to say that the taxable value created by The Woodlands is a significant economic engine for the school district. It is also fair to say that the school district has been effective in providing school facilities and programs for our growing new community. It has been a productive relationship.

Another significant source of revenue for government financing in Texas is sales tax, which is imposed by the state, cities, and certain special purpose districts. The Town Center Improvement District (TCID) has jurisdiction over certain commercial areas in The Woodlands; its sales tax generated about $7.3 million in revenue in 2003. These funds are used for economic development, enhanced security, and marketing. To increase security in the commercial area and nearby communities, TCID engages in contractual agreements with the Montgomery County sheriff's department and with the neighboring cities of Shenandoah and Oak Ridge. Thus, a portion of sales taxes generated within The Woodlands flows to county agencies and neighboring jurisdictions as payment for services or other obligations.

There is also a cooperative program among TCID, Shenandoah, and Oak Ridge to enhance the landscaping along Interstate 45 within the jurisdiction of each entity. The Woodlands Operating Company and several municipal utility districts also contribute resources to highway beautification. Working in concert with the state's department of transportation, the initiative has directed approximately $1 million to the project, which involves the reestablishment of native vegetation.

Economic growth and commercial development within The Woodlands has increased the value and marketability of commercially designated land fronting Interstate 45 for the adjacent communities of Shenandoah and Oak Ridge. This spillover of value has provided opportunities for each city to capture a share of commercial development at an accelerated pace, and, in turn, enjoy enhanced property tax and sales tax revenue. Both cities manage this opportunity wisely, but Shenandoah has achieved exceptional results. In 2003, Shenandoah (population 1,500) collected $2.8 million in sales tax from businesses that were not there just a few years ago.

The growing population in The Woodlands has influenced the political landscape within the county. Currently, there are 197,626 voters registered in Montgomery County and 51,887 of them, or 26 percent, live in The Woodlands. According to Carol Chedsey Gaultney, Montgomery County's elections administrator, in the 2002 general election, 38 percent of the registered voters in Montgomery County voted. The voter turnout in The Woodlands was 46 percent.

Voters in The Woodlands generally support countywide bond issues for infrastructure improvements and bonds to build new school facilities and repair old ones. Even the retirees in The Woodlands support school bonds, while their contemporaries in other jurisdictions tend to oppose additional school taxes. This may be the case, at least in part, because extended families live in The Woodlands and retirees are voting for school improvements that benefit their grandchildren.

Voters in The Woodlands tend to be Republicans rather than Democrats, but I am not sure that is a function of living in The Woodlands. That trend has been present throughout the county and state for a number of years. Today, very few residents are Democrats. In fact, Dr. Wally Wilkerson, who at one time was the only publicly identified Republican in the county, actually had to run against and win over an opponent for his post as county party chairman. Things change!

The increasing voter strength enabled the election of more Woodlands residents to county, state, and federal positions. Currently, Woodlands resident Kevin Brady serves as a U.S. congressman representing the Eighth District. State Senator Tommy Williams and State Representative Rob Eissler are residents of The Woodlands, as are a majority of the Conroe Independent School District's elected school board members.

As The Woodlands' population and influence increased over time, there was growing concern by some in the county who feared a shift in power and resources. This fear tended to support a north-versus-south emotional division within the county, with Conroe to the north of the San Jacinto River and The Woodlands and other communities to the south of the river. Fortunately, reasonable people on both sides of the divide saw the perils of this unfortunate issue and made significant efforts to reunite the county and school district into effective units of government service. The wounds of battle have not fully healed, but the mending process is well advanced.

Today, many in Montgomery County see The Woodlands in a new light. Many county residents work in The Woodlands. Many shop, dine, or attend entertainment functions here. People who grew up in other parts of the county have moved to our community and are raising their families here. Others attend the community college or University Center. Conversely, some residents of The Woodlands have elected to move to other parts of

Montgomery County or enjoy the amenities of Lake Conroe. Other Woodlands residents serve on countywide charities and foundations, use the county airport, or own businesses within Montgomery County.

One way we made sure to maintain good relations with the various communities in Montgomery County, including the people of The Woodlands, was to pay a lot of attention to the local news media, which has tremendous influence on the information that residents receive. This is especially true for new residents who don't have any historical perspective. They rely on local newspapers for information about the community, local politics and issues, what's happening in the area, and what the future holds.

We recognized the power of the press early on, so we interacted with the local newspapers—*The Villager, The Woodlands Sun,* and the *Conroe Courier,* which now is called *The Courier*—on a regular basis. We felt it was important to keep staff reporters fully informed about what we were doing.

We were not trying to shape what they said, but we were trying to give them accurate background information, which they seemed to appreciate. We'd do that by sending press releases to them, but, more important, we would hold news briefings, which I participated in.

As time goes by, we all learn that we don't live on an island and that there are great benefits to be realized from working together for a common purpose. The Woodlands and Montgomery County are moving forward together.

Chapter 23

HOMETOWN HEROES

———————— • ◆ • ————————

In conjunction with The Woodlands' 25th birthday in 1999, "Hometown Heroes" was formed to honor those who contribute to the community. This is a joint effort by The Woodlands Operating Company and *The Villager* newspaper. In its inaugural year, 25 honorees were selected; new honorees have been added to their ranks in succeeding years. The process is open and encourages nominations through advertisements in the local paper. A panel of judges is chosen from past winners. Thus far, 45 individuals have been honored.

Similarly, the Town Center Improvement District now hosts an annual Public Safety Appreciation Awards dinner in the Grand Ballroom of the Marriott Waterway Convention Center. This popular event is sponsored by a large number of local businesses and is designed to honor law enforcement professionals, firefighters, paramedics, and mounted patrol personnel who provide outstanding service to the community. It gives recognition but also provides an opportunity for residents to meet and learn about these dedicated professionals.

The local chamber of commerce holds an annual Volunteer Appreciation Luncheon to emphasize the "importance of volunteers and the impact individuals make on a community or society." The full spectrum of volunteer organizations operating in The Woodlands is recognized.

Even with organized programs to honor those who make a visible difference, there are hundreds of other individuals who quietly contribute to the quality of community life without formal recognition. Several are identified throughout the chapters of this book, but there are still others who deserve our appreciation. For example, George Krenek, now in his 70s, is recognized as an expert craftsman when it comes to hanging doors. Krenek hung doors in the first custom homes in The Woodlands and is still sought after by high-quality builders. By his own count, he has hung 20,000 doors in homes here. The motto on his business card is "Let George DO IT—He did it for 48 years."

And there is Jerry Kirkpatrick and his wife, JoAnn. They have built custom homes in The Woodlands for many years, including the first one. Even with an active and demanding business, they have found time to serve as foster parents to some 60 newborn babies awaiting adoption.

Or there is Bill Kendrick, a forester who has worked for The Woodlands the better part of 30 years. He has supervised and agonized over the preservation and planting of more native trees and shrubs than Johnny Appleseed ever did.

These are just a few examples to illustrate the dedication and value of those who contribute. There are many, many more.

Part V

THE WOODLANDS
AFTER MITCHELL

On June 13, 1997, the *Houston Chronicle* ran a story with the headline, "Mitchell Selling The Woodlands." A photograph taken after the press conference where the sale to a partnership of Fort Worth–based Crescent Real Estate Equities and Morgan Stanley Real Estate Fund II was announced shows George Mitchell walking away from the event. His shoulders are slumped. He's the picture of dejection. Mitchell did not want to sell his baby. He felt he had no choice.

Mitchell first started thinking about selling The Woodlands in 1996. His company, Mitchell Energy & Development Corporation, had long been bedeviled on Wall Street because of its structure. It was an energy company, but it was also a land development company. And it was a publicly held company, with its shares listed on the New York Stock Exchange. The price of any stock depends on many factors. Is the company profitable, and by how much? What is the company's cash flow? What about the level of debt? The Mitchell Energy & Development Corporation stock had long sold at a discount to others in similar businesses. Two factors accounted for the discount. First, Mitchell had always believed in using other people's money for expansion. The company usually had substantial debt.

But there was another, and more important reason. Many, if not most, holders of individual stocks don't take the time to study closely the companies in which they purchase shares. Instead, they rely on the opinions of stock analysts whose job it is to research and assess companies and issue recommendations on the current and future value of their stock. The analysts long had a problem with Mitchell Energy, and specifically with its mix of businesses. While in the past, many energy companies had been active in land development, for most of them it was such a small part of their business that land development was mentioned in their annual reports, if at all, in a footnote. Land development accounted for a significant portion of Mitchell Energy. The analysts who followed energy companies really did not have the expertise to evaluate the land development portion. And those who followed land develop-ment were at sea when it came to energy stocks.

As usual, at the time of the sale Mitchell Energy had considerable debt, which affected its stock price. Unlike many heads of energy corporations, Mitchell believed in keeping his com-pany highly leveraged, but not unreasonably so. A high level of debt never really concerned him. It was his philosophy to borrow a lot, but he was always confident he could repay his loans. But it was clear the company would be stronger without as much debt on the balance sheet.

Chapter 24

SALE OF
THE WOODLANDS

———•◆•———

I n 1996, the board of directors of Mitchell Energy & Development Corporation agreed
that it was time to get out of either the land or energy business. Mitchell went along with
the decision, despite the fact he personally owned enough shares in the company to over-
rule the decision.

"I didn't want to sell The Woodlands," Mitchell said in a 2004 interview. "The Woodlands
is a great project and I was very proud of it. And, of course, I had done a lot of work in energy, and that was very exciting, too. But I hated to sell The Woodlands, not only because it's
more visible, but also because it probably has a greater effect on [people] compared to what I
accomplished in energy."

But at that time Mitchell could not sell the energy portion of Mitchell Energy &
Development Corporation because of a number of lawsuits pending in Wise County in north
Texas, the site of the natural gas strike that put his company into the big time and him on the
list of the 400 richest Americans. The suits claimed that Mitchell's gas wells were polluting
the water wells of many residents and demanded as much as $200 million in damages. Later,
Mitchell prevailed when the courts found that his company's activities were not responsible
for any pollution. But in 1996, with those suits hanging over the company, the energy portion of Mitchell Energy was virtually unsellable. No one wants to buy a lawsuit.

"I couldn't sell the energy company, so I had to make a decision, either sell the energy company or The Woodlands [Corporation], because both of them were very capital intensive,"
Mitchell said. "So I had no choice but to sell The Woodlands. I would have kept The
Woodlands and sold the energy company. But I sold The Woodlands and put the money back
in energy. Then I sold the energy company about three years later. . .but I would rather have
kept The Woodlands."

Mitchell, whose wealth was substantial, might have bought The Woodlands himself from
Mitchell Energy. But there were severe constraints on doing so. Much of his wealth was tied
up in stock of the company named for him. He would have had to sell enough stock to come
up with the sale price—The Woodlands Corporation sold for $543 million—or borrow
against it. And Mitchell was getting older. He had ten children. No one lives forever and

dying in the United States without good estate planning meant much of his wealth could go to the federal government in estate taxes. Tying up a substantial part of his wealth in largely illiquid land just didn't make sense. Mitchell once told me that if he had been 50 years old in 1997, he would not have sold The Woodlands Corporation.

The decision to sell The Woodlands Corporation came shortly after Mitchell Energy & Development Corporation suffered a major tragedy. Don Covey was head of Mitchell Energy's oil and gas exploration and production business. He was flying to London to meet with the carrier who handled insurance for the corporation when he died of a heart attack. Mitchell needed a replacement for Covey. Bill Stevens had just retired as the chief executive officer of Exxon, a much larger company. Mitchell made Stevens president and chief operating officer of Mitchell Energy & Development Corporation over both the energy and real estate businesses, a position of greater scope than Covey had held. Up until that time, energy people ran the energy part of the business and George ran the real estate part of the business, although he was the ultimate decision maker for energy, too. I was the equivalent of Don Covey on the real estate side. But there was no overall president of the entire corporation until Bill Stevens came along. Stevens had had experience with Exxon in observing Friendswood Development Company and its rather insignificant contribution to the Exxon Corporation's bottom line. He was not a champion of an energy company being in the real estate business. However, the circumstances of Mitchell Energy were different in that real estate and energy were about equal assets within the company, which really confused the analysts on Wall Street. With Exxon, there was very little confusion, because Friendswood Development Company represented such a small percentage of the company's total value.

It was apparent that for the Mitchell Energy stock to advance in value on Wall Street, there would need to be a separation between energy and real estate. The change could be engineered as a spin-off, an outright sale of assets, or a restructuring to divide Mitchell Energy into two companies. I was not privy to all the discussions that took place, but the Mitchell board decided that the best course of action would be to sell the real estate operations, either the assets or the corporate entities that owned them, and keep the energy company. When that decision was made, we set about organizing ourselves to divest of the assets quickly but at a fair price. It was not a fire sale.

While The Woodlands Corporation was the dominant entity in Mitchell Energy's real estate holdings, there were many other assets housed in another subsidiary, Mitchell Development Corporation of the Southwest. The company hired investment bank Goldman Sachs to help it evaluate Woodlands' properties. Bill Stevens played a key role both in the separation of the two operating units and in the organization and implementation of a plan to dispose of real estate assets.

Within the real estate division, we set up a working team that included Michael Richmond, executive vice president; Jeff Harris, senior vice president for administration and accounting; George Lake, vice president for finance; Vicki Armstrong, controller; and myself. We catalogued and valued the many real estate assets. We also engaged two outside experts: Buzz McCoy, a former senior executive with Morgan Stanley, and Stan Ross, vice chairman of Ernst & Young, along with his accounting firm.

It was quite an exercise. We had a large portfolio of very diverse assets, ranging from country clubs and a mortgage company to a title company; from undeveloped land to developed land to office buildings and retail centers. A host of assets in The Woodlands were subject to leases, contracts, liens, and loans. The properties outside The Woodlands were also diverse but simpler in terms of ownership. We divided the assets into two packages. There was The Woodlands package and another package for assets outside the new town. We sold the non-Woodlands assets separately—not through a financial adviser, but with our own resources using appraisers and industry standards to establish values. In some cases, we used outside brokers, in others we didn't.

Mitchell had long had his fingers in a number of pies. The assets outside The Woodlands included 30,000 acres of timberland in Montgomery County, the San Luis Hotel in Galveston, several vacation developments on the west end of Galveston Island, a retail center, a large amount of undeveloped land, and a 3,000-acre property near Steamboat Springs, Colorado, which Mitchell had hoped to develop into a resort community.

We sold the timberlands. At that time, the timber market in the United States was very good. Timber prices were quite high and we really had very little trouble finding a number of buyers. We would have sold all 30,000 acres to one purchaser, but we didn't find one capable of or interested in buying the entire parcel. We broke it up into a number of major land parcels, ranging in size from 2,000 to 15,000 acres each. The timberlands were sold in probably four or five different transactions before The Woodlands was sold.

We also sold the San Luis Hotel, which was a happy day. The hotel had never made money for the company. In fact, its ownership was more or less an accident. Years earlier, Mitchell had been convinced that there was both oil and natural gas beneath the close-in waters of the Gulf of Mexico fronting Galveston Island and within Galveston's city limits. But the Galveston City Council refused to grant him a permit to drill offshore, citing fears about pollution and damage to the city's tourist trade. No matter. Mitchell bought property rights on the water, behind the seawall the city had built after the great hurricane of 1900. The property itself had been part of the U.S. Army's coastal fortifications for many years. It had huge concrete bunkers built to house coastal artillery—designed, perhaps, to drive off the British fleet if it had ever decided to invade the United States. The guns never fired a shot in defense and changing circumstances made them obsolete. The guns were dismantled and the federal government sold the property. The huge bunkers were—and are—still there. Trying to dismantle them would have been financially ruinous. Mitchell bought the bunkers and the land around them. He told the Galveston City Council that if they would not let him drill offshore, he would drill directional wells from the bunker site. Under Texas laws, the city council could not stop him from drilling on the site. Faced with the threat of drilling rigs right on the beachfront, the council granted Mitchell permission to drill several miles offshore.

Unfortunately, the hotel and condominium he built on the former artillery site never made money for Mitchell and given what he spent on the construction and the rather short resort season on the island, it probably never would. Construction costs were high because the buildings had to be built around and on top of the massive concrete bunkers. We built the adjacent condominium tower at a time when the real estate market was absolutely at the

bottom, so our losses in the condominium alone were significant enough to postpone profitability to quite some time in the future. Michael Richmond, then the executive vice president of The Woodlands, was quite familiar with the hospitality part of the business and he
looked for a buyer for the San Luis Hotel. The most likely buyer was Tillman Fertitta, who,
like Mitchell, was born on Galveston Island. He was the son of Vic Fertitta, who operated
restaurants and a hotel. Fertitta was chief executive officer of the Landry's Restaurant chain,
which he eventually built into a national powerhouse.

The San Luis Hotel and condominiums sold quickly. Fertitta said what he would pay and
we were happy with that number. The transaction was done. Fertitta bought it well below our
cost basis. The incentive to sell it was to shut off the operating losses that it sent into our
books every year and to avoid spending capital for needed upgrades.

While the other real estate assets were sold to separate buyers, selling The Woodlands
Corporation was a package deal. Its assets included:

- Approximately 14,000 acres of undeveloped land in the master-planned
  community;
- The Woodlands Executive Conference Center Resort and The Woodlands
  Country Club with its four golf courses;
- Total or partial interest in 1.4 million square feet of office space, a million
  square feet of research technology space, and 2,300 apartments;
- Partial ownership of Mitchell Mortgage Company and Stewart Title
  Company of Montgomery County;
- Easement use fees and a realty sales operation;
- WoodTrace, a proposed 2,850-acre master-planned residential golf commu-
  nity in northwest Houston;
- Certain financial assets, contracts, and leases;
- The franchise value of a nationally recognized, successful master-planned
  community;
- An experienced staff of professionals heading The Woodlands Corporation;
  and
- A going business with positive cash flow.

We set up a war room in one of the office buildings owned by Mitchell Energy and assembled the information about The Woodlands. There was very limited access to the room. We
were forced, for legal, business, and community relations reasons, to hold the preparation for
the sale in strict confidence. Goldman Sachs prepared a confidential memorandum offering
The Woodlands for sale. It was released to potential buyers in March 1997. It anticipated that
the corporation would be sold for cash, but also stated that a stock sale could be arranged,
subject to favorable tax rulings and the financial strength of the acquiring company. It also
noted that officials of Mitchell Energy & Development Corporation would provide briefings
and access to the war room to make sure those invited to bid would have a good understanding of the offering. After bids were submitted, Mitchell Energy would choose one
prospective buyer with whom it would negotiate.

Just assembling the massive information was a challenge for everyone involved. There were hundreds of leases, thousands of accounts, the inspection of millions of square feet of office and technology buildings, numerous leases in a regional mall half owned by The Woodlands Corporation, a mortgage company, interest in a title company, and a lot of real estate and real estate–related businesses to evaluate. The top officers of the company essentially had to take on two jobs. We had to continue running the company while also preparing it for sale. To make matters worse, once the negotiations with one buyer started, due diligence had to be completed and the sale closed in 45 days.

In addition to the increased workload, the top officers of The Woodlands Corporation found themselves in an awkward position. We had all signed contracts to stay on after the sale. When helping structure the offering for Mitchell, Goldman Sachs pointed out the value of employees and the senior management team and they recommended to Mitchell that he put together an incentive package that would keep key people available to the new owner for a period of time. All members of that small group were offered a compensation package that would pay us a bonus for staying six months after closing. The new buyer didn't have to keep us employed. All we had to do was volunteer to be there, and if we didn't perform, we'd get fired. That gave the new buyer an opportunity to get to know us—and for us to get to know them—and to avoid a vacuum should senior management people leave en masse after the sale. So in effect, we were working for both our present and future employers. It could have been an untenable position. Bill Stevens took the pressure off us. He told us that our job, as long as we were still employed by Mitchell Energy, was to provide adequate and appropriate information to the acquiring party so that they could make a fair evaluation. We were not to negotiate with them or reject requests for anything they needed. Our small team handling the sale appreciated his candor, because we had to make the transition from Mitchell Energy to the new buyer. It was a thoughtful thing Stevens did.

There were two finalists, the Rouse Co. and the Crescent–Morgan Stanley partnership. The Crescent partnership had the higher bid and it sent in a team of executives for the due diligence portion of the process. As the time approached for the closing, Crescent–Morgan Stanley identified a number of issues about deferred maintenance and other matters. They viewed those as a valid reason either to extend the period for due diligence or to adjust the price. Bill Stevens and George Mitchell refused to renegotiate. Mitchell didn't want to sell anyway and he was not about to reduce the price to accommodate the sale. I got a call from a Crescent representative on the weekend before the transaction was to close asking if I would try to convince Mitchell to reconsider his position on the matter. I told them that I would make the call. But I didn't call George. I called Phil Smith, chief financial officer of Mitchell Energy, who confirmed that Mitchell probably wouldn't agree to discuss the deal with me or anyone else. I don't know if Smith called Mitchell or not, but the closing did occur at the original offer price and within the time frame set forth in the agreement.

A good case can be made that George Mitchell sold The Woodlands at exactly the wrong time. The cash sale price of $545 million was within the upper range of values anticipated by Goldman Sachs and Ernst & Young. But that $545 million sale generated an after-tax loss for Mitchell Energy & Development Corporation of $67 million. That loss can be chalked up to two significant reasons: (1) The sale occurred before The Woodlands' assets had reached financial maturity (reported profitable returns to Crescent and Morgan Stanley bear out this circumstance); and (2) George Mitchell's charitable nature and his belief that the community required contributions of assets and funds to make it a better place, *i.e.,* the Cynthia Woods Mitchell Pavilion, funding and land grants to the Houston Area Research Center, the John Cooper School, the University Center, and other institutions. These contributions, or long-term investments, by Mitchell created value that could be recovered over time from future sales, but no current income to the company per se. Mitchell sold The Woodlands with the belief that the sale was likely premature, but did it for broader business reasons.

In 2003, Devon Energy acquired Mitchell Energy & Development Corporation for $3.1 billion. That same year, Mitchell was ranked number 139 on the Forbes 400 list of wealthiest individuals. So The Woodlands wasn't a bad investment for Mitchell. Sale of The Woodlands Corporation and other real estate assets added market value to the energy company and supported the very successful sale of Mitchell Energy to Devon just four years later. Had Mitchell retained both energy and real estate assets, the sale of the energy company to Devon would have been more difficult. A buyer would have run into the same problem of valuing a company in two dissimilar lines of business.

Of course, if he had kept The Woodlands, it might well have been an even better one. Building a master-planned community as large as The Woodlands requires a huge upfront investment. The payoff is usually years down the road. Mitchell sold just as the payoff was on the horizon. But the loss of future profits from The Woodlands Corporation was more than made up for by the stock market. The market value of Mitchell Energy stock improved significantly after the real estate sale.

Upon the closing of the sale to Crescent–Morgan Stanley, our management team had several objectives. We wanted to introduce the new owners to the community and make sure they knew all about the assets they bought. We needed to reshape our operations to achieve the new owners' objectives. We felt we had to both reassure the community that George Mitchell's vision was intact and reinforce our network of relationships with regulatory agencies, elected officials, and community leaders. And finally, we knew if we were going to accomplish these objectives we needed to establish our credibility with the new owners.

Crescent–Morgan Stanley kept most of the existing management team at The Woodlands when it completed the sale. The new owners put in place a financial bonus program for key employees who would stay for several years. This worked for a time, but gradually those employees moved on. By late 2003, the majority of their positions were filled by new people.

Changes were made in the way The Woodlands operated, but they occurred gradually. Land use covenants, development plans, existing regulatory approvals, contracts with third parties, and agreements with homebuilders and contractors meant that changes would be gradual. Like a large ship, shifting directions quickly in The Woodlands was impossible. Crescent–Morgan Stanley understood the value of George Mitchell's vision. They did not, however, share his passion. They saw the Mitchell vision as a vehicle to achieve the financial goals of their investors and shareholders, but they chose a somewhat different approach to achieving it.

It was important for residents to understand that the sale of The Woodlands involved only its name and assets, not the assets of the community such as the pavilion or its governmental structure. These remained beyond the direct control of Crescent–Morgan Stanley. Residents continued to raise their families, buy and sell homes, educate their children, and enjoy community amenities. Businesses continued without interruption. Resident volunteers and the institutions they supported continued to weave the tapestry of community fabric, just as they had done under Mitchell's ownership. This human element provided continuity as the company and its assets transferred from one owner to the other. Residents became more alert to even minor changes. They became more active protectors of George Mitchell's vision.

The new partners formed an executive management committee to set policy for their new acquisition. Each had three votes on the committee, but Crescent was the managing partner so it oversaw day-to-day affairs. However, Owen Thomas, managing director of Morgan Stanley and a trustee of the Urban Land Institute, recognized the value of the management team already in place at The Woodlands Corporation. He insisted that Morgan Stanley approve any major change to our team.

The way The Woodlands was managed changed after the sale. Members of the executive management committee changed frequently. Morgan Stanley, for the most part, appointed bright, young asset managers of varying experience. Crescent's appointments were usually employees or business associates. For the first time during the life of The Woodlands, absentee owners controlled it and its management team had little direct contact with the decision makers. Under its new ownership, the corporation was governed by a committee. It was quite a contrast to the hands-on management style of George Mitchell, who had both a personal and corporate interest in the long-term success of The Woodlands, sometimes at the expense of quarterly earnings. Crescent did name to the committee one person, Harry Frampton, president of the western division of East West Partners, who had a real and positive impact on management during the early months of the new ownership. Frampton was an experienced community developer and had a financial relationship with Crescent in some of his projects in Beaver Creek, Colorado. Frampton served The Woodlands well and became an ally as we attempted to help the new owners become acquainted with what they had bought and how to manage it. Frampton is now chairman of the Urban Land Institute. Shortly after the acquisition, with the urging and support of Frampton, we organized a two-day workshop to help the new members of the executive committee gain a better understanding of the community development process and its connections to the value of assets in The Woodlands. Outside participants in the two-day workshop were all ULI members. Gadi Kaufmann, CEO of Robert Charles Lesser & Co., served as facilitator. Others included Drew Brown, president of DMB Associates, Inc.; Bill Bone, CEO of Sunrise Colony Company; Dan Van Epp, then president of the Howard Hughes Corporation; and Tom Lee, CEO of Newhall Land and Farming Company. The process worked. Unfortunately, its effect did not last long because of the frequent turnover of members of the executive committee.

Morgan Stanley is a huge financial institution, so one would expect oversight of a property like The Woodlands Corporation to be handled by asset managers. Thomas is well versed in the community development business but was available only on a limited basis due to his other responsibilities at Morgan Stanley. Therefore, asset managers played an important role for Morgan Stanley. Crescent Real Estate Equities, however, is a real estate investment trust governed by federal tax regulations that limited its role in certain kinds of business activities including land development and specific real estate operations, both among the principal business activities of The Woodlands. Legal and corporate structures had to be created to allow Crescent to manage the assets it now owned. Diagrams of the organizational and legal structure resembled the illustration on the back of a refrigerator. Luckily, one does not need to understand it to use the icemaker. All of these changes were invisible to the people who lived in The Woodlands, but they did consume a great amount of management time and emotion during the transition. The Crescent team was stimulated by, and quite good at, structuring legal and financial transactions. They seemed to have more interest in the deal and less interest in managing what they bought. Perhaps this was because of the tremendous number of deals that consumed Crescent throughout the 1990s.

The new ownership did, however, cause concern in The Woodlands community. Some of it was justified, but most simply was normal reaction to change. For example, an article in the *Conroe Courier* in April 1998 described some residents' unhappiness with the new owners: "Community meetings have had huge turnouts in the past few months," the newspaper reported. "Residents have made impassioned pleas for help to stop construction of basketball courts, office buildings, a sports stadium, and anything else that might come between them and their quality of life, not to mention property values. Some residents have read into these basic community disputes a new callousness on the part of The Woodlands developer. One resident at a recent meeting said it was difficult to trust company officials now that 'Uncle George' Mitchell, The Woodlands founder and principal visionary, was no longer at the helm. They feared since Mitchell sold The Woodlands to Crescent Real Estate Equities and its partner Morgan Stanley, the human, the caring element of the developer had been replaced with a dollar-driven one."

We held many news conferences and community meetings to respond to these kinds of concerns. I pointed out that the construction of the great Paris cathedral of Notre Dame took 400 years. But driven by a clear vision of what needed to be accomplished, it now stands as an architectural and spiritual marvel. So, too, would The Woodlands survive and excel if the new owners made a reasonable commitment to respect George Mitchell's vision. I recall at the initial news conference announcing the sale of The Woodlands, Mitchell told those gathered at the event that he was convinced that the new owners cared about the community and embraced its vision. In response to this show of support, an executive from Crescent pledged a donation of $1 million to the Cynthia Woods Mitchell Pavilion for construction of an additional performing arts theater in The Woodlands. Sadly, that pledge was not kept, and Mitchell has often expressed disappointment about it.

Crescent's initial appointment of one of its own as chairman of the executive committee was a disappointment. This was a person with little experience in community development and a management style that included less than perfect people skills. He questioned the wisdom of having a YMCA in The Woodlands, arguing that it caters to poor people. Actually, The Woodlands' YMCA is very popular with people from all walks of life and has over 6,000 members. He criticized long-term employees who proudly worked at the Conference Center and Resort, calling them worthless for working at the same jobs for so long. He stayed for less than a year; fortunately, not many people in the community came in contact with him during his tenure. Later executive committee appointments by Crescent were much better. I stepped aside at the end of 1998. Michael Richmond succeeded me and served until the end of 2002. Richmond carried forward those development programs already underway and initiated important new objectives. He kept intact the core management team that included Steve McPhetridge, Tim Welbes, Alex Sutton, John Landrum, Karen West, Robert Heineman, Eric Wojner, and Vicki Armstrong. Even though the transition to new ownership had been challenging, business activity increased during that time. Anadarko constructed and occupied its 30-story headquarters in Town Center. Chevron Phillips Chemical Co., a major employer, moved its operation to The Woodlands, as did CBI. New home sales increased from 1,000 in 1997 (year of sale) to 1,600 in 2001. The new Carlton Woods Country Club featuring a Jack Nicklaus Signature Golf Course opened on schedule; a new Gary Player Signature Course was added to The Woodlands Country Club. New public schools have opened. The Woodlands Waterway is advancing as a major commercial amenity. A 350-room Marriott hotel and convention center has opened. Restaurants and retail facilities have opened and a new hospital has been constructed. From a development standpoint, the new owners have made significant progress since taking over in 1997. Most of the bruises and scrapes have been from internal organizational and operational battles. For the most part, George Mitchell's vision has been strong enough to endure the changes in management, and the residents continue to help protect it. Credit goes to the team of company professionals and volunteer leaders in the community for making the transition a success.

There was one major departure from the original plan set by Mitchell. His philosophy was to build and hold. Crescent and Morgan Stanley's philosophy was to buy and sell, so they disposed of a lot of the income-producing portfolio that we had put together. And there is nothing wrong with that at all. I think George eventually would have had to sell some assets to fund other development activity. Properties do reach peak value and the right thing to do is to sell them and invest in something else. But having said that, there was a great value to The Woodlands community development program in owning the office buildings, retail centers, and apartments. If you manage a portfolio rather than a single property, you could reduce profits on one and build value for another corporate enterprise. In one retail center, we had a tenant who operated a frame shop. The owner of the shop, Peter Lampros, also exhibited and sold artwork in addition to running his framing business. He was also a very good chef and catered meals for selected people. Groups would buy the opportunity to have a catered meal at this shop. They would invite their friends and it was an entertaining activity. There was some profit for Peter, but it was a community building experience. The new owners sold controlling interest in that retail center to a university endowment trust. The trust was solely concerned about the income from its new property; it had little interest in community building. The trust didn't profit from home sales or benefit from the country club revenue. So the university's endowment trust raised rents in the center, and in the process, pushed out Lampros, who couldn't afford to pay the higher rent. I'm not sure how much space he occupied, maybe

3,000 square feet. That space remained vacant for five years. Not only did the trust lose the cash flow they were getting from Peter, the development process lost a small but vital piece of community building activity. That's just an example of why I think it would have been more difficult to develop The Woodlands had we not controlled a significant amount of income-producing properties.

While I am convinced that had Crescent–Morgan Stanley started The Woodlands in 1974, instead of George Mitchell, it would have been a failure, it's equally clear that during their ownership in 1997 they were successful in creating value, generating a profitable cash flow, and advancing elements of Mitchell's vision.

On December 31, 2003, Crescent sold its 52.5 percent financial interest in The Woodlands to the Rouse Company for $202 million in cash with the new buyer assuming $185 million in debt, according to public announcements. Morgan Stanley remained as a 47.5 percent financial interest after the sale. Crescent announced it made a gross gain of about $87 million from the sale of its majority share interest in The Woodlands. But that tells only a very small part of their profitable story. Over the seven years Crescent and Morgan Stanley owned The Woodlands, the combination of aggressive asset sales, successful operating results, and project refinancing likely produced approximately $500 million in cash distributions to the partners. This, in addition to Crescent's announced $87 million gain on the sale of its interest, provided a handsome return on their investment in The Woodlands—a return that some estimate to be in excess of 30 percent. They were good at harvesting cash.

Chapter 25

FUTURE OF
THE WOODLANDS

——— • ◆ • ———

I n December 2003, The Woodlands took another step on its road to the future when the
Rouse Company bought the majority financial interest from Crescent and assumed operational control. In a way, it was a return to the new town's beginnings. Much of the early
planning for The Woodlands came from George Mitchell's observations of Columbia, the
new town built in Maryland by the late James Rouse. In The Woodlands' early years, Mitchell
recruited many executives from Rouse's company.

The acquisition by Rouse gave it an interest in 8,400 gross acres of land in the master-
planned community, of which approximately 4,300 acres are earmarked for residential development and 1,200 acres for commercial use located primarily along Interstate 45 and adjacent to the 1,100-acre Town Center, which is now only half built out. Also included in the
purchase are seven office buildings containing 520,000 square feet, the conference center and
resort with three related golf courses, the 350-room Marriott hotel, and various miscellaneous
assets. The 8,400 acres remaining for development exceeds the total acreage in Reston, so
there is much remaining to be done to complete The Woodlands.

Tom D'Alesandro, the current chief executive of The Woodlands Operating Company, as
it is now known, was hired for that position while Crescent was the managing partner. But
he has close ties to the Rouse Company. Both his father and grandfather were mayors of
Baltimore, James Rouse's hometown. And he'd known James Rouse from his childhood.
Before coming to The Woodlands, D'Alesandro was an executive with the new town of
Reston, Virginia, which was founded by Robert E. Simon in the 1960s.

D'Alesandro expects The Woodlands to be substantially completed by the year 2015
or thereabouts.

The Rouse Company is committed to Mitchell's vision of an ecologically enhanced new
town, its executives say. But it is moving away from his plan of mixing various economic
groups in the final developed areas. In one respect, that's realistic. Building homes for low-
income residents depends on securing housing subsidies from the federal government. And
the feds have drastically cut back those subsidies. Another reason for the change comes from
standard development practices. A cliché in the development business says you make your

profit on the last lot sold in a subdivision. It's also true that the affluence of those who choose to live in The Woodlands has been increasing over the years.

"The Woodlands is now fairly upscale," D'Alesandro told me in an interview. "When we look at the Houston market overall, 40 percent of the housing sold there is priced below $150,000. Our pricing of new homes starts at $160,000, so there's 40 percent of the market we don't even deal with. Our average home is $270,000, so we're almost double the average price."

D'Alesandro is seeing the same move to an upscale customer happening at The Woodlands Mall. A recent expansion brought in such upscale retailers, D'Alesandro notes, as "Anthropologie, Williams-Sonoma, P.F. Chang's China Bistro, Cheesecake Factory, and Barnes & Noble. The mall is about ten years old now and a lot of the first wave of leasing is expiring. Old tenants are leaving and General Growth [owner of the mall], is replacing them with stronger merchants. The mall will continue its shift to upper-scale fashion merchandise." For the reason why, D'Alesandro suggests looking at household income levels in The Woodlands. "Today," he says, "the average is about $87,000, which is very strong on a national level. But the new homebuyer moving into The Woodlands has a household income of $114,000."

As of the writing of this book, work is ongoing for Market Street, a completely new shopping experience adjacent to the existing mall. It will have an upscale grocery called The Woodlands Market, operated by the Texas-based H.E.B., and will feature both the chain's regular groceries and its very successful Central Market concept, which offers fresh and gourmet food.

What's happening today in The Woodlands, D'Alesandro believes, is a natural progression of post–World War II housing patterns in the United States. In the postwar economic expansion there was optimism because we had the depression and the war behind us. Cities, he points out, were overcrowded in part due to limits on construction in the 1930s and 1940s. Suburban expansion "really began in the 1950s. With the [federal program to build] highways, you began to have the Levittown-style single-use suburbs. They were only residential; there was no open space and no integration of uses. It was just cookie-cutter housing, and people like Simon and Rouse in the late 1950s and early 1960s said there has to be a better model, and there was.

"They were saying we really could plan cities. We've seen the unintended consequences of some of the big cities, [that resulted in] overcrowding and the desire to flee." But people, notes D'Alesandro, "were fleeing from one problem to another. So part of the thinking was to create an environment that, when it was mature, would have a balance of built and natural environments, of employment and housing and recreation." The new town builders "were [not] planning utopias."

This new kind of developer launched projects that would provide something more satisfying than the settlement patterns found in cities. Among new town builders, says D'Alesandro, "There was a commitment at the beginning to excellence in design, environmental quality, and creating a balance to live, work, and play."

That's the kind of balance he hopes to achieve in building out Town Center, which up until now has been the commercial heart of The Woodlands.

"We went out to see who are the very best architects today," D'Alesandro said. "We're working now with three firms. There's Cooper, Robertson & Partners who planned Battery Park City, which is an extension of lower Manhattan. They just had a landfill that the Port Authority owned, and it was absolutely a blank slate. They created the street pattern, the open space pattern, and the building configurations. They didn't design each of the buildings, but they created the framework. And they also did the plan for Disney's Celebration. We brought them in to work on the residential component of the Town Center.

"Then we worked with Sasaki Associates, which worked with me in Reston Town Center. They won the design competition to build the Olympic Village in Beijing for the 2008 Olympic Games. They did the Dallas Arts District in downtown Dallas and the National Arboretum."

The Sasaki firm is helping The Woodlands design land use patterns for Town Center. Public open spaces in downtown areas are community-defining places, D'Alesandro said. The Woodlands Town Center has been divided into residential, office, hospitality, and retail areas near public squares; Sasaki is helping the developer frame those squares and redefine them. D'Alesandro's team is also working with a firm called Street-Works, designers of a mixed-use project called Mizner Park in Boca Raton, Florida.

The objective of all this planning, he says, is to integrate residential and retail into the same areas. "In Reston Town Center, we put office above retail in a way that created a public place, so that it wasn't just a suburban office development. Mizner Park and Reston Town Center were designed as alternatives to the typical suburban fragmentation."

So how is this planning actually going to look? "Well, you're going to have to see it on foot. Most of The Woodlands is viewed at 35 miles an hour. When you come to the Town Center. . .[it's] a place that's enjoyable to be experienced on foot." The plan to turn Town Center into a pedestrian-friendly place involves more than just giving people a place to walk. It also involves a design challenge—keeping them from being bored while walking.

"If you think about a typical office building, it may be 200 feet long. People get bored if something's not happening every 30 feet—a bay, a balcony. If you go inside any mall, every 15 to 30 feet something else is happening. A different material is used in the window treatment, the signage, and awnings. That's the world of retail, where you have to keep people interested. [Mall owners] have to keep people interested in walking a quarter mile from Sears to Foley's. If they had dead space, say 200 feet of what looked like a typical suburban office building between Foley's and one of the other department stores, it would be like Death Valley. No one would walk it." Transferring that idea to the street, he continues, "buildings have to have a pedestrian vernacular, which means they have to break down into 15-, 20-, or 30-foot bays, or have something happening every 20, 15, 30 feet. That's part of what we did at Reston Town Center. Even though you have office space above, the ground level needs to have something interesting to walk past.

"How are the buildings along the Waterway going to feel comfortable to walk around and be more animated than the typical suburban building? We're looking at bringing an urban vernacular to the Waterway corridor, so that people enjoy walking from one use to the other."

At the time of this book's writing, the residential areas of Town Center were just getting started. These areas will look very different from the residential villages. "It's going to be more pedestrian oriented," D'Alesandro says. "They'll have sidewalks on both sides of the street, and trees, all of which encourage pedestrians."

One of the major differences is how Town Center will treat access to public spaces. "In The Woodlands," explains D'Alesandro, "you have sections of the golf courses that are public and sections that are private. There are pieces of it that you have a public view of. [But] you're not really encouraged to walk around. Access is difficult."

Town Center residential areas won't have consecutive house lots. Instead, they will have numerous small areas open for public access, to encourage pedestrians. Some residential areas will face the Waterway, and a few lots will go all the way to the water's edge. But that will be the exception. There will be a public pathway along most of the water's edge and there will be trails that take that pathway into interior lots. This system will create view corridors for those who don't live right on the water, while establishing points of access for residents to get to the water for a walk or a jog.

The residential area in Town Center will be named Watervale. There will be between 1,500 and 2,000 townhomes on narrower lots. Unlike most of the villages in The Woodlands, there will be no culs-de-sac. In addition to the townhomes, there will be other types of residential construction. "We think we can probably do about ten different types of housing—townhouses of different shapes and sizes and configurations, conventional condominiums, loft condominiums, and some single-family homes." Single-family homes need much more land than do multifamily ones. So while only about 10 percent of the area will be earmarked for single-family dwellings, they will take up about half of the land, D'Alesandro said.

Looking back on his experience developing Reston's Town Center, D'Alesandro thinks that The Woodlands Town Center has greater potential. The Woodlands Town Center already has a far stronger infrastructure today than Reston. You have the Cynthia Woods Mitchell Pavilion and the Marriott, a full-service convention hotel. You've got the mall generating 12 million visits a year and the Tinseltown Theater with 1.5 million visits a year. "We can play off of these other strong users and strong destinations and just improve on them. The negative here is the economy. We are working with a weak economy. Houston continues to lose jobs as far as I can tell. But we're setting the track, so to speak, so that when Houston does rebound, we're going to be in an excellent position," he said.

Still, D'Alesandro believes that there are many pluses about the Houston economy. First, Houston has a relatively low cost of living. For example, a person making $100,000 a year and living in New York City would need to make only $36,863 annually in Houston to maintain the same lifestyle.

The Woodlands' proximity to Houston's main airport, Bush Intercontinental, also helps. D'Alesandro says that recent studies have found that the best determinant of new job formation is expansion in hub airports. "So the expansion that's occurring at Intercontinental has tremendous positive implications for Houston and The Woodlands." D'Alesandro says that the town can continue to count on getting a large percentage of the families moving to the

Houston area from elsewhere. "We get an incredible amount of relocations. Some 50 percent of our houses are sold to people from out of state. If you're moving to Texas from California or New York, and you're thinking about moving to a place that you understand, The Woodlands is viewed as acceptable."

The other challenge to the future of The Woodlands is development of its last village. Once named Harmony Bend, it has now been renamed the Village of Creekside Park. For the first time, The Woodlands is going to be developing a residential village in a separate county (Harris), in a separate school district (the Tomball Independent School District), and with a separate community association.

D'Alesandro agrees it will be a challenge. But, he adds, "We really don't sell the village as a village. We sell The Woodlands. Whether you move to Panther Creek or Grogan's Mill or Alden Bridge, you're in The Woodlands. Crossing the county line is not as important as a school district. You know, my kids are not going to be going to the same school system as the other kids. This is what I'm scratching my head about and I don't know what the right answer is. I'm thinking of doing two things. One is to begin now to celebrate Creekside Park and to really start to promote it as the Village of Creekside Park in The Woodlands with the newest schools and the newest library. You don't want to lose the brand, but you begin to create the identity of the village in a stronger way."

D'Alesandro said he is also looking at how the Rouse Company promoted the last village for sale in its new town of Columbia. "When they launched the last village, it was the biggest thing that ever happened to Columbia. And part of what they did was to tell people that the Rouse Company had 30 years of experience developing Columbia and all of the lessons they've learned they've put into this final village—this is the grand finale. They made it seem like you better get on board this train." One obvious way to sell Creekside Park, D'Alesandro says, is to target current residents of The Woodlands who are empty nesters and therefore would not be worried about being in a different school district.

The remaining development of The Woodlands should be in good hands with the addition of the Rouse Company and its extensive experience in developing significant master-planned communities, including Columbia, Maryland, and Summerlin, near Las Vegas. And Tom D'Alesandro's experience with the very successful Reston Town Center is a great fit for what remains to be done in The Woodlands Town Center.

There is a reservoir of community support for the continuation of George Mitchell's vision. But there are also some future challenges brought on by changing times. For example, membership in the historically productive human network of residents (those "pioneers" who moved to the new town when it was barely a town at all) and company employees is changing. This is a natural process for an endeavor that extends for almost a half century. George Mitchell and many of his team are no longer associated with the development company. Pioneers have moved on or are not recognized by the current owner or newer residents of The Woodlands. New residents will move in and assume positions of leadership in institutions that form the community's framework. This is a healthy renewal of human resources. The new ownership has the opportunity to benefit from existing community relationships, but it must cultivate new ones as well.

It appears that Rouse could face some challenges not encountered by previous owners. The apparent higher cost basis of the assets it acquired from Crescent and the already established trend toward more upscale development with aggressive pricing could slow the pace of new construction and affect community development and marketing decisions. As staff functions are being reassigned to the Rouse Company headquarters in Columbia and jobs are being eliminated at the local level for greater cost efficiency, morale within The Woodlands Operating Company is an understandable concern. Many experienced long-term employees are no longer at the company and a smaller number of new employees need to build a productive relationship with the community. To some it may appear that a new absentee owner has moved in with a heavy hand. It will be up to the Rouse staff to demonstrate otherwise.

But all future decisions may not be left to Rouse. Just as this book was going to the printer, General Growth Properties, Inc., the second-largest owner of shopping malls in the United States, announced plans to purchase all outstanding shares of the publicly traded Rouse Company for $7.2 billion and to assume $5.4 billion of its debt. The proposed acquisition likely was motivated by General Growth's interest in Rouse's 37 regional malls and other retail properties. The Woodlands and other master-planned communities owned by Rouse are just a part of a much larger portfolio of properties. Because General Growth has little experience in community development, it remains to be seen how its purchase of a 52.5 percent financial interest in The Woodlands will affect staffing and operational policy within the community, assuming the transaction is consummated as proposed. One option—which is only speculation at this point—would be for General Growth to spin off Rouse's community development projects. However, one observation is clear: this proposed sale has caused much less discussion than did George Mitchell's sale in 1997.

As Tom D'Alesandro correctly pointed out, developing the final village in a separate county and school district will be an additional challenge for Rouse and Morgan Stanley in going forward. Not only do governance and schools present special issues, so too does the cost of infrastructure. For the past two decades, The Woodlands Corporation has simply extended existing water, sewage, and drainage utilities to new villages as they are developed. But with the seventh and final village, all new infrastructure must be built, increasing costs. And this last village will focus extensively on more expensive housing surrounding a Tom Fazio Signature Golf Course. This amenity has great value, but competition offered by similar golf courses in other parts of The Woodlands, coupled with public school concerns, could slow the absorption pace in the new Village of Creekside Park.

Beyond the challenges of new development opportunities, perhaps the most important issue for the community to focus on is that of future governance. Most of the property in The Woodlands lies within the extraterritorial jurisdiction of the city of Houston, which means that the city has the unilateral right under existing state law to annex The Woodlands. Several years ago, the city and "the community" entered into an agreement whereby the city would not annex The Woodlands until 2014, essentially providing adequate time to agree on a system of governance that would mutually benefit the city and The Woodlands.

A committee has been formed in The Woodlands under the leadership of the several community associations to study alternatives and recommend an approach to future governance. Local residents would have to agree on the approach, as would Houston officials. So we are now asking ourselves, "How will we govern the community after the developer leaves the picture?"

My personal view is that I'd like to see the committee and the city consider an alternative whereby state legislation would institutionalize the kind of governance we have now. Absent a change in state law, I don't think Houston is going to give up the advantages of being able to tax property in The Woodlands. By the same token, I don't think it's going to be practical for the city to annex The Woodlands in the near future. For one thing, it would have to skip over a lot of territory beyond the existing city limits. I'm hopeful that there can be a form of limited annexation that would allow Houston to collect a limited tax from The Woodlands that would go to fund regional things that benefit our residents, like the Port of Houston, the airport, museums, flood control, and regional air and water quality programs. In exchange for that limited tax, residents of the community would have the right to vote on policies that affect these regional resources. It also would allow our community to continue to tax and govern itself on local issues like police and fire protection, parks and recreation, wastewater and solid waste disposal, and the like. The form of governance we have in The Woodlands today has served us well for many years and we should not walk away from it. We must also support a healthy Houston. A stronger central city will mean stronger suburban areas.

While there are still some ten or more years remaining until The Woodlands is fully developed, the project has nonetheless reached its final phases of completion. When George Mitchell owned The Woodlands Corporation, its remaining development life was quite substantial and Mitchell made decisions and investments based on a very long-term outlook. "Things will improve in a year or two," he would say when we got off track, and they usually did. Under Mitchell's leadership, the corporation made contributions to community amenities that could be recovered only in the very long term.

The current owners are faced with a different timeline and their development decisions will necessarily be of a short-term nature. It is impractical to expect that they will make investments that will not produce a return or be recovered within the remaining development life of The Woodlands. They have a responsibility to their shareholders and owners, too. That does not mean they will shortchange their obligations to the community, but they will likely be less generous than Mitchell.

This suggests that community leaders and institutions must continue and even expand their role in community affairs as we go forward. This is a healthy exercise. Someday, the developer will be gone and if it has done a good job, a system of institutions for managing the community will be in place, supported and managed by elected or appointed resident and business leaders. We are now well along with that transition and the quality of life we enjoy in the future will hinge on how well we do.

Control of The Woodlands Community Association has passed to residents. Control of the other community associations will transition to resident control as development progresses. A board governs the Town Center Improvement District with a majority of noncompany representatives. All of the Municipal Utility District boards are composed of elected residents of the community. Institutions such as the YMCA, places of worship, public and private schools, community college, hospitals, and the chamber of commerce are operated outside the control of the developer, as are entertainment venues, restaurants, and retail shops. Some 3,000 business and others employ more than 30,000 people in The Woodlands. Covenants are in place to govern land use, protect the environment, and address quality controls. In fact, we have become a functioning "city." The developer will continue to play an important role for a period of time, but it will be less dominant than Mitchell's role during the initial years.

I recall a brief presentation George Mitchell made to the annual meeting of The Woodlands Community Association several years after he sold the corporation. He concluded his remarks by telling the assembled residents that they would have to help him watch the progress of the new owners "to make sure they do a good job." His message was clear: The baton has passed. The obligation belongs to the community. Rouse and Morgan Stanley can use our help and we need theirs during the remaining development phase.

Other than a few specific skirmishes, there has always been a productive relationship between the development company and the community. There has never been a widespread "not in my backyard" mentality or a no-growth sentiment like that found in other parts of the country. If that productive relationship is nurtured and preserved, the future of The Woodlands looks especially bright. It really boils down to the human side of development.

Chapter 26

LESSONS LEARNED

———— • ◆ • ————

The Woodlands today is 30 years old, with another ten years or so remaining for the current owners to advance George Mitchell's vision. So what can we learn from The Woodlands? What lessons may be useful to others?

First, great master-planned communities are vision led. The Woodlands was. So were Columbia, Reston, Irvine, and others that achieved similar success. Each had a visionary leader with a passion for the endeavor and a willingness to trade short-term profits for long-term benefits. That doesn't mean they paid no attention to economics. An enterprise like The Woodlands must be guided by market-wise decisions to succeed in a competitive environment. The Woodlands' march toward profitability was hampered in part by a lack of adequate financial controls and organizational discipline during its turbulent startup in the early 1970s, the OPEC oil embargo, high interest rates, and Houston's severe economic downturn in the mid-1980s. Those events delayed profitability. But the long-term nature of master-planned communities exposes them to such economic vagaries.

If properly designed, master-planned communities use land more efficiently and offer a better alternative to urban sprawl. I believe that this has been demonstrated by The Woodlands. Its development plan sets aside approximately 6,700 acres for open space and preserves valuable environmental assets. Of the remaining undeveloped land, 5,000 acres is planned for commercial or institutional uses, leaving 15,300 acres for a projected final residential population of about 125,000 people. Much of the exurban development surrounding The Woodlands has residential densities that would consume approximately 100,000 acres to accommodate 125,000 people, which could not accommodate a cost-efficient system for delivering basic community services such as utilities or postal services. The average higher residential density at The Woodlands has not harmed sales. Residential sites are large enough to accommodate individual homes and are complimented by an abundance of common open space.

Great master-planned communities succeed by building communities rather than focusing on land development. They emphasize the human side of development. This doesn't mean they ignore good engineering practices, architecture, building construction, or other physical aspects of the development process. But they recognize that there must be a thoughtful process in creating a place that is more than simply one where people may choose to live or work, but is a real community where residents feel connected to their neighbors.

The Woodlands experience shows that successful master-planned communities provide positive benefits beyond their borders. While it is fair to say that Montgomery County would have gained population and jobs as nearby Houston expanded, The Woodlands influenced the quality and timing of growth and economic expansion within the county. By 2003, with 25 percent of the county's population, The Woodlands holds 37 percent of its taxable property. A similar situation is true within the school district, where The Woodlands accounts for 43 percent of the students and pays 60 percent of school property taxes. Commercial development in The Woodlands has produced a spillover effect of value to property in adjacent jurisdictions. And a significant number of new jobs within the county are located in The Woodlands. This is not just a one-way street, however. The county, school district, and other jurisdictions provide valuable facilities and services to The Woodlands. There are just no losers. It is a productive relationship.

From its inception and prior to the sale of its assets in 1997, The Woodlands Corporation followed a rather simple planning process and business strategy. Of course, implementing that process required complicated individual transactions, contractual agreements, regulatory approvals, engineering challenges, planning discussions, and financial arrangements. Some were quite difficult and consumed considerable resources, but the principles upon which we operated were straightforward. We also conducted frequent market surveys with community residents and prospective customers. The survey results helped confirm, shape, and improve community building blocks, although our fundamental development principles remained in place.

The land assemblage, ultimately encompassing 27,000 acres of forested property, was divided into seven residential villages with 5,000 acres designated for commercial development. There was an aggressive attempt to create a significant employment base within the community with a target of one job per household. Community design was conceived in "harmony with nature," employing a functional natural drainage concept and extensive tree preservation. Twenty-five percent of the land was preserved as natural open space or used for recreational activities. Each village included a similar diversity of housing and a neighborhood retail center anchored by a grocery store. Places of worship, schools, and parks were positioned in each village to take advantage of shared parking. Pathways within greenbelts connected residential neighborhoods with village amenities. Major thoroughfares within the community were constructed as limited access corridors with wooded medians and meaningful roadside vegetation easements to protect views and serve as buffers. Vegetation within floodplains and along stream channels was protected to thwart erosion and serve as wildlife corridors and open space.

Signs were limited in number, size, shape, color, and location. Town Center at The Woodlands was designed to serve as the downtown for the entire north Houston region with a population of approximately 1 million people. It was positioned adjacent to Interstate 45 to avoid intrusion into residential villages. Facilities within Town Center were planned as regional destinations, including shopping, entertainment, restaurants, hospitality, and health care. A university-supported research program initially anchored the Research Forest with significant involvement from institutions of the Texas Medical Center. A high-quality education system was a significant community building block and included public and private schools, a community college, and university learning opportunities. Golf was perceived as a major recreational amenity and business opportunity. Community governance was structured to transition to resident leadership as development progressed. Architectural review and control would reside with the developer until substantial completion of the town. Public funding for infrastructure was critical to the financial success of the development. Our focus was on quality and attention to detail, requiring personal involvement of the entire management team. Market sensitivity would influence our decisions. The Woodlands would be a community where people could live, work, play, and learn. It would be an asset for both the Houston region and Montgomery County.

From a strategy standpoint, our company functioned as a land developer for the residential business, selling finished lots and building sites to qualified and financially capable homebuilders with a proven track record. With the exception of custom homes, our company advertised and marketed the community, and builders advertised and marketed their homes. The Woodlands Corporation developed, owned, and managed most rental apartments, neighborhood retail centers, and speculative office buildings, selling commercial sites only to unique users who would agree to construct facilities that added jobs, economic advantages, or specific services to the community. All land sales included use restrictions and building requirements. Our business plan called for a major portfolio of income-producing properties within The Woodlands so that when land development was complete, the company would benefit from an ongoing cash flow produced by a viable, residual business. This extensive ownership of commercial income property also permitted us to take advantage of trade-off opportunities in competitive situations. For example, we had the flexibility of reducing rent in one of our office buildings to attract a tenant that would bring jobs to the community because those jobs would produce potential homebuyers and lot sales. These homebuyers would become customers in our retail centers or country club members at our golf facilities, increasing revenue opportunities for the properties owned by our company.

While not required to do so, many of our employees and most of the management team elected to live in The Woodlands. They participated in civic and social programs in the community, sent their children to neighborhood schools, and met neighbors in the grocery store or at the post office. They paid local taxes, traveled local streets, and attended special events. They were visible in the community, so when contentious issues arose in The Woodlands, our company was not viewed as an uncaring absentee owner. When issues did arise, it was more difficult to get angry with your neighbor who worked at the development company. George Mitchell's vision and leadership played the key role, but much of our success with The Woodlands is attributable to our exceptional team.

By following this relatively simple planning process and business strategy, The Woodlands assembled an impressive portfolio of income-generating assets and landholdings. Under George Mitchell's ownership, it became the top master-planned community in Texas and among the top five in the United States, with more than 1,000 new home sales per year.

Community development is based on four fundamental components: land, money, people, and trust. It starts with the land. Often, buying a particular piece of land isn't a rational, planned decision. Sometimes it's a matter of convenience. A large mass of land becomes available at an affordable price. The transaction can be achieved quickly. Developers don't always determine the ideal location first and then go seek land there. Sometimes the opportunity to acquire land comes along first, and its future use is determined after purchase. That's initially what happened in The Woodlands. George Mitchell recognized the profitable opportunity afforded by acquisition of his original 2,800 acres of land—it later became a part of The Woodlands. He also understood the emerging market forces that would enhance its potential for community development. He was not lucky. He was smart. Most of the other master-planned communities initially supported by HUD Title VII loan guarantees failed because their land was in the wrong place.

Money is obviously important, but not only for the reason one might think. Adequate capitalization gives the developer flexibility. If you're undercapitalized, you sometimes don't have the flexibility to achieve long-term goals. Your decisions are driven by short-term cash needs as opposed to long-term planning. George Mitchell was in the fortunate position of having money, both corporate and personal wealth. He used it wisely. He didn't flaunt it, but he had the flexibility to achieve long-term goals and planning. And even with that wealth, The Woodlands came close to almost breaking both Mitchell and his company. The dual challenges of land and money can sometimes be resolved by a partnership between landowners and the community developer. That reduces the amount of capital necessary by making the land partner share the risk and rewards with the developer. But partners must be chosen carefully and exit strategies provided for both parties. These are very long-term arrangements and things will change along the way.

And there are people. They are an important part of the equation. The people on the development team are vital, whether they are on staff or are professional consultants who provide advice. But important people also include residents of the community, business associates, and clients who lease office space. How you deal with them is an important element of community development. Master-planned communities require years, even decades, to mature. They require long-term relationships. It's not like selling an automobile where you have a customer who buys a product, drives it away, and relies on the warranty to make sure it performs well. Your customers are people who move into the community. The decisions you make affect their daily lives for years and years. You create associations that impose and collect fees that provide services in the community. Every resident has an interest in how effectively and efficiently those services are provided. People pay taxes. They send children to school. Community building is deeply involved in the lives of families and people throughout the development process.

And finally, there is trust. That is an intangible quality that is earned through words and deeds. It is the element that grants permission to proceed. Trust supports creditability in dealing with regulatory agencies, environmental organizations, community residents, clients, professional consultants, and others. We all know that trust is hard to gain and easy to lose. Protect it every day.

So what are the factors that, if done well, give a developer the chance to succeed? What will help the developer to achieve profits and provide residents of the community a living environment they will enjoy? The fundamental thing that every good developer must do is look closely at the market before making decisions. Conduct market research. It's a good investment. At The Woodlands Corporation, we spent much time and effort on market research, interviewing our customers and existing residents, trying to understand what they wanted and how we could deliver it. On the other hand, always remember that the plan will need to be adjusted with circumstances as you learn from your own mistakes. In the Houston region, that's no great problem because government-planning controls are flexible. In other jurisdictions, the approvals process is so rigid it doesn't allow a great deal of flexibility to change, which requires going back through public hearings and having approvals modified.

Successful developers also define and communicate their message, and not just to the public, residential, and business communities. It's equally important that the message be spread within its own team of professionals. Particularly in the early stages of The Woodlands, that was a problem. Mitchell pulled together outstanding people from Columbia, Irvine, and other ongoing new town projects around the country. But it took time for that group to become a team and talk to each other. It was during those early days when there was not a good communications mechanism that some of the floundering took place. There were other problems, but the lack of both communication and teamwork was of paramount importance.

Successful master-planned communities focus on quality. Quality starts with a commitment by the developer and extends through the entire process from the recruitment of the development team and selection of professional consultants and advisers to the design and construction of facilities, advertising and marketing programs, and the way one deals with people. Achieving high-quality results requires the personal encouragement of senior leadership in the organization. Attention must be given to detail. Do not allow the excitement of the big picture to obscure the small things that will make a new community come to life.

The use of public funding to pay for public infrastructure was critical to the financial success of The Woodlands. Public funds came in the form of state and federal grants, sale of tax-exempt bonds by special purpose districts, and the construction of public facilities by government agencies, or special purpose districts such as those used to build roads, school districts, community college districts, and other political subdivisions. Altogether I would estimate approximately $500 million has come from such sources to fund the construction of public facilities, including schools, county buildings, major thoroughfares, overpasses, wastewater treatment plans, water plants, utility collection and distribution systems, and parks. Infrastructure is generally funded by the public agencies and public sources within counties and cities in the state, so this was not a special favor to The Woodlands. But what was challenging was to get so much done on a schedule that would accommodate the community development process. To accomplish this, The Woodlands Corporation often donated or discounted rights-of-way and sites for plants, schools, and public buildings. In addition, we advanced millions of dollars to utility districts and other similar entities, and deferred repayment until the community tax base was sufficient to support the sale of tax-exempt bonds.

That is the advantage of a large master-planned community. The Woodlands did not use someone else's tax base to finance local water, sewer, drainage, or road improvements. To repay debt, special purpose districts whose jurisdiction was limited to property within The

Woodlands sold bonds and imposed taxes only on property in the community. I remember reading an article in *U.S. News and World Report* several years ago that took suburban developers to task for pirating wealth from urban centers by connecting to city-owned utilities; to pay for the necessary expansion of the utility's capacity, bonds were sold and the city's residents were taxed. Now that may be the case for small developments on the edges of some cities. But in jurisdictions that allow the creation of special purpose districts such as those used in The Woodlands, the larger master-planned communities can develop a tax base that does not have to depend on the "mother city" and thus does not burden existing taxpayers.

Good market research helps to define what potential residents want in a new community. Good communication helps the development team deliver what customers want and lets potential residents know it is available. So what do they want? A list of community building blocks—those things that residents expect and demand—emerged as the process of developing our new community advanced. In The Woodlands, education, personal safety, the environment, and open spaces were always at the top of every survey we did among residents over some 25 years. Sometimes education was first, sometimes personal safety, sometimes the environment. But those were always the top three. They were things that touched the everyday lives of our residents.

Public education drives suburban development with its promise of better-quality education than that found in central cities. The Houston Independent School District is making significant progress in improving its schools, but it still has a way to go. We put a lot of time and effort into The Woodlands schools. We worked with the local school districts. We donated school sites or sold them at less than our cost. We donated to school programs. We had several employees who served on the school board. Many employees have served on committees of the school district. We also focused on private education through the founding of the John Cooper School, which has an outstanding college preparatory program. We also had limited involvement in the founding of The Woodlands Christian Academy, with its focus on religion and a good education. We provided help to the founding of a community college, which has become a very valuable asset for the people who live here. But it is also valuable in recruiting businesses to locate here through job training programs. And, of course, there's the University Center. It's one of three in the country where multiple universities offer degree programs in a facility that's located on the campus of the community college. You can go from kindergarten to a university degree without leaving the community.

From the beginning, we focused on personal safety and it is still a focus. The Woodlands is a very safe place to live. There is crime in the community, but as a percentage of the population, it is very low. That's not by happenstance. It's because of the community associations that fund additional services to protect people who live here through agreements with the Montgomery County sheriff's department. There's an agreement with a private security organization, the Alpha & Omega Royal Courtesy Mounted Patrol, in the commercial areas.

There are neighborhood watch programs where people can create their own neighborhood organization to address safety issues. There's a reporting system from individual homes to a block captain to the sheriff's department, so that if something does happen, there's a communication procedure in place. The Woodlands is physically designed in such a way that it's confusing to criminals who don't live here. It's hard to find your way around in some neighborhoods. It was not designed for public safety, but it worked out that way. Our small, individual neighborhoods don't have through-streets, which means there's only a single access point for entry and exit.

The third issue of importance always high on every resident survey is the natural environment and open space. Popular opinion is straightforward: save the trees. It's not a battle cry, although we have had battles. It's a uniting statement, not a divisive one. I visit the third-grade class in Galatas Elementary School every year and I read a book by Shel Silverstein called *The Giving Tree*. It's an opportunity to talk to the third-graders about the environmental program in The Woodlands, using the book as a way to open the conversation. I ask them what they like about The Woodlands, and almost without exception the trees come up high on their lists, too. I believe that The Woodlands experience clearly demonstrates that an environmentally sensitive development plan adds value and enhances marketability of a community. The residents profit and so does the developer.

There are other building blocks for a successful development. Transportation and mobility are among them. Streets and signal lights that control traffic flow without causing congestion are fundamental components to the initial development in any new town. And as traffic increases, it's the first thing that you get complaints about.

But mobility goes beyond that. We opened The Woodlands in 1974 during the gasoline crisis, when people were sitting in lines waiting to fill up their tanks and paying higher prices for the privilege. We organized carpools to help to defray expenses for people who commuted to Houston every day. The next step was organizing vanpools. We helped to secure grants and also provided some initial funding to acquire several 12-passenger vans. And we allowed parking at some of our office buildings so those vanpool riders would have a common place to leave their cars and meet the van. The next step in mobility was to work with the Brazos Transit Authority, which receives federal funds, to provide bus service. There are now 67 bus trips a day from The Woodlands to major work locations in the central business district of Houston, the Galleria, and the Texas Medical Center. There are two park-and-ride lots with bus operations, each with parking for 1,000 cars. It's a very efficient way for people to get from here to their work locations and it takes 2,000 cars off Interstate 45 each day.

We also reduced the number of commuters by creating jobs in the local community. That's really the solution. There are now 30,000 jobs in The Woodlands. If you can get people to live close to where they work or work close to where they live, you cut out a lot of commuting. Future mobility plans here include local shuttle buses, trolleys, and water cruisers on the Waterway in Town Center.

People also want good amenities and recreation. But they are lower on the list of priorities for local residents because they are expected as part of the package. The most popular recreational facility in The Woodlands is the pathway system, which is a network of greenbelt walkways constructed along major thoroughfares. The adjacency of cars and pedestrians is actually a public safety feature, because passing automobiles are in sight and at night the streetlights help light the pathways. Of course, fields for soccer, baseball, football, and other organized sports for children are popular, as are village swim centers. These all build family ties and a sense of community.

Other amenities in the community include a very significant swim and athletic center that is an Olympic training center. One of the first projects built in The Woodlands, it has served the community well. It's the training center for our high schools' swim and diving team. The Russian swim team worked out here before competing in the Atlanta Olympics. Golf is another important amenity. There are now six golf courses in The Woodlands and a seventh under construction. Signature courses are designed so they are challenging for the pros but also accommodate weekend golfers. Several are available for public play, while others are only for club members.

Good shopping is always important. Our goal was to be the regional downtown for all of north Houston, with a population of a million people. It would also be the downtown for the residents of The Woodlands. It was located on Interstate 45 to provide easy access for people from outside the community so that they did not drive through our residential neighborhoods to get there. There are grocery-anchored retail centers for daily shopping needs in each village.

Housing in The Woodlands was planned from the outset to be affordable for a diverse population. It was not intended to be just for the rich or the poor, but to mirror the population of the greater Houston area. Residential offerings range from subsidized rental apartments to very expensive estate homes. The existing villages were designed to support a full range of housing options. There isn't the more affordable village or the most exclusive one. You aren't identified as being wealthy or less than wealthy by your address.

The uniqueness of the housing in The Woodlands is due to the design of the neighborhoods and the care taken to save the trees around the homes and along the streets. Housing has never been at the top of the things mentioned by residents because it's something that people expect to find when they come to a place like The Woodlands. It's an expectation they have, and they wouldn't come in large numbers if there weren't a diversity of architectural styles and high-quality construction. Providing affordable housing choices has created a more diverse, stronger community and encouraged some businesses to locate here because all of their employees can live in the community.

Housing designed to attract and accommodate seniors expanded our market reach and has encouraged extended families to coexist in The Woodlands. Four generations of some families live here. A community is much stronger when grandparents and grandchildren walk along the same pathway.

Community governance was and is important. The Woodlands was in an unincorporated area of a rural county when it opened. The county had limited ability to provide municipal services. We had to organize ourselves to provide government in this setting. We did it through utility districts, community associations, volunteer groups, and agreements with the county and adjacent towns and cities. It has worked well and encouraged a host of residents to serve in elected or appointed positions of meaningful service to the community.

Festive events and an institutional structure to support them are important in every community, but even more so in a new one. The events bring people together. It makes them feel good about where they live. People need an opportunity to participate and express themselves. At first, The Woodlands Corporation organized a lot of the events. It served as a facilitator, catalyst, and provider of initial financial support. Now the community organizes its own events, from the Fourth of July celebration and the winter holiday season festivities to political rallies. There are special performing arts events at the Cynthia Woods Mitchell Pavilion and other places in the community. There are social clubs, civic clubs, religious organizations, the Rotary Club, the Kiwanis Club, and the YMCA—institutional activities that people have established to entertain and educate themselves.

For the past 30 years, I have been an observer or a participant in happenings at The Woodlands. Not many people get the opportunity I have enjoyed and I thank George Mitchell for that. It has been a unique and rewarding experience. Perhaps the greatest reward is overhearing a conversation where residents of the community tell each other they like living here. Our two grown children and their spouses have chosen to live here and raise their children here, and that is really special, too.

Many people have worked to make The Woodlands a better place to live and I have known most of them. My regret is that I could not include all of them by name in this book.

If we had known at the beginning what we all know now about building a new town, we could have done a better job, but the surprises would be gone. Perhaps this book will serve those who remain in The Woodlands to complete the job, or it will inspire others who seek to develop another community where people live, work, play, and learn.

INDEX

A

AARP, 77
Adams, Ruth, 74
Alcoholics Anonymous, 77
Alden Bridge Village, 103, 169
Allison, Bob, 65
Alpha & Omega Royal Courtesy
    Mounted Patrol, 178
Amoco, 6, 7
Anadarko Petroleum Co., 65, 130,
    163
Anheuser-Busch, 136
Anthropologie, 166
Ardry, Robert, 31
Armstrong, Vicki, 156, 163
Army Reserve, 6
Association for the Advancement of
    Mexican Americans, 119
Austin Bridge, 48

B

Ballentyne, Maria, 98
Baptist General Convention of
    Texas, 75
Barnes, Ben, 112
Barnes & Noble, 166
Baylor College of Medicine, 90,
    123
Bensten, Lloyd, 18
Black, Jack, 91
Bomke, Linda, 4
Bone, Bill, 161
Bowen, Ted, 90
Brady, Kevin, 150
Brasher, Louis, 18
Brazos Transportation Authority,
    126–127, 133–134, 142,
    179
Brenneman, Greg, 98
Brown, Drew, 161
Brown, Lee, 86–87
Browne, Richard P.: and Cynthia
    Woods Mitchell Pavilion,
    support of, 142–143; and
    dispute over future of The
    Woodlands, 52; and
    involvement in concept of
    The Woodlands, 17, 25,
    28; and involvement in
    Town Center, 126–127;
    and planning of The
    Woodlands, 30–31

Buckalew, Don, 104
Buffalo Bayou, 33–34, 54
Buffalo Bayou Preservation
    Association, 33–34
Bumgardner, G. David, 27, 47–48
Bush, Barbara, 104, 105
Bush, George, 34, 100
Bush, George H.W., 98
Bush, George W., 34, 100

C

Calleri, Salvatore T., 45
Carlton Woods Country Club, 163
Carter, Jimmy, 56
Carter, Leland, 51–52
Caudill, Rowlett, Scott (CRS), 16
CBI, 130
Champion Paper Company, 24
Chase Manhattan Bank, 43, 51
Cheesecake Factory, 166
Chevron Phillips Chemical Co.,
    130, 163
Christie, Merlyn, 7, 9
Christie, Mitchell & Mitchell, 9,
    23
Church of Latter-Day Saints, 76
CISD. See Conroe Independent
    School District
Clark, B.F. "Budd," 9, 48, 51
Coca-Cola, 136
College Park Village, 41, 104
Congress, U.S., 67
Connelly, John, 112
Conroe Courier. See Courier, The
Conroe Independent School
    District (CISD), 76,
    93–97, 148–150
Conroe Regional Hospital, 90
Continental Airlines, 98
Continental Oil Co., 52
Cooper, John, 97
Cooper, Robertson & Partners, 167
Coordinating Board for Higher
    Education, 99
Corps of Engineers, 6, 34
Couch, Dean, 25
Courier, The (previously Conroe
    Courier), 151, 162
Covey, Don, 156
Crabbe, Buster, 50
Creekside Park Village, 104, 169

Crescent Real Estate Equities, 65,
    85, 113, 138, 153,
    159–165
Crittenden, Laura, 18
CRS (Caudill, Rowlett, Scott), 16
Cynthia Woods Mitchell Pavilion,
    88, 126–127, 131,
    142–143, 160–162, 181

D

D'Alesandro, Tom, 165–170
D.E. Harvey Builders, 65
Deison, R.A. "Mickey," 11, 47, 79,
    147
Del Webb Co., 113
Deretchin, Joel, 66, 67, 83–86,
    115–120, 145, 149
Devlin, Bruce, 139, 142
Devon Energy, 160
Dillard's, 128
DMB Associates, 161

E

East West Partners, 161
Edwards, Jimmy, 99
Eissler, Rob, 150
Environmental Protection Agency,
    U.S., 66
Ernst & Young, 156, 159
Everhart, Ralph, 45
Exxon, 58, 156

F

Faith Together, 78
Fazio, Tom, 104, 139, 170
Fehn, Gil, 110
Fertitta, Tillman, 158
Fertitta, Vic, 158
Foley's, 128
Ford, Gerald, 137
Frampton, Harry, 161
Friendswood Development
    Corporation, 99, 156

G

Galatas Elementary School, 66, 103, 179
Galveston City Council, 157
Galveston Country Club, 11
Gaultney, Carol Chedsey, 150
Gay, Joyce, 9, 144
Gebert, Don, 71–78, 88
General Growth Properties, Inc., 166, 170
Gensler Architects, 65
George Mitchell & Associates, 13
Georgia-Pacific, 13
Ginsburg, Hanna, 33–34
Gipson, Carlton, 113, 136, 139
Gipson, Robert, 92
Gladstone Associates, 17
Glass Menagerie, The, 62
Goldman Sachs, 156, 158, 159
Grace, Robert, 45
Greater Houston Partnership, 65
Grogan Cochran land, 13, 14, 16, 24
Grogan Cochran Lumber Company, 11, 38, 103
Grogan's Crossing Village, 103, 112
Grogan's Mill Village, 38–39, 45, 102, 103, 169
Grogan's Mill Village Association, 74
Grogan's Point, 112–113

H

Hailey, Sam, 104
Harmony Bend Village, 104, 169
Harris, Jeff, 156
Harris Development Company, 111–112
Hartsfield, Robert J., 16, 18, 34
Harvard University, 32
H.E.B., 166
Heineman, Robert, 32, 36–39, 41, 47, 125–127, 163
Henderson Junior College, 22
Hendricks, David, 18, 46, 51
Hershey, Terry, 33
Hewitt Associates, 130
HGA. See Houston Golf Association
Hoffman, Philip G., 98–99
Holmes, John, 91

Homart, 25, 128–129
Hometown Builders, 58, 112
Hope, Bob, 137
Housing and Urban Development Department, U.S. See HUD
Houston Advanced Research Center, 88, 121–124, 145
Houston Area Research Center, 122, 160
Houston City Council, 79
Houston-Galveston Area Council, 133
Houston Golf Association (HGA), 135–138, 142
Houston Independent School District, 178
Houston Metropolitan YMCA, 140
Houston Symphony, 143
Howard Hughes Corporation, 161
Howard Research and Development, 45
HUD (U.S. Department of Housing and Urban Development): and affordable housing requirement, 115–116, 118–120; approval of development plan, 43, 46; and fire and rescue station, feasibility of, 146–147; and loan guarantee, 21; Office of New Community Development, 51, 67; problems with Panther Creek, 40; relations with The Woodlands, 66; and Title VII of HUD Act of 1970, 15, 176
Hughes, Howard, 64
Hughes Christensen, 130
Hughes Tool, 64–65
Humana Corporation, 90

I

Independent Insurance Agents of America, 137
Indian Springs Village, 103
Institutional Planning Committee, 71

Interfaith Woodlands Religious Community, 73, 74, 75, 76–78, 88, 117
International Real Estate Federation, 9
Irvine Company, 55
Ivins, J. Leonard "Len," 45–46, 47, 48, 49, 51, 55

J

Jamail's, 40
JCPenney, 128, 129
Jimmy Swaggert Ministries, 29
John Cooper School, 88, 98, 160, 178
Jolly, Walter, 91

K

Kaufmann, Gadi, 161
Kelly, Charles, 18, 71
Kendrik, Bill, 152
King, John O., 34
Kirkpatrick, Jerry, 152
Kirkpatrick, JoAnn, 152
Kiwanis Club, 181
Knievel, Evel, 137
Knox, Ned, 104
Krenek, George, 152
Kutchin, Joe, 143

L

Lake, George, 156
Lampros, Peter, 163–164
Landrum, John, 163
Landry's Restaurant, 158
Law, Bill, 100
Ledwell, Tom, 26, 27, 28–29
Lee, Ed, 54, 55–56, 97, 146
Lee, Joe, 139
Lee, Tom, 161
Lennar Homes, 114
Lesch, Jack, 89
Lieberman, Harris, 111
Life Cell and Surgimedics, 123
Life Form Homes, 111
Lively, Charles, 21–26, 29
Lone Star Gas Co., 23
Louisiana State University, 122
Love, Ben, 128

M

Maceo, Rose, 5
Maceo, Sam, 5
MacKie, Kamrath and Pickford
    Planning Development
    Associates, 15
Maggert, Jeff, 139
Magnolia Independent School
    District (MISD), 93–96
Magnolia School Board, 96
Magnolia Volunteer Fire
    Department, 95
Mahost, Larry, 18
Mann, Robert, 27
Marriott Waterway Hotel and
    Convention Center, 130,
    152, 168
Marsh, Owen, 78
Marshall, James, 32
Mayo, John, 8
McAlister, Jim, 13–20, 47
McCoy, Buzz, 156
McCullough, J.L. "Mac," 94, 104
McDonald's, 37
McHarg, Ian, 17, 31, 33–35,
    37–38, 42
McIntyre, Margery, 91
McPhetridge, Steve, 61–66, 140,
    144, 163
Memorial Hermann Hospital, 130
Memorial Hospital System, 91
Mervyn's, 128
Methodist Hospital, 90–92
Meyer, Randy, 58
Middleton, D. Scott, 41
MISD (Magnolia Independent
    School District), 93–96
Mitchell, Christy, 5, 7
Mitchell, Cynthia, 16, 143–144,
    145
Mitchell, George: and affordable
    housing and affirmative
    action, 115–116; and art
    in public places, 144–145;
    and Cynthia Woods
    Mitchell Pavilion,
    142–143; early years, edu-
    cation, first business ven-
    tures of, 1–12; and future
    of The Woodlands, 165,
    169, 171–172; and golf
    club, establishment of,

135–136, 138; and gover-
    nance issues regarding The
    Woodlands, 79–87; and
    health care funding, 90;
    and HUD experience,
    13–20; and interfaith
    community, 72–78; land
    acquisition by, 21–29; and
    lessons learned, 173,
    175–177, 181; and nam-
    ing of streets and neigh-
    borhoods, 102–105; and
    planning and the environ-
    ment, 30–42; and prepara-
    tions to build The
    Woodlands, 45–52; rela-
    tions with neighbors,
    147–148; and research
    complex, 121–124; resi-
    dential development phi-
    losophy of, 112–113; and
    sale of The Woodlands,
    153–164; and schools,
    93–101; and Town Center,
    development of, 125–132;
    and turnaround, begin-
    ning of, 53–58
Mitchell, Johnny, 5, 7, 22–23
Mitchell, Katina, 4
Mitchell, Maria, 5
Mitchell, Mike, 4
Mitchell, Scott, 32, 57, 111
Mitchell, Todd, 124
Mitchell Development Corporation
    of the Southwest, 156
Mitchell Energy & Development
    Corp.: corporate culture
    of, 55; evolution of name
    of, 13; formation of, 3,
    7–9, 11–12; interests sold
    in, 65, 85; land acquisition
    by, 21–29; and prepara-
    tions to build The
    Woodlands, 45; and
    research center funding,
    122; and risk of The
    Woodlands, 20; and sale
    of The Woodlands,
    153–160
Mitchell Mortgage Company, 158
Mobil Land Company, 113
Monicle, Bruce, 92

Montgomery County Hospital
    District, 90
Montgomery County Youth
    Services, 77
Moreland, Bill, 90
Morgan, George T., Jr., 34
Morgan Stanley Real Estate, 65,
    85, 113, 138, 153,
    159–164, 170, 172
Moritz, Pat, 57–58, 113
Municipal Utility Districts
    (MUDs), 80–81

N

Nash, Barbara, 53
Natural Gas Pipeline of America, 8,
    23
Nelson, Ted, 53
Nelson, Willie, 138
New York Stock Exchange, 153
Newhall Land and Farming
    Company, 161
Newton, Isaac, 145
Nicklaus, Jack, 104, 113, 139
Nixon, Richard, 50
North Harris Community College,
    100, 124
North Harris Montgomery
    Community College, 100

O

Oil Drilling, 7, 8, 9, 13
Organization of Petroleum
    Exporting Countries
    (OPEC), 32, 50, 134, 173
O'Sullivan, Jack, 74
Overeaters Anonymous, 77
Owen, Rigby, Jr., 91

P

Pace Entertainment, 142
Pacesetter Homes, 21
Page, Mike, 80–83, 96
Palmer, Arnold, 139
Palmer Course Design Company,
    139
Panther Creek Village, 27, 40, 59,
    103, 112, 169
Pappas, Plato, 18, 19, 46, 48, 143
Paraskevopoulos, Savvas, 4
Parker, Carl, 95

Peerless Engineering Company, 52
Pereira, William, 30–32
Peyton, Pat, 91
P.F. Chang's China Bistro, 166
PGA. *See* Professional Golfers Association
Pickelman, John, 100
Pirates' Beach, 11
Pirates' Cove, 11
Player, Gary, 104, 139
Porter, Skip, 122
Powell, Boone, 127
Powell, Colin, 104, 105
Powell & Carson Architects, 127
Prairie View A&M, 101
Price, Jack, 45
Professional Golfers Association (PGA), 135, 142
Pulaski, Louis, 8

Q
Quail Valley Country Club, 135, 136

R
Research Forest, 41, 121–124, 174
Rice Institute, 6
Rice University, 32
Richmond, Michael: and infrastructure financing, 81; and interfaith community, 76; and positive cash flow in The Woodlands, 61; and preparations to build The Woodlands, 46, 48; and Research Forest, financing of, 122; and sale of The Woodlands, 156, 158, 163; and Town Center financing, 128–129
Ride, Sally K., 104
Robert Charles Lesser & Co., 161
Robinson, Frank, 130–132
Rogers, Len, 52, 55, 75
Roman Catholic Diocese, 27
Ross, Cerf Standford, 15–16
Ross, Stan, 156
Rotary Club, 181
Rouse, James, 17, 30–31, 165–166
Rouse Company, 30–31, 45, 159, 164, 165, 169–170, 172

Royal, Darrell, 138
Russ, Terry, 136, 139
Ryland, Jim, 110
Ryland Homes, 110–111

S
Sadler, Adam "Barb," 149
St. Luke's Community Hospital, 104
St. Luke's Episcopal Hospital, 90, 92
Salcetti, Bob, 110
Sam Houston State University, 99, 101
San Jacinto River Authority, 80, 81
San Luis Hotel and Condominium, 12, 157–158
Sanders, Doug, 137, 138
Sasaki Associates, 167
Sears, 128
Seay, Ed, 139
Shatner, William, 50
Shell Oil Co., 11, 137
Simon, Robert E., 165–166
Sinatra, Frank, 143
Smith, Barton A., 148
Smith, Phil, 159
Smith, R.E. "Bob," 14
South Texas Junior College, 99
Southwestern Gas & Pipeline Company, 51
Southwood Community Hospital, 91
Sprout, Sally, 144
Stanolind Oil and Gas Co., 6
Sterling Ridge Village, 103
Stevens, Bill, 156, 159
Stewart Title Co., 29, 158
Stolz, Otto G., 51
Street-Works, 167
Sunrise Colony Company, 161
Sutton, Alex, 163
Swanson, Matt, 145
Szescila, Andy, 64–65

T
Target, 59
TCID. *See* Town Center Improvement District
Texaco, Inc., 52
Texas A&M College, 5, 6

Texas A&M University, 22, 99, 101, 122
Texas Board of Education, 96
Texas Department of Highways and Public Transportation, 26, 133
Texas Department of Vital Statistics, 29
Texas Education Agency, 93
Texas Legislature, 82, 86–87, 95, 99, 130
Texas Medical Center of Houston, 41, 90, 121–122, 174, 179
Texas Parks and Wildlife Department, 25
Texas Railroad Commission, 21
Texas Senate, 95
Texas Southern University, 99, 101
Thomas, Owen, 161
Thompson, Morris, 13
Tinseltown Theater, 168
Title VII of HUD Act of 1970, 15, 176
Tomball Independent School District, 97, 104, 169
Tough, Coulson, 98, 99, 104, 105, 144, 145
Tower, John, 18
Town Center, 41, 125–132, 134, 165–169, 174
Town Center Improvement District (TCID), 82, 105, 130–132, 149, 152, 171
Trade Center, 41
Transco Energy Company, 144

U
UH. *See* University of Houston
University Center, 100–101, 104, 150, 160, 178
University of Houston (UH), 7, 98–99, 101, 148
University of Houston Downtown, 101
University of Oklahoma, 122
University of Pennsylvania Department of Landscape and Regional Planning, 33
University of Texas, 5, 122, 138
Urban Land Institute, 41, 161, 168
U.S. Congress, 67

U.S. Corps of Engineers, 6, 34
U.S. Department of Housing and
    Urban Development. *See*
    HUD
U.S. Environmental Protection
    Agency, 66

V

Van Epp, Dan, 161
Vance, Harold, 7
Veltman, Jim, 18, 34
Vetter, David, 105
Vetter, David, Sr., 105
Village of. *See name of specific
    village*
Villager, The, 151, 152
Vinson & Elkins, 9, 80
Von Hagge, Robert, 139, 142
Vuy, Ron, 12

W

Wahlberg, Paul, 136–137
Ware, Dancie, 12, 143
Welbes, Tim, 163
West, Karen, 96, 163
Wharf, The, 40
Wheatcroft, Dick, 72, 73
White, Bill, 87
White, Mark, 99
Wilkerson, Wally D., 104,
    147–148
William L. Pereira Associates, 17
Williams, Andy, 137
Williams, Bob, 56
Williams, Tommy, 150
Williams-Sonoma, 166
Williamson, Charles Lee, 75
Williamson, Mike, 90
Willis, Don, 65
Wilson, Charles, 50
Wingert, Lynn, 29
Woodlands Association, 83–84
Woodlands Christian Academy, 98,
    178
Woodlands Commercial Owners
    Association, 83
Woodlands Community
    Association, 45, 83–84,
    171–172
Woodlands Community Services
    Corporation, 85

Woodlands Corporation: and
    affordable housing and
    affirmative action,
    115–120; and art in pub-
    lic places, 144–145; corpo-
    rate culture of, 55; and
    Cynthia Woods Mitchell
    Pavilion, funding of, 143;
    in dispute with HUD, 49;
    in dispute with Roman
    Catholic Diocese, 27; and
    environmental covenants,
    39; evolution of, 3, 4; and
    future of The Woodlands,
    165, 171; and governance
    issues, 81–87; and health
    care facilities, funding of,
    88–92; HGA, agreement
    with, 138; initial success
    of, 60–68; and interfaith
    communities, develop-
    ment of, 71–78; and les-
    sons learned, 40–41,
    174–175, 177, 181; and
    marketing decisions, 36;
    and naming of streets and
    neighborhoods, 102–105;
    and neighbors, relations
    with, 146–151; and
    research center, funding
    for, 122; residential pro-
    gram of, 110–111; sale of,
    155–164; and schools,
    94–100; Town Center,
    development of, 126–132;
    turnaround for, 55–59;
    YMCA, support of, 140
Woodlands Country Club, 158,
    163
Woodlands Executive Conference
    Center Resort, 137, 139,
    158, 163
Woodlands Hospital, 58, 91–92
Woodlands Mall, 83, 128–129,
    131, 166
Woodlands Medical Center, Inc.,
    88
Woodlands Operating Company,
    149, 152, 170
Woodlands Religious Community
    Inc., 72, 73
Woodlands Sun, The, 151

Woodlands Waterway, 126–127,
    163, 167, 168, 179
Woods, Cynthia, 7, 16
Woods, Tiger, 139
Worksource, 77
Worley, Ben, 45
Wyrick, Bob, 18

Y

YMCA, 77, 140–142, 162, 172,
    181
Young President's Organization, 14,
    22

Z

Zonagen, 123